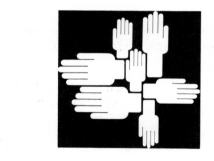

Career Education in the Middle/Junior High School

RUPERT N. EVANS · KENNETH B. HOYT · GARTH L. MANGUM

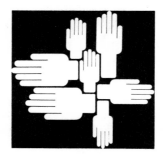

Olympus Publishing Company ⊛ Salt Lake City, Utah

Contents

LIST OF FIGURES

Preface

This is the third volume of our career education series which began with *Career Education: What It Is and How to Do It*, followed by *Career Education and the Elementary School Teacher*. This middle/junior high school volume is followed shortly by *Career Education for the Gifted and Talented Student* and a revision (after seven printings) of the original volume. These, with our manpower publications, represent deeply held convictions as to:

(1) The centrality of work in life and society

(2) The need for concept to be fleshed out with solid "how to do it" suggestions

This same concern for the basic quality of life and the essentiality of implementation — of "social engineering" to improve that quality — is reflected in early childhood education (see *Your Child's Intellect*, Olympus Publishing Company, 1973) and parent training, implemented in both the printed page and audio-visual presentations. Parenthood, too, is a career, the most basic one of all, and human development is society's greatest challenge.

With those premises, the middle and junior high school assignment of self- and social exploration becomes a critical role in the development of the personality, the economy, and the society. It is our hope to contribute modestly with this volume by helping educational administrators and teachers at that vital level be more effective in two essential aspects of that human development task: the development of values and the discovery of talents related to achievement and service.

Dr. Garn Coombs, Associate Professor of Education at Brigham Young University, contributed mightily to the concepts and factual information of chapters 1 and 4, as well as constructively criticizing other chapters. Examples were taken from the works of many people in many states whose originality and energy are to be commended. Sybil H. Clays and G. Donald Gale of Olympus Publishing Company turned the concepts and examples into book form for straightforward reading. The authors express gratitude, but claim full responsibility for the product.

Career Education in the Middle/Junior High School: Introduction to the Concept

During the painful years of pre- and early adolescence, the query most persistently in the mind of every youth is: *Who am I?* It is a time of uncertainty and even anguish, of looking inward, of probing to identify talents and take stock of assets, of self-testing, looking to further decisions: *What am I like? Why? What can I become? What am I to do to be worthwhile? How do I get there from here?* The school is only one of the institutions in life and society which attempt to influence and meet the needs of youth. But the institutions, including schools, which make the greatest contribution to the early adolescent are those which support these tentative probes at self-identity and the development of a personal value system. High among that list of exploratory probings are career considerations. Probably only social and sexual roles and skills are of greater concern. *What am I going to be?* (particularly to American youth) is still synonymous with *What will be my occupation?* rather than with the deeper question: *What type of career would be best for me?*

Exploration, then, is the appropriate emphasis for education in the middle schools and the junior high schools which encompass these years, and career education is an essential

9

part of it. In turning attention to the exploration of possible career roles, career education may do a service to the education of all adolescents. It may serve as a reminder that exploration — of self, of society, and one's role in it, including the working role — is the name of the game for ages ten through fifteen. It is the purpose of this book to argue and demonstrate that career education can make a vital contribution to the needs of youth at that age...that in fact a middle school or junior high curriculum which does not contain some of the components of career education cannot fulfill its assignment. The first chapter sets the stage by reviewing — as an introduction for the uninitiated and as a review for the practitioner — the definitions, goals, principal stages, and components of career education. These are explored at greater length in *Career Education: What It Is and How to Do It* and *Career Education and the Elementary School Teacher* but are summarized here as reference points to proposed middle/junior high activities. It also reviews the role and purpose of the middle school and junior high and illustrates the parallels between that assignment and the content of career education. Later chapters provide illustrations and examples of "how to do it" in service to the pre- and early adolescent.

CAREER EDUCATION: WHAT IT IS

Definitions of career education are numerous, and there is no official one. Ours, developed in *Career Education: A Handbook for Implementation* and *Career Education: What It Is and How to Do It*, is now widely used and appears to be as good as any. More importantly, there is a reasonably solid consensus on the general objectives, principles, and content of career education and the stages in which it should occur. We see career education as:

> ...the total effort of public education and the community aimed at helping all individuals to become familiar with the values of a work-oriented society, to integrate these values into their personal value systems, and to implement these values into their personal lives in such a way that work becomes possible, meaningful, and satisfying to each individual (Hoyt *et al.*, 1972, p. 1).

The definition identifies the actors and the goals in career education. The objectives which mark the way to achievement of the goals of career education, stated in their most simple and direct form, are to help all individuals (a) have reasons to want to work, (b) acquire the skills required for useful work, (c) know how to obtain work opportunities, and (d) enter the world of work as a successful and productive contributor. Career education can be understood only if this set of goals and objectives is kept clearly in mind.

Among the concepts within the realm of this definition, the following are of fundamental significance:

(1) The term "public education" means education available to the public and from which the public may choose. Thus career education is not limited to the kindergarten through twelfth grade public school system. Rather, it encompasses the public schools, but is extended beyond the twelfth grade to include all of post-secondary education, including community colleges, post-high school occupational education institutions (both public and private), degree-granting colleges and universities, and all adult education.

(2) Career education involves the *joint effort* of public education and the community. It is not something that schools can do by themselves. The school of *hard knocks,* as represented in the broader community, is joining with the school of *hard books* as represented by the formal education system, to become the total learning environment of career education.

(3) Career education is for all individuals — the very young child and the adults of the community, the intellectually able and the mentally handicapped, males and females, those who will attend college and those who will not, the economically affluent and the economically disadvantaged, and those from rural and those from urban settings.

(4) Career education seeks to help individuals become familiar with a wide variety of work values now present in this society and to choose some set of work

values that will be personally meaningful to each individual. It seeks to impose no single standard form of work values on any individual. While it clearly seeks to help each individual adopt some form of work values, it does not aim to coerce him into doing so. It does aim to teach the advantages and disadvantages of choosing or not choosing different sets of work values.

(5) Career education is vitally concerned with helping individuals *implement* their own personal work values. To do this demands that in addition to *wanting* to work, individuals must also acquire the skills *necessary* to work, and having done this, must then find work that is both meaningful and satisfying to them. Thus jobs, in a generic sense, are not career education's goal. Rather, the capacity to work at productive activity that holds personal meaning and satisfaction for the individual is the ultimate goal of career education.

As general underlying principles for career education:

(1) Preparation for successful working careers shall be a key objective of all education.

(2) Every teacher in every course will emphasize the contribution that subject matter can make to a successful career.

(3) "Hands-on" occupationally oriented experiences will be used as a method of teaching and motivating the learning of abstract academic content.

(4) Preparation for careers will be recognized as the mutual interaction of work attitudes, human relations skills, orientation to the nature of the workaday world, exposure to alternative career choices, and the acquisition of actual job skills.

(5) Learning will not be reserved for the classroom, but learning environments for career education will also be identified in the home and the community, and in employing establishments.

(6) Beginning in early childhood and continuing through the regular school years, allowing the flexibility for

a youth to leave for experience and return to school for further education (including opportunity for upgrading and continued refurbishing for adult workers and including productive use of leisure time and the retirement years), career education will seek to extend its time horizons from "womb to tomb."

(7) Career education is a basic and pervasive approach to all education, but it in no way conflicts with other legitimate educational objectives related to citizenship, to culture, to family responsibility, and to basic education.

(8) The school cannot shed responsibility for the individual just because he or she has been handed a diploma or has dropped out. While it may not perform the actual placement function, the school has the responsibility to stick with the youth until he has his feet firmly on the next step of his career ladder, help him get back on the ladder if his foot slips, and be available to help him onto a new ladder at any point in the future when the old one proves to be too short or unsteady.

Our definition states career education's goal and potential contributions more than its substance. The child and youth progressing through a career education system during his or her formative years would traverse five components, each of which is equally essential but which are listed here in order of the extent to which they are a primary responsibility of the schools:

(1) The classroom in which all possible learnings are articulated in terms of the career applications for both understanding and motivation

(2) The ultimate acquiring of vocational job skills, whether they are learned on the job, in a structured classroom situation, or from general life experiences

(3) Career development programs for exposure to occupational alternatives and for derivation of a work ethic and a set of work values, allowing the individual

to visualize himself or herself in various work settings and to make career decisions which appear to promise the preferred life-style

(4) Interaction among the training institutions, employing institutions, and labor organizations to provide more fertile learning environments than the schoolroom

(5) The home and family from which the individual develops initial attitudes and concepts

These five components interact, in career education, as intervention strategies, beginning no later than kindergarten and continuing through the adult years, to provide positive assistance to persons in their career development. Thus career education, while concerned with the continuing process of making work possible, meaningful, and satisfying to the individual, includes special attention to assisting persons as they move toward vocational maturity — the choice of a primary work role. By emphasizing a broad career development emphasis, career education seeks to ready youth for acceptance of the probability that each will, in all likelihood, change primary work roles (vocations) during their lifetimes.

Thus we can speak of vocational maturation as an integral part of the total process of career development. As part of the career development process, vocational maturation can be pictured as occurring in growth stages which, in sequential order, includes (1) awareness of primary work roles played by persons in society, (2) exploration of work roles that an individual might consider as important, possible, and probable for himself or herself, (3) vocational decision making (which may go from a highly tentative to a very specific form), (4) establishment (including preparing for and actually assuming a primary work role), and (5) maintenance (all of the ways in which one gains — or fails to gain — personal meaningfulness and satisfaction from the primary work role he or she has assumed).

Career education theorists generally see the awareness, exploration, and decision-making stages as coincidental and consistent with what tends to be occurring in the broader maturation of youth at the elementary, middle/junior high school, and high school levels of the education system. As one of many devices to aid this sequence, the U.S. Office of Education has designed and promulgated fifteen occupational clusters into which all occupations can be conceptually subsumed; these are as follows:

(1) Agri-business

(2) Natural resources

(3) Business and office

(4) Communications and media

(5) Consumer and homemaking education

(6) Construction

(7) Environmental control

(8) Fine arts and humanities

(9) Health

(10) Hospitality and recreation

(11) Manufacturing

(12) Marine science

(13) Marketing and distribution

(14) Personal services

(15) Public services and transportation

The Office of Education's proposal is that elementary school youth be exposed to all fifteen clusters in developing awareness of the world of work, but that they select fewer occupations for deeper exploration at the junior high school level, ultimately leading them to choose and train in one occupation at the senior high school level or beyond. However, there are many alternative ways to cluster occupations and other effective ways to accomplish the awareness, exploration, and decision-making objectives.

Career education identifies a lengthy set of prerequisites for successful careers and attempts to contribute to their attainment: good mental and physical health, human relations skills, a commitment to honest work as a source of income, and a willingness to accept the discipline of the workplace and to be motivated toward achievement in the work setting. It also requires all of the basic skills of communication and computation and a fundamental familiarity with the concepts of science and technology, as well as actual or potential skills attractive to employers and in demand in the job market. Selection of such skills requires sufficient knowledge of the opportunities available in the labor market to make valid, though tentative, choices and the decision-making skills required for choices. Opportunities to use these skills also require an understanding of the workings of the labor market and an ability to compete successfully in it.

To give substance to the process of career education, each of the five components deserves brief discussion here.

A. Role of Teachers

Efforts of classroom teachers to emphasize career implications as part of good teaching are a major component in the new career education drama. In brief, this component aims to help students see some relationships between that which they are presently studying and the possible careers they may choose to follow. As such, it represents a form of educational motivation for the teacher to use in *conjunction with* any other motivational devices that have worked effectively in the past.

Career education does not seek to use this form of educational motivation to replace other effective motivational procedures that classroom teachers have always used. However, this form of motivation should appeal to all students some of the time and to some students almost all of the time, if it is incorporated with all other forms of educational motivation, so that students can learn more substantive content. For the teacher to emphasize the career implications of substantive content holds great potential for helping all students discover reasons for learning that are directly related to the world of work outside education.

This form of educational motivation is not intended to detract from the actual amount of time students spend in absorbing substantive content. Rather, the *time* required for providing this motivation comes from the total pool of time and effort available to every teacher for student motivation.

Thus career education in no way seeks to "water down" the substantive content of education. Instead, it seeks to assure that more such content will be meaningfully assimilated by the individual student.

B. Vocational Skills Training in Formal Education

The goal of this component is to provide students with occupational skills required to work successfully. The phrase "vocational skills training" rather than "vocational education" is used in part to emphasize the fact that the teacher of any subject in any classroom can provide vocational skills training for the prospective engineer or mathematician or skilled worker, just as a machine shop class is vocational skills training for the prospective machinist, the chemistry class for the pharmacist, and the home economics class for the *haute couturier* (Antonellis and James). In part, this phrase is used to emphasize the direct and substantial contributions of basic educational skills to occupational competence. That is, both teachers and students should recognize that when the student learns to read, he is acquiring skills that will be required for and useful in the work he will eventually pursue as an adult.

At least three false assumptions must be eradicated: (1) that students do not begin to ready themselves for work until after they leave the middle school and the junior high; (2) that at the secondary level, only that part of the school called "vocational education" exists to prepare students for work; and (3) that only students who lack the potential for successful college completion are getting ready for work while they are in the elementary and secondary schools.

Education as preparation for work must become an important goal of all who teach and all who learn. To provide this emphasis adds to the meaning and meaningfulness of all education without in any way detracting from any other worthy educational goal. At the same time we need to provide opportunities for specific vocational education in occupations which the school can teach most effectively. The notion that only middle-class occupations deserve attention in the school program is particularly pernicious and divisive.

C. *Career Development Programs*

This component, involving the efforts of all educators and those of many persons outside education, aims to help students understand themselves in terms of their values, interests, abilities, and accomplishments. Moreover, it seeks to help students see relationships between these kinds of self-under-standings and understandings of possible educational-occupational opportunities that are likely to be available to them. Finally, it seeks to help students make some kind of occupational or career decisions based on these kinds of understandings. In short, it represents career education's attempt to emphasize and make meaningful the inherent right of each individual to lead his own life, to control to the maximum extent his own destiny, and to see himself as the worthy and worthwhile person he is.

It should be clear at the outset that during the elementary school years, the career development component seeks no firm occupational commitment on the part of any individual. Rather, it seeks to help the student think about himself in relationship to the world of work and to try to picture himself as a possible contributing member of that world. In the middle school and junior high, the youth begins to focus on more specific interests, but is never encouraged to lock himself in or to reach more than tentative decisions. Even in the senior high school and beyond, flexibility, adaptability, and keeping open as many options as possible are emphasized, even though choices must be made and implemented.

D. *Efforts of the Business-Labor-Industry Community*

This component assumes that neither students nor educators can learn what they need to know about work or about the relationships between education and work by insulating themselves from the real world of work outside education. Observational work experience and work study opportunities for students and for those who educate students — teachers, counselors, supervisors, school administrators — would be an integral part of the education process.

For middle school students, this component is implemented primarily through observations of the world of work gained through field trips and through bringing business, industrial, and labor representatives into the middle school classroom. In the junior high, some work experience and broadened work observation are possible. This component also seeks to provide the teacher with opportunities to gain knowledge regarding the world of work outside education through actual work experience, as well as through observations made in that outside world. In part, this component seeks to supply those students who are leaving school for work with the means to make a successful transition from school to work. For all, it seeks the opportunity for exploration and realistic choices about the level of schooling to pursue and its relation to life-work and life-styles.

E. Home and Family

This component recognizes both the right and the responsibility of parents to care about and to influence attitudes which their children develop toward work, toward education, and toward the relationships existing between work and education. It sees the home as a place where work values and the dignity of all honest work can be taught. Furthermore, it recognizes that in addition to helping students get ready to earn money, we must also help them get ready to spend it, and so assigns a consumer education role jointly to the home and the school. Finally, it recognizes the need to help parents develop and apply means of positively assisting in the career development of their children in ways that will enhance rather than detract from the goals of career education.

THE NEED FOR CAREER EDUCATION

Multiple forces merge in the demand for career education. Society views with concern the high incidence of youth unemployment, the special employment problems of minority youth, the "opting out" of many youth from traditional norms, campus unrest, signs of worker alienation within employment, high educational expenditures, and rapidly rising productivity among competing nations with consequent balance of payments. Career education is not expected to provide a cure-all for these ills; but there is hope for positive contributions.

As for the education system — most criticism has been leveled at the "school for schooling's sake" tendencies and the worship of the college degree as the only really respectable entrance way into the occupational world. It is to be expected that to the educator, education might become an end in itself. However, society, which pays the bills, looks to education as a means to some larger and more important end. It is not enough for the elementary school teacher to concentrate upon preparing the youth for the junior high and so on up the educational ladder. Society expects preparation for something outside the schools — for successful living, including making a living. Success in the job market is not the only objective of education, but it is the one many parents and legislators recognize most readily.

The more than tenfold increase in education investment in a quarter century is enough to give most taxpayers pause. The college preparatory track is readily observed as the favored one by most school administrators, teachers, and staff. Only about 20 percent of jobs are filled by college graduates, yet educators and administrators attempt to justify college budgets to the taxpayers primarily as a way to prepare youth for a more attractive place in the occupational structure. Some reaction to continued emphasis on college attendance as more respectable than other avenues into work is to be expected. More harmful than the monetary cost is the social implication of telling four-fifths of school-leaving youth that they are somehow of lesser worth in society than those who attain a college degree.

Career education seeks to redress these imbalances without attacking the value of either academic education or college attendance. It holds that the schools must have as their goals contribution to the development of youth into the kind of adults who can find the greatest satisfaction and make the most useful contributions in their lives. To identify one of those ends in successful and satisfying working lives helps prevent mistaking means for ends. It helps keep the college role in perspective by declaring it to be only one of the respectable and effective alternatives available in preparing for life and life's work.

Advocacy of career education is also closely connected to a rising concern for the meaning of work in the lives of people. Unrest, dissatisfaction, even alienation have been evident in recent years, though it is still unclear whether the incidence is greater than in the past. Much of the debate as to what is happening to work values and worker attitudes starts with a confusion of terms.

Work must be defined as productive effort aimed at producing goods and services that will be beneficial to one's self or others. Whether or not one is paid for the work and whether or not one enjoys it are irrelevant to the definition. Anyone who thinks that a young person of today works less than she or he did at that age should not neglect to count the hours of homework and voluntary service activities of the younger set. There is nothing in the definition or reality of work to suggest that it must demand pay. A work ethic implies societal norms exerting pressure to undertake work. To say with some that the Protestant (or Puritan) work ethic, which allegedly built this country, is disappearing is not to charge that no other work ethic is taking its place. The previous work ethic was allegedly instrumental in the rise of capitalism because (1) it justified accumulation of wealth — salvation was by grace of God, not act of man, but the elect of God could prove their positions by demonstrating God's blessing to them in financial ways; and (2) it encouraged work and saving and discouraged conspicuous consumption — a perfect recipe for capital formation and economic development. But for a consumer economy, as contrasted to a capitalist one, excess savings can do positive harm. Work to enjoy work; serve through work; and work to spend — each is a form of work ethic. One *ought* to go to college and become a professional is as much a work ethic as one *ought* to work hard, save his money, and become a capitalist, or one *ought* to go to work early and work hard as a craftsman or industrial worker.

Work values lack the sense of "oughtness" of the work ethic. Even "I don't like work!" is a work value. Career education says: Each individual should be led to develop his own work values after becoming fully aware of the alternatives and the implications, rather than have them dictated.

As to whether the work role is diminishing among human values — there is no evidence, only speculation. So long as a feeling of self-worth is an essential *element* in personal happiness and is based largely on others' estimates of the individual's worth, and so long as our tendency is to judge each other largely in terms of our achievements, a life that does not include work is unlikely to be very satisfying to the individual or of worth to society.

"Career" itself is a confusing term. To us, it refers to the sum total of all the work done by a person in his lifetime. It may be a satisfying or an unsatisfying career, a more or less ideal career, but a career it is. It differs from an occupation in that an occupation is a component of a career at a point in time. A person's occupation or vocation is his major work activity at any point in time, whether paid or unpaid; and a career may be made up over a lifetime of many occupations or vocations.

Leisure is even more difficult to define. It is more than rest or pleasure. It carries with it the connotation of discretion — what a person chooses to do with his time when he is under no economic or other compulsion outside himself. A part of leisure may be spent in volunteer work, while commuting to work is hardly leisure (though it may be pleasurable).

Career education, then, attempts to help students understand the work ethics imposed by society; develops their work values based on their own personal interests in full awareness of society's demands; helps them become aware of the world of work and its values; explores the alternative occupations and careers available; and chooses, prepares for, and ultimately begins and pursues a career, including the possibility of occupational change and the hope for productive use of leisure during that career.

From career education, a stronger commitment to productive activity might emerge. There might be greater consistency between goals and action among youth. The later consequences of earlier choices might become more apparent. Attitudes and abilities of youth might be more attractive to employers, while youth might become more skilled at manipulating the labor market. Greater career satisfaction and fewer families in the poverty ranks might be a result. Among developing work values might be a greater commitment to service. Wiser career choices might lead to greater satisfaction with life-styles. More nearly ideal careers might emerge. There is no way to be certain that any or all of these objectives will be achieved. But there is little question that the probabilities should improve.

Despite these advocacies and possibilities, career education is not universally endorsed. There are those who argue that there is a declining amount of work to be done in society because of technological developments. Though totally without support from data, the myth is persistent. There are "humanists" who fear that a career emphasis will destroy "liberal education," failing to recognize that one cannot really claim to understand human society and his relation to it without an understanding of the work nexus. Increased emphasis on one aspect of life and society need not imply neglect of others. Some minority group representatives fear that career education could be used to foreclose college attendance for the poor, the visually different, and other groups against which society has often discriminated in the past. Their fears arise from career education advocates' arguments that college is not necessarily the best career preparation for everyone. "Just as we begin to get access to college educations, you say it isn't needed." The concern is understandable. Any educational program can be used as an agent of discrimination. However, career education's intent is to open options, not to close them. Career education does not argue against college training but only against the notion that other options and those who choose them are somehow "second class."

ROLE AND GOALS OF THE MIDDLE/JUNIOR HIGH SCHOOL

A critical point to be recognized by advocates, critics, and investigators alike of career education is that while it seeks to elevate career development concerns among education's legitimate goals, it does not intend to replace or supersede those goals. The junior high and the middle school have assignments in the development of young human beings which are not encompassed by career education, though career education can assist in the achievement of many of them and should conflict with none of them. Career education is *not* synonymous with vocational education, though it includes that as a key component. Perhaps it is worthwhile to include an illustration we have used before to clarify that career education, in our view, should not be expected to absorb all education. Nor should it all be expected to occur within the walls of the school. All teachers should teach some things that are of value in vocational education, career education, and the remainder of education, though each of the three types of education has successively broader goals (Figure 1).

Let us now review the role and goals of the junior high and middle school to make sure that approaches taken in career education do not conflict with but indeed support the existing curricula. The more prevalent junior highs, grades seven through nine, aim their attention at the years best described as "early adolescence," roughly ages twelve to fifteen; whereas the middle schools begin with grades five or six and continue through grade eight, therefore encompassing ages ten to fourteen and including those generally described as "pre-adolescent." Formerly, the eight-year grammar school (later followed by four years of high school) presumed that the bulk of the students would end their formal education with the eighth grade. In the grammar school they were to learn the three Rs plus enough about geography, history, music, and so on, to function reasonably well as citizens and members of society. The high school was a "prep" school to prepare the few who were headed for college. Indeed, at the beginning of the century, 80 percent of high school graduates did enter college, compared to the 50 percent we consider so remarkable today.

However, as the transition from family farming to industrial wage and salary employment reduced the economic role of youth, rising wealth made it possible to forego youth's present labor and invest in its future productivity. As the world became more complex, requiring longer study to understand it, universal high school became the goal and graduation the norm. (Society failed to give a clear change of signals, and many in education went on acting as if preparation for college were still the primary goal of high school.) Given mass high school attendance, the eight-year grammar school to four-year high school transition seemed too abrupt. The youth moved from home — where tutelage by parents and siblings was highly personalized — to a classroom (and sometimes the entire school) under the full-time attention and guidance of one teacher. Though the number of peers to replace the siblings expanded greatly, there was not a sharp break from the family setting. Then at the end of the eighth grade, the student was suddenly thrust into a highly impersonal setting of numerous specialists, each emphasizing subject matter, but he or she lacked enough time exposure to effectively pursue personal development. Providing essentially the same format for an age spread from six to fourteen or older but a sharply different format for fifteen to eighteen became an anomaly.

Later, the system changed almost universally to six years of elementary school followed by three years of junior high and three years of senior high. The junior high was to provide the transition needed to separate the early adolescent from the child, to ease into the subject matter approach, and to smooth the sharp edges of the dropout-prone entrance into the high school.

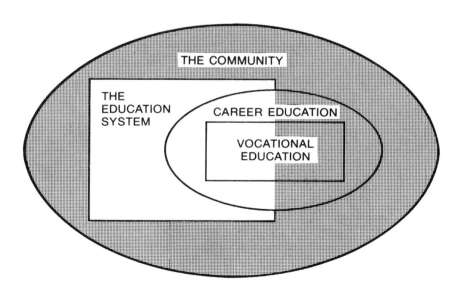

FIGURE 1. Career Education's Place in Education

But critics charged that the junior high was ill-designed for the task. It tended to take its title too seriously and was in fact a "junior" high school guided by subject matter specialists. The major difference, many complained, was that the junior high student had less discretion in the choice of classes. The middle school was offered as an alternative. Puberty was tending to arrive earlier; urbanization, television, and travel were producing a more sophisticated student; high schools were too committed to preparation for college, with the colleges pushing subject matter, as well as entrance requirements, and the junior high curriculum becoming crowded with subjects passed downward by the high school. A four-four-four or five-three-four division, it was argued, more closely supported the trends of personal development. Team teaching, flexible scheduling, individualized instruction, programmed learning, etc., could combine the advantages of and provide transition between the self-contained classroom of the elementary school and the specialization of the high school. Departmentalization could begin among the faculty and increase in the upper grades, yet be bridged by team teaching. Specialized courses which would be taught in a departmentalized structure in high school could be taught in an interdisciplinary manner in the middle school, with their subject matter interrelated and mutually supporting. A guidance program especially designed for the pre- and early adolescent was to be a typical middle school component along with a program of intramural sports and social activities less intense and competitive than that inherited by the junior highs from their older brothers.

Middle school advocates, of course, describe their system in terms of the ideals they hope to attain:

(1) An effort to combine the best features of the elementary school and its self-contained classrooms with the best aspects of the specialization of the secondary schools.

(2) At least three grades to provide for the transition from elementary methods to high school instructional procedures. Grades six and seven must be included, with none below grade five or above grade eight.

(3)   A movement toward departmentalization, more pro-
      nounced in each higher grade, to effect the change
      from the elementary self-contained classroom to the
      departmentalized structure of the high school.

(4)   Flexible approaches to instruction — team teaching,
      flexible scheduling, individualized instruction, inde-
      pendent study, programmed learning, and such other
      procedures as will help children learn how to learn.

(5)   Special courses, required of all students, usually taught
      in a departmentalized structure in such fields as indus-
      trial arts, home economics, foreign languages, art,
      music, and typing. These may be taught in an interdis-
      ciplinary manner such as unified arts, humanities, or
      exploratory fields.

(6)   A guidance program that is a distinct entity, espe-
      cially designed for the pre-adolescent and early adoles-
      cent, and one that is comprised of more than tests and
      record keeping.

(7)   An instructional program that emphasizes self-under-
      standing and includes units on the special concerns of
      young adolescents.

(8)   An observable, definite, and planned emphasis upon
      greater student self-direction and self-responsibility
      for learning. This requires extended use of independent
      study and student selection of activities of the indi-
      vidual's own choosing and design.

(9)   A faculty that is specifically trained for this age group
      and this sort of school. If this kind of teacher is un-
      available, then it is necessary to have teachers with
      both elementary and secondary certification or, at the
      very least, some teachers of each type.

(10) A program of interscholastic sports and social activ-
      ities that is substantially limited from that commonly
      found in the traditional junior high school (Howard
      and Stoumbis, pp. 198–99).

In actuality, the differences between the junior high school
and the middle school appear to be more in concept than in

practice. It is difficult to generalize. Some middle schools are only junior highs begun early; others merely approach the idea. Some junior high schools have every innovation advocated for middle schools, and others model themselves too slavishly after high schools — which try, in turn, to emulate colleges. Middle schools can be stodgy and junior highs innovative and exciting, or vice versa, depending more upon the philosophies and energy of teachers, administrators, and parents than upon concept. Only the age structure is fixed and that, given trends in physical and social development of children and youth, may signal the outcome of the contest between the two alternatives.

The critical point is the exploratory assignment of both types of schools, reflecting the needs of the age group they serve. Over twenty years ago, Havighurst identified ten developmental needs of adolescent youth which would probably still be well accepted:

(1)   To achieve new and more mature relationships with boys and girls the same age

(2)   To attain a feminine or masculine role socially

(3)   To attain emotional independence of adults

(4)   To accept one's physique and use the body effectively

(5)   To reach an assurance of economic independence

(6)   To choose and prepare for an occupation

(7)   To prepare for marriage and family life

(8)   To develop intellectual skills and concepts necessary for civic competence

(9)   To want and attain socially responsible behavior

(10) To acquire a set of values and an ethical system as a guide to behavior (Havighurst, 1953)

But the pre- and early adolescent is not ready to launch full-scale into all of these. Every child and youth will differ, but in general the child should be secure in his self-esteem as the recipient of the love of his family and the warmth of a familiar teacher and classrooom. Just learning the rudimentary psychomotor and social skills of life absorbs energy and attention. A little later, chemical changes of the physical body, the buffetings of society outside the home, and enforced awareness of a complex world produce the uncertainties and self-doubt which lead to the question of early adolescence: *Who am I?*

Youth of this age are "increasingly able to draw conclusions from few and less concrete situations than are necessary in teaching...lower elementary school children. They learn fairly rapidly how to apply rules to specific situations and they become more skillful in solving problems in the mind" (Inhelder and Piaget, p. 332). They are capable of abstract thought but too concerned with themselves to give high priority to subject matter content in the use of that reasoning ability. That questing for self-image will continue throughout life. However, the maturing personality will make peace sufficiently with itself to look beyond and outward into the world and seek to understand it as well. Thus we have the differentiated assignments of various levels of education — basic skills and self-awareness in the elementary grades, exploration of self and society in relation to that self in the middle/junior high school, with the accumulation, evaluation, and application of knowledge assigned primarily to the secondary and post-secondary phases.

The three major functions of the junior high school have been listed as:

(1) To attack the common problems faced by young adolescents in our society, employing and improving command of basic skills and knowledge from many sources for this purpose

(2) To enrich and differentiate learning by exploration of vocational and other individual interests

(3) To assist the early adolescent to make satisfactory personal-social adjustment (Faurce and Clute, p. 16)

The exploration advocated for early adolescents is defined as "the technique of leading students to discover and explore their particular interests, aptitudes, and abilities so they would be able to make wise decisions regarding educational and vocational opportunities" (Howard and Stoumbis, p. 25). It should not be limited to a few courses, but should extend into every

subject in the curriculum. Exploration is to be provided by
a variety of in-class and extracurricular activities and accomplished by flexible methods of teaching, giving students opportunities to plan and choose those learning activities that are
interesting to them. Such exploration "helps keep students
in school and provides opportunities for students to find themselves in vocational, social, personal, recreational, and avocational pursuits" (Gruhn and Douglass, pp. 31–32).

The educational assignments of the middle school and the
junior high school are clear in theory, though — as in any
human endeavor — they sometimes get lost in practice. Many
pressures tempt both schools from their priority exploratory
assignments, but career education is exempt from that charge.
Students, having been preprogrammed by parents and rela-
tives, are old enough to ask: What am I going to be when I
grow up? But they are still too young and limited in experience to make firm career choices, and are restrained by law
from most forms of employment. Thus exploration of self in
relation to careers and work is the principal task of career
education at this stage.

All subjects taught in the middle/junior high school take
into consideration the characteristics of early adolescents,
including a desire to explore one's self in relation to possible
life-styles, vocations, and achievements. Career education is
not an addition to the curriculum and course content. It is
a process through which this exploration can occur so far as
productive achievement, career choice, and career performance
are concerned.

APPLYING CAREER EDUCATION CONCEPTS IN THE MIDDLE/JUNIOR HIGH SCHOOL

The concept that exploration and self-assessment are a
primary educational need of the pre- and early adolescent is
a key to grasping the role of career education in the middle
school/junior high years. But if that recognition goes no farther
than to encourage exploration of occupational alternatives,
career education's potential contributions will have been
shortchanged, and education in general will have been done
a disservice. The adolescent is yearning most to explore and

understand himself. The relevance of the outer world at this age lies not so much in what it can offer in terms of opportunities as in what it can "tell me about myself." Statistical data about job opportunities or even substantive knowledge of job content is less important than intuitive knowledge of the broader implications of a career. Every occupation carries with it more than pay, working conditions, and certain performance requirements. There is involved a total package of locations, acquaintanceships, values, self-identity, prestige, income, residence, standards of living, and amount and types of leisure-time activities which are best described by the term "life-style." All these are a part of the total when choosing the occupations which make up a career (or what one stumbles into in the absence of choice). The emphasis in career exploration should be on: What kind of life-style fits me? But youth can learn much more than that from career education properly done.

Whether one prefers involvement with people, data, or things is a relatively elementary level of career consciousness: Do I learn better through abstractions or by concrete experiences? Do I prefer to be a leader or a follower? Am I given to an all-absorbing interest in a dedicated pursuit of some goal, be it wealth, knowledge, or status? Do I have strong status needs? Am I prepared to pay the price of high achievement? Am I by nature intense or casual, competitive or cooperative, outgoing or inward looking? Is there reason for me to value one life-style over another? All of these are self-assessment questions to which career education can contribute answers.

Too often in practice, education becomes perversely structured relative to the psychological needs of adolescence. The elementary school treats the individual as a whole and unique being. The student spends the full day in familiar and integrated surroundings, the family and neighborhood, the classroom with the same teacher and fellow students, and knowledge at least can be and usually is incorporated as an interrelated continuum. School projects interrelate a variety of subject matters. Development of personality, the imparting of fundamental knowledge shared by all members of society, and the development of sound intellectual and social habits are the emphasis. Classroom learning is more likely to be from experience than is true in later school years. Content tends to be specific. Career education melds in smoothly under the direction of a committed teacher. Content can be related to real world activity, including adult role examples. The teacher has the exposure to probe the child's talents, abilities, and learning styles. Diagnosis and prescription are possible. It is now generally recognized at this level that intelligence is not fixed, that a variety of learning styles exists, and that success experiences and self-esteem are keys to freeing later learning ability. These potentials of the elementary school environment may not be entirely realized, but they are there. And career education can be smoothly introduced and can contribute to them.

Yet just when a widening exposure to the world begins to challenge the student's sense of wholeness, the school too often chooses to fragmentize him into the tight compartments of subject matter disciplines. With self-discovery as the need but separation into 45-minute rotating exposures to subject matter disciplines as the prescribed pedagogy, the need for career education is even greater but more difficult to design and initiate. Surveys of career education practices in middle schools and junior high schools find the exploration assignment taken seriously insofar as occupations are concerned, but too little self-exploration by youth of their own values in relation to work.

The U.S. Office of Education's fifteen career clusters are the focus of the exploration. Excellent programs of awareness in the elementary school and exploration in the middle/junior high school examine the occupations that cluster around the industries and major economic activities of these fifteen clusters. However, too often it is the clusters which get explored and not the needs and values of youth in relationship to the clusters.

One possible approach is to deal with occupational clusters which have industries as their focus. However, it is also conceivable to cluster occupations around aspects more meaningful to self-exploration: location (Where do I want to live?), personality (Do I prefer working with people, data, or things?), working conditions (Do I prefer inside or outside work, and so forth?). The results of the best of the cluster exploration programs are admirable. Students do learn a great deal about the world of work, but career education's potential for self-discovery is too often neglected, and the components beyond career exploration may be ignored. It is in visualizing herself or himself in an occupation, in trying on in imagination, if not practice, the entire life-style surrounding an occupation that the youth begins to understand himself, his preferences, and his potential. It is in testing his self-discipline, his commitment to a goal, his preferences for service and for material reward that the youth begins to test his developing values. For some, it is the career relevance which provides the motivation to try seriously to learn and achieve, and thus test academic mettle. For most, there is self-discovery in hands-on experience and in the learning of productive skills. In a time of growing independence and pulling away, increased understanding of home as a producing and consuming unit as well as a social and emotional unit may be an important and lasting perspective.

Yet there are advantages in the junior high school structure. It is true that it does tend to fragmentize the learning experiences, but it also has the advantage of exposing youth to a broadening range of adults of varied backgrounds and intellectual standards. Subject matter specialists can be more learned in and enthusiastic about their disciplines and often, but not always, about their relevance to the real world. Concentration on the rudimentary skills of reading, writing, spelling, and arithmetic can now give way to application in geography, history, social studies, science, and mathematics. Home economics and industrial arts can open avenues for exploration of hands-on physical skills, often a relatively new experience to those from white-collar homes. Art and music are equally new worlds to explore for many, and foreign languages can provide cultural explorations as well as mere memorization.

All of these are potential worlds to explore. But they can and should be vehicles for self-exploration as well. Where can I fit? What fits me? What is important to me? What is possible for me? What is probable for me? What must I do to get where I would like to go? — all are questions which should be raised and explored by the youth with the help of the teacher.

The stages and components of career education, then, are not merely tools for occupational choice and preparation. They are implements of self-exploration and academic motivation.

While teaching academic principles, the teacher can also emphasize the career relevancy of mathematics, English, science, history, geography, or social studies to motivate the students to learn of the world of work. Citizens' duties, parents' responsibilities, indeed any adult role in the real world (for which youth yearn) can also motivate and illustrate. Employing establishments and labor organizations can provide learning environments and experiences. But so can noneconomic community institutions... public agencies, legislatures, community action agencies, and so on ... as providers of services to the community as well as employers.

A workplace can be a stimulating learning environment, as can a museum. Any area, atmosphere, or locus that combines freedom and excitement with the information and the discipline necessary for learning is a proving ground. Vocational skills can be part of self-discovery, yet recreational and avocational skills are necessary too. And although the family and the home will always fill a vital role in the child's total education, youth will always strain against restraint, attempting to pull away from it.

At the middle/junior high school level, new actors appear on the educational scene with vital roles for career education. Across the broad range of teachers to which the youth are now exposed, all have personalities as well as subject matter to offer. Every teacher of elective subjects is a vocational teacher to someone in every class: the art teacher for the prospective artist, the music teacher for the prospective musician, the industrial arts and home economics specialists for careers that are manifold. Who knows who will be "turned on" by whom? Some academic skills are so integral to particular careers — mathematics for the engineer, for instance — that they too are vocational for some.

Of particular importance are three potentially new contributors to career education — the shop teacher, the home economics teacher, and the counselor. The role and need for the counselor in career education are obvious. Less obvious is the fact that more of the hands-on and real world orientation must leaven the lumps of academic teaching. The counselor — properly trained and committed — is the logical source of statistical data, but only with recent work experiences can the more intimate flavor of interpersonal, man/machine, and other relationships be passed on to the student. The industrial arts and home economics teachers are more likely to be world-of-work oriented than teachers of more academic subjects. Yet they can also offer a practicable, hands-on setting around which the academic subject matter can be melded and purveyed in a team-teaching setting.

In the chapters which follow, we illustrate, through concept and example, the potential and problems of career education for the ten to fifteen age group. The structure of the chapters consists of illustrations of the potential contributions of each of the faculty in the middle/junior high school to the attainment of career education's objective:

> ... helping all individuals to become familiar with the values of a work-oriented society, to integrate these values into their personal value systems, and to implement these values into their lives in such a way that work becomes possible, meaningful, and satisfying to each individual (Hoyt *et al.*, 1972, p. 1).

REFERENCES

Antonellis, Gerard P.; and James, George B. *Cross Discipline Planning.* Salt Lake City: Olympus Publishing Company, 1973.

Faurce, Roland C.; and Clute, Morrel J. *Teaching and Learning in the Junior High School.* Belmont, California: Wadsworth, 1961.

Gruhn, William T.; and Douglass, Harl R. *The Modern Junior High School.* New York: Ronald Press, 1956.

Havighurst, Robert J. *Human Development and Education.* New York: David McKay Co., Inc., 1953.

Howard, Alwin W.; and Stoumbis, George C. *The Junior High and Middle School: Issues and Practices.* Scranton, Pennsylvania: Intext Educational Publications, 1970.

Hoyt, Kenneth B.; Evans, Rupert N.; Mackin, Edward F.; and Mangum, Garth L. *Career Education: What It Is and How to Do It.* Salt Lake City: Olympus Publishing Company, 1972.

_____; Pinson, Nancy M.; Laramore, Darryl; Mangum, Garth L. *Career Education and the Elementary School Teacher*. Salt Lake City: Olympus Publishing Company, 1973.

Inhelder, Barbara; and Piaget, Jean. *The Growth of Logical Thinking from Childhood to Adolescence*. New York: Basic Books, Inc., 1958.

U.S. Department of Health, Education and Welfare, Office of Education. *Career Education: A Handbook for Implementation*. Salt Lake City: Olympus Research Corporation, 1972.

Nature of Career Development: Middle/Junior High School Years

The practitioner has been deluged with repeated suggestions that the career education curriculum for the middle school years be regarded as "exploratory." What does this mean? Why do people use this term? What is the rationale behind this kind of urging? It is apparent that many now working in middle school career education programs have been thrust into their positions without the benefit of extensive study of the career development literature. It is also apparent that the busy practitioner has little time to study this literature in depth. As a result, there is a need for a summary of viewpoints that practitioners can use, both as an abbreviated method of catching up on the literature and as a guide for any more intensive study they may be able to do. It is the purpose of this chapter to provide such a summary.

Those who study the literature (or even this summary) are likely to be confused unless they clearly understand the distinction between "vocation" and "career." "Vocation" is a term that covers such subjects as occupations, jobs, and positions of employment in the occupational world. It is the principal work role of an individual at any given time. When we speak about "career education," we include more than "vocational education" — even when "vocational education" is viewed sufficiently broadly to include vocations requiring a college degree. Rather, in "career education," we focus on *careers*. In our view, "career" can be defined as the totality of work one does in his or her lifetime. "Work" can be defined as conscious effort aimed at producing benefits for one's self or for others. One's career consists of the totality of one's work, that is of conscious efforts exerted during a lifetime aimed at producing benefits for one's self or for others. Since this includes many kinds of work activities in addition to those involved in one's primary work role, the term "career" is obviously a much broader term than "vocation." Similarly, since "work," as defined here, begins for most persons considerably before the time they assume a primary work role, one's "career" begins in the very early years and continues beyond the time one retires from a position of paid employment.

Although we expand both on the concept of "work" and of "career" in this book, there is no way in which the summary to be presented here can be thoughtfully considered unless these basic understandings are clear. Assuming that we have begun to do so, the materials to be summarized here have been divided into the following major sections: (1) a summary of other comprehensive attempts to review the career development literature, and (2) a summary of selected research studies bearing particularly on career development in the middle school years.

A SUMMARY OF SUMMARIES: FOUR MAJOR CONTRIBUTIONS

For the reader who is unfamiliar with career development literature, there are four basic documents that deserve careful study. In an effort to encourage their study, brief excerpts from each of these four documents are presented. Each of these documents was written by a major leader in the field of career development. Their words and thoughts deserve serious consideration by all.

Donald E. Super

If one person were to be named the "father" of the career development movement, it would be Dr. Donald E. Super,

Professor of Psychology, Teachers College, Columbia University. Super has been writing profusely on this subject since 1950 and has conducted the most extensive longitudinal research studies available to the field. In the first volume of *The Counseling Psychologist*, Super contributed the major writing of two sections: "Vocational Development Theory: Persons, Positions, and Processes" and "Vocational Development Theory in 1988: How Will It Come About?" The remainder of that first volume is devoted largely to critical reviews by other leaders in the field. The entire volume is worthy of the most careful study on the part of all who today are working in the area of career education. Here, only a few brief excerpts from these two sections by Super are presented, along with a few comments concerning their significance.

In the first of these two, Super has defined career as:

> ...the sequence of occupations, jobs, and positions occupied during the course of a person's working life. Careers actually extend beyond either end of the working life to include pre-vocational and post-vocational positions such as those of students preparing for work and of retired men playing substitute work roles (p. 3).

We do not find Super's definition of career to be basically at variance with ours in that he obviously includes unpaid as well as paid positions. All we have done is extend the concept slightly to include all work carried out by an individual — including that done while he or she is not occupying any particular, specified "position." The important point to be recognized, it seems, is that with either Super's definition or the one we have devised, it is clear that *any given individual has only one career*, although he or she may change positions, jobs, or vocations several times during his or her lifetime.

At times, some have accused Super of not including elementary school children in his views of career development. That such accusations are without a factual basis is illustrated by the following quotes from Super's first section referred to above:

> The career model of developmental vocational counseling is one in which the individual is conceived

of as moving along one of a number of possible pathways through the educational system and on into and through the work system. His starting point is his father's socioeconomic status (p. 3).

...This analysis led to the identification of the five familiar life stages: growth (childhood), exploration (adolescence), establishment (young adulthood), maintenance (maturity), and decline (old age) (p. 4).

Thus, while much of Super's writings are concerned with the exploration, establishment, and maintenance stages of career development, he certainly does include early childhood in his conceptual view.

Many of Super's views have obviously been influenced by the work he has carried out, over many years, in his famous "career pattern study." While much interested and concerned about the career development of junior high school age boys, Super has, on the basis of his study, apparently come to a general conclusion that specific vocational choice planning is not appropriate during the middle years. The following quotes, from the first section of *The Counseling Psychologist*, illustrate this point:

...the level of vocational development attained by these 9th grade boys strongly suggested that they were not ready to make sound vocational or *prevocational* decisons. They had not attained an understanding of themselves or of the work which would justify deciding on curricula leading toward certain types of occupations rather than toward others...(p. 5, emphasis added).

...These data suggest, furthermore, that the realism of the late teens is more the reality of the self, of its abilities and interests, than that of opportunities beyond the realm of personal experience (p. 5).

...Only 16% of the 12th graders had the same specific occupational preference as in 9th grade, and 22% aimed at the same field of work at a different level. Only 13% were strongly committed to their vocational preference, 18% were only moderately committed, and more than 68% minimally (p. 5).

...Until there is more compelling evidence, it seems necessary to conclude that the vocational development of 8th and 9th graders [career pattern study data] and that of 10th graders [study findings] have not progressed sufficiently for directional vocational decision-making. Even in the 12th grade [study data] there appears to be only a limited basis for sound directional vocational decision-making in the majority of students. *Exploration is more relevant than training* (p. 6, emphasis added).

More than any other individual, Super, because of his career pattern study, is responsible for policy decisions leading to the middle school years as being regarded as "exploratory" in today's current career education programs. It is readily recognized by those acquainted with this study that the research was essentially conducted on white, middle-class suburban boys, and thus may not be universally applicable in its conclusions. At the same time, it is difficult to conceive that conclusions would be opposite in nature for other possible subpopulations of middle school age students.

It should be further recognized by those now working in the career education movement that Super's research was conducted in the absence of a comprehensive career education program. We do not yet know what conclusions it may be legitimate to draw thirty years from now, assuming that longitudinal studies are conducted in environments where a kindergarten through adult career education emphasis has been present.

Henry Borow

For many years, Dr. Henry Borow, University of Minnesota, has engaged in scholarly studies of career development research. In 1965 he presented a paper at the Airlie House Conference on Vocational Aspects of Counselor Education titled "Research in Vocational Development: Implications for the Vocational Aspects of Counselor Education." Borow very carefully attempted in that paper to summarize research findings that could be said to represent knowledge in the area of career development. Thus it seems appropriate here to quote several excerpts from his paper. Using a 41-item research bibliography, Borow includes the following generalizations:

> A number of motivational traits and response styles are acquired in the early formative years of personality development which, while not yet converging upon occupation, would appear to shape the course and effectiveness of the broad career pattern.... Among these may be mentioned coping and mastery behavior, habits of industry, personal autonomy, and achievement orientation (p. 74).

The research literature on which Borow based this generalization forms much of the rationale for career education activities in the elementary school:

> Children appear to acquire powerful prestige stereotypes of occupations from the general culture without having to learn them formally or deliberately. ...Children thus assimilate negative views of many occupations as they move through middle and late childhood (p. 75).

The research Borow refers to as a basis for this generalization points to the middle school years as those when children are most apt to acquire the occupational stereotype biases of the adult culture. Certainly, if this is true, many implications exist for the nature and goals of career education programs at the middle school level. He further states:

> Younger children do not appear to distinguish between occupational aspirations and occupation expectation. For a second or third grader to want a certain vocation is tantamount to having it...self-estimated and objectively determined scores on interest, aptitudes, and values, *in that order*, converge on one another between the ninth and twelfth grades.... Many studies agree with Schmidt and Rothney's finding that vocational choices fluctuate fairly commonly during the high school years...devoting the counseling of junior high school students to an evaluation of the wisdom of stated vocational choices or to the working out of specific vocational choices seems unjustified...academically less successful students and those of low socioeconomic status [scale] down their

expectations considerably more than is typical of academically successful students and of subjects from higher-level socioeconomic backgrounds (p. 76).

While the research Borow quotes in making these generalizations includes Super's career pattern study, his research goes considerably beyond Super's study and largely confirms the latter's generalizations quoted earlier. The final quotes from Borow, for those who are inclined to criticize Super's samples, seem particularly germane:

> The quantity and quality of occupational information generated by children at both elementary and secondary school levels are distressingly poor... children of high intelligence and upper social class membership are somewhat better informed about their preferred occupations than are other samples of students... a national sample of boys aged 14 to 16 years reports that only 18 per cent of the subjects possessed a clear picture of the steps which would have to be taken to qualify for their chosen field... in general, the rate of vocational development is associated with social class status. Culturally disadvantaged and delinquent youth evince slower and more sporadic development... (p. 78).

The kinds of evidence Borow quoted in making the above generalizations clearly form part of the rationale for need for career education programs for *all* students. The evidence also points to a need for special provisions in career education programs for disadvantaged students that, as of now, has not been much in evidence in career education programs throughout the country.

> ...it is very questionable whether objective and factual occupational information *per se* is as potent a determinant of occupational preference and aspiration as the broadly framed images of jobs as social ways of life.... Respondents in both American and British surveys cite outside work experience as highly influential in the making of definite overt vocational decisions, especially so when the outside jobs have been in a field related to the preferred occupation.... In Slocum and Empey's studies in the state of Washing-

ton, students were more likely to point to outside work experience than to persons as the single most important factor in choice...(p. 79).

The above generalizations are based on a considerable body of research and form much of the basis for the career education rationale, placing high emphasis on a project approach to career education that exposes students of middle/-junior high school age to work and to workers outside the walls of school.

Samuel H. Osipow

Dr. Samuel H. Osipow, Professor of Psychology, Ohio State University, has been both a valuable contributor to and summarizer of the research literature in the field of career development. Two of Osipow's attempts to summarize current knowledge in career development seem especially appropriate to be recommended to readers of this book. The first is "What Do We *Really* Know about Career Development?" and the second is "Implications for Career Education of Research and Theory on Career Development." Although the second paper incorporates much of the basic content found in the first, we quote from both papers below, identifying them as we go. In addition to the concepts embodied in these excerpts, Osipow does a masterful job of summarizing some current major theories of career development in the second paper. Since we will attempt no such concentration on career development theories here, readers interested in that topic are especially urged to study Osipow's paper for a summary view and a list of basic references.

In the second paper he asks us: "What do these theories tell us about vocational development that is significant?" and then proceeds to explain:

> ...there is something systematic about career development although it may be culturally defined to a large extent...preferences come about in a developmental manner which may be facilitated by the particular tasks that an individual is confronted with by significant institutions...while, in general, career pref-

erences move in a narrowing direction, in adolescence they are still broad, relatively undifferentiated, and rather changeable...a reasonably good technology exists which permits certain large-scale predictions to be made about vocational environments that might be suitable to individuals.

And in the first paper, he informs us:

Career development is characterized by change...of two types. One type [is] within the individual, as a function of his age and experience, [the other] external to the individual...as a function of changing economics and changing occupations....The early emphasis and attention to early career development continue during maturity.

...Career choice is typically accompanied by anxiety in our culture...people worry about making a mistake with respect to the choice of their career....Gribbons and Lohnes...found that although much growth in readiness for vocational planning occurs between eighth and tenth grade, a great many decisions are based on irrelevant information and facts.

...Abilities play an important role in career development...certain kinds of work require minimal and distinctive kinds and levels of abilities....In our culture the role of interests in career choice tends to be overemphasized....In point of fact, people are more likely to end up doing what they are capable of doing than they are to end up doing what they like to do if there is some inconsistency between the two...there is some evidence to indicate that preferences, in fact, are influenced by success...instead of the reverse.

...It is important to give proper emphasis to the interaction between the individual and his environment...certain types of individuals are more easily influenced by their environment in their career choice persistence than others...some environments are more likely than others to produce change...environmental types interact significantly with personality types to influence change and persistence...individuals frequently tend to see themselves as having changed in a way that conforms to the environmental norm.

Once more we turn to the second paper to read:

> ... Perhaps the most important ... is the need to develop programming which is not too rigid or too tightly conceived ... the very early and crucial years can be spent, not in leading the child to develop a specific vocational preference, but rather to help him develop certain fundamental attitudes which will enable him to make necessary decisions later on in a more suitable manner ... it is not realistic to expect an individual to choose a career in ninth grade, to train for it, and assume that the issue is forevermore closed ... the stability of field preferences during the high school years suggests a way out of this dilemma by means of education through occupational clusters, the heart of the Office of Education career education programs that are emerging today.

The thirty basic references found at the conclusion of Osipow's paper will, if studied carefully, provide much documentation for his generalizations. It seems to us that in this literature review, Osipow has provided a substantial research base to those career education practitioners who want to keep career options open for middle school age youth, who want to emphasize use of the broader community in career education efforts, and who want to emphasize work values, work habits, and work attitudes in their middle school years career education programs. His entire paper is worthy of very careful study.

Edwin L. Herr

Dr. Edwin L. Herr, Professor of Education, Pennsylvania State University, more than any other single individual, is responsible for introducing the concept of infusion of career education concepts within the total school curriculum. He made this proposal, based on an extensive review of the career development literature, in his paper "Unifying an Entire System of Education around a Career Development Theme." The paper, while not summarized here, is highly recommended to all.

In 1972, Dr. Herr was commissioned by the Center for Vocational and Technical Education, Ohio State University, to prepare the monograph *Review and Synthesis of Foundations for Career Education,* in which he incorporated much of the content of the earlier paper, along with an extensive literature review. The following quotations represent excerpts of generalizations Herr made concerning our assumptions of career development. They are based on his review of the literature related to theories of career development:

> ...Career development is an ongoing process which extends from infancy through at least young adulthood. Thus, the time when programs mounted to intervene in career development should begin is during the first decade of life.... Career development can be described in terms of learning tasks, frequently culturally defined, which are important at each stage of development.... Individuals differ in their readiness for career development [and] these differences...are complex. Differences in readiness suggest the need for different types of experiences to be available at any given educational level.... Career development is modifiable [thus] the structure of the school, the timing of decision points, cultural expectations can each affect the unfolding of career development.... The attitudes, knowledge and skills which make up career development should weave through and be reinforced by many educational experiences and the attitudes of those who monitor the experiences.... A displaced or unemployed adult may be as illiterate in terms of career as an elementary child.

While Herr identifies the above as "assumptions" based on "theories of career development," it seems obvious from the earlier summaries of research presented above that Herr's "assumptions" are, almost without exception, firmly grounded in a research base. His discussion of various theories of career development that precedes these generalizations is well worth reading. Readers of this book will also be greatly interested in Herr's careful analysis of existing programs of career education at the elementary, junior high, and senior high school levels that is found in earlier parts of this monograph. As a useful summary of the historical base, current practices, and popular theories, Herr's monograph should be carefully studied by all those who work in career education.

RESEARCH RELATED TO CAREER DEVELOPMENT
IN THE MIDDLE SCHOOL YEARS

The most definitive longitudinal research program related to career development of persons beginning in the middle school years is the career pattern study by Donald E. Super. Some conclusions from this study were quoted in the preceding section of this chapter. The definitive research, while too voluminous to be reviewed here, can be found in a book authored by Super and Overstreet. Rather than undertake a very lengthy review of this research, we find it more appropriate to refer readers to this book.

Gribbons and Lohnes

A second longitudinal career development research program is that originally initiated by Warren D. Gribbons, who was later joined by Paul R. Lohnes. This is known as the "career development study" and is often contrasted in the literature with Super's career pattern study. The basic reference here is a book written by Gribbons and Lohnes titled *Emerging Careers*.

The first of these is an article by Gribbons reporting early results of the study. The basic sample consisted of 111 eighth grade students (57 boys and 54 girls). Gribbons administered an eight scale instrument which he calls "readiness for vocational planning" to these students when they were eighth graders and again when these same students were in tenth grade. He found statistically significant differences on each of the eight variables, indicating, in general, a greater "readiness for vocational planning" on the part of tenth graders than for those same students when they were in the eighth grade. He also found several of the eighth graders to be above the tenth grade norms, and several tenth graders below the eighth grade norms — thus demonstrating rather convincingly that large individual differences in career development do in fact exist for students of varying ages, and that there is no single pattern universally applicable to any grade level. He concluded from these data that some eighth graders are ready to make vocational decisions.

This tentative conclusion was reinforced by further research (Gribbons and Lohnes, 1965, pp. 248–52). In this research, using the same sample of students, these men report student choices of twelve different kinds of work values as given when the students were eighth graders, then as tenth graders, and then as twelfth graders. They found that of the twelve kinds of work values, "interest" and "satisfaction" ranked as the top two at all three grade levels. They found some sex differences in work values, with girls more "people oriented" and boys more "extrinsic-reward oriented," although correlations of work values at each of the three grades were around 0.50. While some shifting in work values was seen between eighth and twelfth grades, there were also important patterns of consistency which, to us, appear to be brought about largely because of the relatively high ranking for "satisfaction" and "interest" at all three grade levels.

After examining the data reported in this 1965 study, Gribbons and Lohnes were led to conclude:

> Our interpretation of our data is that the constancy it shows bespeaks a maturity of self-concepts early in the eighth grade sufficient to justify close attention from counselors at that time while the shifts testify to a healthy maturation during adolescence...boys and girls appear to be rather alike in their employment of vocational value categories...it would seem that counselors should assist young people at an early age to an increased awareness of their personal value hierarchies, to the improvement of their values, and to the integration of their values and their aspirations and plans.

The third study reported on nine-year career patterns followed by these same 111 persons from whom initial data had been collected when they were eighth graders (Gribbons and Lohnes, 1969, pp. 557–62). In this study, they looked at four predictors of adult occupational aspirations and achievements (sex, socioeconomic status, I.Q., and vocational maturity) as they operated over a nine-year period. They used a single scale which represented a combination of their eight previous readiness for career planning scales as the measure of vocational maturity. Their findings indicated that sex and readiness were the strongest predictors from the eighth through the twelfth grades, whereas socioeconomic status and intelligence became the better predictors of adult occupational aspirations and achievements in the years following high school graduation. In discussing their findings, they observe the following:

> It is, of course, well known that socio-economic status and IQ are among the best predictors of adult occupational aspirations and achievements. What is seen in this data is how in early adolescence the variables of sex and vocational maturity (or planfulness) take precedence over these reality factors.

On the basis of their data, they concluded that vocational maturity scaled in early adolescence (eighth grade) *is* related to career aspirations on into early adulthood in ways that complement the relations of sex, socioeconomic status, and intelligence.

It should be noted that Gribbons and Lohnes report no data contradicting Super's cautions regarding specific vocational planning with youth during the middle school years. Rather, their data have led them to plead for greater attention to problems of work values among middle school age youth, greater systematic assistance in value clarification on the part of school personnel at the middle school level, and greater flexibility in career development programs reflecting the marked individual differences in vocational maturity indicated by the data they have collected from the 111 subjects in their longitudinal study. It seems to us that their career development studies lend definite credence to the concept of vocational maturity as a developmental phenomenon and pose definite challenges to persons working in career education programs, at the middle school level, to devise means of furthering vocational maturity among their students.

Examples of Research Demonstrating the Presence of Occupational Stereotypes

Several of the research generalizations mentioned earlier indicated that, by the time students reach the middle school years, they have essentially the same kinds of occupational stereotypes biasing them in favor of some occupations and against others as do their parents and other adults. Here, we will illustrate, with two studies, the kinds of investigations that have led to this generalization.

One type is aimed at comparing the prestige rankings assigned various occupations by youth as opposed to adults. An example is a study in which fourth, eighth, and twelfth grade students were asked to rank twenty occupations on a prestige scale and to express their interest in entering each (Simons, pp. 332–36). The prestige rankings given by these students, separately by sex and grade level, were compared with those that other researchers had obtained earlier for a variety of adult samples. For boys, even at the fourth grade level, prestige rankings correlated 0.868 with adult prestige rankings and rose to 0.937 by the eighth grade level. While girls in the fourth grade showed only a moderate rank correlation (0.538) with adult rankings, these correlations increased to 0.936 by the eighth grade.

It is studies such as this that have led some career development experts to contend that youth learn about occupational stereotypes as they progress through school. These studies do not, of course, prove that they learned such occupational biases while in school or from their teachers. They do, however, point to a need for the school's career education program to actively work to reduce occupational stereotyping where possible.

A second type of study in this area is one aimed at examining directly possible contributions schools are making toward giving students the same kinds of occupational stereotypes seen in the adult society. An example of this is a study at the elementary school level (Tennyson and Monnens, pp. 85–88). In this study, the researchers examined elementary school readers commonly used in grades one through six in schools throughout the United States. After studying 13,344 pages of 54 readers published by six different companies, they discovered that when occupations are mentioned, professional and managerial occupations are discussed most frequently. They concluded that a marked discrepancy existed between the frequency with which various occupations were mentioned and the proportions of people working in them, and that these textbooks are creating stereotypic images which are both unrealistic and unrepresentative. Further, they could find no differences in materials published by these six major publishing houses. Apparently, all were doing about the same thing.

This is an example of the type of study that has led people in career education to plead for a broader and more comprehensive view of the worth and dignity of all work to be presented to children beginning in the early elementary school years. In addition, this kind of study reinforces the suspicions of those who believe that the schools themselves are currently contributing to the presence of occupational stereotyping and could, if operating a comprehensive career education program, possibly use their influence on children in more positive and beneficial ways.

Examples of Research Demonstrating Socioeconomic Status of Parents on Occupational Choices

The influence of socioeconomic status, as reflected primarily in parental occupations, on the occupational aspirations of youth has been widely researched. The generalization made by the career development movement is that definite positive relationships do exist here — that the occupational aspirations of pupils will bear a positive relationship to the occupations in which their parents engage. We will illustrate the kinds of studies on which this generalization is based, using a few research investigations carried out with students at the middle school level.

One example is a study reported by Krippner in 1963 (pp. 590–95). In this study, data were collected from 351 seventh and eighth grade students, during the 1960–61 school year, in a junior high school located in an upper middle-class Chicago suburban community. Students were asked to state the occupations of their father and their mother, to state their own tentative occupational choices, and to report the occupational choices that represented what their parents would like them to choose. It was found that statistically significant relationships existed between father's occupational level (using Roe's classification system) and the preferences of both boys and girls for various levels of occupational choice. Further, it was found that statistically significant relationships existed between the occupational preferences of girls and their mothers' occupations (where mothers were employed outside the home).

Essentially, this demonstrates that where parents are engaged in occupations that require a college degree, their children tend to have occupational aspirations that also call for them to go to college. This, of course, is not a new revelation to practicing counselors who have observed this happening for years. It does illustrate, however, the need for an emphasis in career education for broadening the occupational horizons of all students to maximize their freedom for choosing careers from the widest possible range of opportunities. Career education does not seek either to ignore or to destroy this relationship. Rather, it seeks to make it possible for this relationship to be modified if this is what students really choose to do.

A second study, illustrating the opposite end of the continuum, involved a study of 179 ninth grade girls enrolled in a technical high school in a large midwestern city (Lee and King, pp. 163–68). The school was situated in a relatively low socioeconomic community with a large black population. Most of the fathers were engaged in unskilled and semiskilled labor. Of the mothers, 92 were houseworkers and unskilled workers. No data were collected directly from parents. Instead, only the girls themselves were questioned. After analyzing and discussing their statistical findings, the authors say:

> The overall picture for girls seems to be this: Mother and father come from the same occupational level, but the girls aspire to occupations having more prestige than either of them. Fathers want their daughters to enter higher level occupations than the mothers do, but the girls side with the suggestions of their mothers in their own preference of occupational levels. However, when the girls determine their life's work, they expect to exceed the actual occupations of both father and mother, but the girls do not expect actually to reach the occupational level that their mothers wish them to, or that they (themselves) prefer. All this occurs in a setting in which both mother and father wish their daughters to attain an occupational level that carries more prestige than one attained by the

parents. The girls are not influenced one way or the other by having their mothers work outside the home.

Translated, what these researchers found was that, while both parents and their daughters from low socioeconomic levels desire to have these girls engage in occupations at higher prestige levels than those of their parents, the girls themselves do not actually expect to move up as far as either they or their parents feel is desirable. Again, this illustrates both the very marked influence of parental occupational level on occupational plans of their children and the challenge for career education to extend greater freedom of occupational choice to all students. As with the students in Krippner's study, we cannot hope to eliminate the influence of level of parental socioeconomic status, but we can certainly be aware of and work actively to give the student a wider variety of options.

An early study (Steinke and Kaczkowski, pp. 101–03) examined occupational choices of 100 ninth grade girls, their mothers' preferences for their daughters' occupational choices, the mothers' current occupations, and occupations of the grandmothers. Afterward, the researchers introduced an eight-week unit on occupations and then reassessed occupational preferences of these ninth grade girls. Prior to the unit, they found a 76 percent agreement between occupational preferences of these girls and the preferences their mothers had for them.

Of all factors they studied as influencers of occupational choices of these girls, they found "parents" to be the greatest influence. After the eight-week unit, they found 29 of the 100 girls had made changes in their occupational preferences, with such changes being described by the authors as "consistent with the mothers' occupational preferences." This of course is exactly the opposite of what we would consider a desirable outcome of career education. If we cannot effectively provide alternatives to parental occupational levels as an influence of their children's occupational choices, we certainly shouldn't reinforce it! Other positive results are reported in chapter 3, which is devoted specifically to descriptions of career development programs as part of career education.

The natural tendency for parental expectations to increasingly influence occupational preference of their children is illustrated in a study reported by Perrone in 1967 (pp. 268–74). He had initially administered a value-orientation instrument to 196 seventh and eighth grade girls and to parents of those girls. This study involved a second administration two years later to these same groups. He found that expressed work values of both students and their parents changed during the two-year period, that differences between work values of boys and girls tended to become greater, and that both boys and girls tended to express work values correlating higher with work values expressed by their parents than he had found when these students were in the seventh and eighth grades.

Again, we see demonstrated the fact that when no active career education program is in operation, both sex stereotyping of occupations and the influence of parental socioeconomic status seem to have increasing influence on occupational values of youth during the secondary school years. Perhaps when career education programs are evaluated, we should consider "success" to be present when these correlations simply remain unchanged over a period of time! This study well illustrates both the seriousness of the problem and the operational difficulties we face in trying to solve them.

Samples of Research Illustrating Career Development as a Growth Process

Almost without exception, career development theorists have pictured career development as a maturational process beginning in early childhood and continuing through the adult years. A considerable body of research evidence exists which demonstrates that this is one theoretical concept that can be backed up by some fairly solid evidence. Here, we will illustrate this kind of research by again drawing on a few studies that have involved students in a middle or junior high school setting.

Helen Astin reported in 1968 on a major study involving 7,061 girls from the Project Talent data bank in which career choices made by these girls while in ninth grade were compared with those they made one year after the time they were due to graduate from high school (pp. 961–66). In addition to simply demonstrating change over time, Astin also studied the effect of aptitude and interest measures on the direction of such changes. She found that girls who changed their career choices in fields that require college degrees on the average scored lower on scholastic aptitude tests than did girls who maintained their career choices in such fields during this five-year period. Similarly, when she studied vocational interests, she found that girls who changed their interests tended to score lower on vocational interest measures in the areas of their initial choices than did girls who maintained their interests in such fields. Both of these findings, in addition to illustrating changes over time, also indicated a move toward increased realism on the part of these girls. If this kind of positive result can be observed in the absence of a comprehensive career education program, it would certainly seem that even more dramatic positive results should be obtainable when evidence is finally in on the results of career education programs that were solidly conceived and operated effectively from kindergarten through early adulthood.

A study bearing more directly on the concept of career development as a maturational phenomenon was reported by Montesano and Geist in 1964. These researchers, using the Geist "picture interest inventory," collected data from 30 ninth and 30 twelfth graders. They then asked these students to state their occupational preferences and their reasons for choosing such occupations. Their results indicated that the twelfth graders used a greater variety of reasons for occupational choices than did the ninth graders. This led them to conclude that their results lend some credence to the concept of vocational "development" as maturation.

Some studies in this area — rather than being longitudinal in nature, involving multiple data collections over a period of years from the same group of subjects — are cross sectional in that the same questions are asked of subjects of varying ages. One example of this type of study is a cross-sectional survey reported by Hollender, involving students in grades six through twelve. All these students were asked the question: What occupation do you plan to enter? His findings indicated that:

(1) Significantly more girls than boys reported having made vocational choices.

(2)   The percentage of boys reporting definite vocational choices was greater in both elementary school and in senior high school than during the junior high school years.

(3)   Students who scored higher on scholastic aptitude tests made more vocational choices, on the average, than did students who scored low on such measures.

(4)   Roughly 30 percent of these students entered adolescence undecided about their career choices, and by the end of the senior high school, about 30 percent were still undecided.

(5)   Decisiveness of vocational choice appeared to be much more closely related to grade in school than to age of the students (which he attributed more to parental than to school influence).

This excellent study illustrates some of the complexities involved in the career *development* concept. For example, it should be of great interest to persons working at the middle school level to discover that fewer pupils had vocational choices there than at either the elementary or the senior high school level. Their development may have been positive enough to cause them to reject some of the fantasy choices made during the elementary school years, but still insufficient to make choices that students in senior high school could make. Furthermore, to discover that roughly the same percentage of students was undecided relative to vocational choice at the twelfth and ninth grade levels does not mean that no career development had taken place, or that the same students were undecided at each level. Both of these examples illustrate why it is imperative to be cautious when interpreting data. This is one study that many readers may want to examine further.

Some aspects of career development do not typically exhibit great variability during the elementary and secondary school years. The most notable illustration is in the case of work values. A study illustrating this was reported in 1972 by Hales and Fenner (pp. 199–203), in which 36 fifth graders, 54 eighth graders, and 26 eleventh graders from a southeastern Ohio town were involved. The students were described by the authors as "disadvantaged." They were given an experimental form of the Ohio "work values inventory" (the inventory itself is described in the article). After presenting the findings, the authors observed:

> ... Results revealed that the development of values related to work is well under way for most children by the fifth grade, and that eighth graders as a group display value profiles not unlike those of their younger counterparts... differences exist between the 12th grade subjects and the 5th and 8th grade subjects on two of the ten scale variables. With these two exceptions, the profiles of all three grade levels are notable for their similarity.

Flores and Olsen, in a study they conducted, report high similarity in "level of occupational aspiration" between eighth graders and students in the eleventh and twelfth grades (pp. 104–12). They were interested in the question of whether or not the level of occupational aspiration of eighth grade students is sufficiently stable to justify choosing for themselves a high school curriculum or program that is designed to contribute toward the occupational goals they stated in the eighth grade. To do so, the researchers administered the occupational aspiration scale designed by A. O. Haller to 31 twelfth graders, 33 eleventh graders, and 36 eighth graders, each sample having a random sample of all students in such grades in the schools in which the study was carried out. This same instrument was then readministered to all subjects that could be found six months later. Thus it was possible to compare both actual level of aspiration scores in terms of differences at various grade levels and stability of the level of aspiration at each grade level. They found no significant differences between eighth graders and the two older samples of students. In discussing their results, they say:

> ... As a result of this study, it can be said that the LOA [level of aspiration] of eighth grade males, since it closely resembles the LOA of eleventh grade males, is probably sufficiently realistic and well formed to allow eighth grade males to make valid choices of seconday school courses and curriculum. Although there

were differences in LOA noticed between the eighth grade males and the two older groups, the impressive factor was the similarity between the two groups.... The results of this study indicate that LOA is probably formed in eighth grade males and is possibly one of the first stable and realistic occupational considerations formed in young people.

We would raise serious objections to the authors' use of the word "realistic" as quoted above. At the same time, it is important to point out the close similarity in *nature* of level of aspiration noted in these three groups of students and in their stability of measurement over a six-month period. Those who study this reference carefully will note that they found *stability* of level of occupational aspiration to be higher for eighth graders than for the two older samples, thereby indicating the possibility that a part of the career development process may be changes at those points in time when one is faced with the necessity of implementing a particular level of aspiration through actions he takes.

An interesting contrast is to be found in two studies Droege has reported in the realm of occupational aptitude testing (1966, pp. 919–30; 1968, pp. 668–72). Droege, who worked for the United States Employment Service, was interested in the practical possibilities of being able to use the "general aptitude test battery" with ninth grade students in career guidance and counseling. During the early 1960s, the employment service conducted an extensive aptitude test, longitudinal maturation study. Droege, in his 1966 article which reported on results of that investigation, said:

> The results show clearly that these individual differences have an adverse effect on aptitude stability, with some individual aptitudes and some OAP's [occupational aptitude patterns] having stability coefficients that are too low to be considered useful in counseling in lower high school grades.

He also found difficulty establishing suitable stability coefficients for the aptitude test scores with his ninth grade samples with only those for factors G, V, and N being consistently 0.75 or higher for both boys and girls at the ninth grade level. He further found, as expected, steady increases in mean aptitude scores between ninth through twelfth grade samples of students and demonstrated rather convincingly that the *maturation* effect was greater than the *practice* effect. In his 1968 study, he investigated the aptitude test intercorrelation matrices collected from ninth grade samples, compared with those obtained from twelfth graders, and found the intercorrelation matrices essentially similar in nature. On the basis of that study, he observed:

> A reasonable conclusion to be made from these results is that, although there are some small changes in the interrelationships of GATB aptitudes from the ninth to the twelfth grade, the overall picture is one of relative stability of aptitude interrelationships from the ninth to the twelfth grade.

Thus while the 1966 study demonstrated that scores of ninth graders on aptitudes are expected to increase, on the average, each year up to the twelfth grade (at least), and that ninth grade aptitude scores have realitively low stability, when total aptitude patterns are studied, the intercorrelations found at the ninth grade level are similar to those found at the twelfth grade level. The vocational maturation concept is extremely well illustrated here.

These six examples were chosen not only because they involved middle school age students, but also because they illustrate something of the complex nature of the total career development process. It does not appear to be orderly and neat in all of its aspects.

Two additional examples may be used to further illustrate this point. The first is a study of disadvantaged Appalachian youth in four rural eighth grades in the state of Kentucky (Asbury, pp. 109–13). In this study, a combination of a vocational maturity measurement, an occupational aspiration scale, and scores on standardized intelligence and achievement tests was obtained from these students and then contrasted with national norms. While these students were found to be significantly below the national norms on measures of vocational maturity, intelligence, and achievement, they were not significantly different on measurements used to measure level of occupational aspiration. This may point to a need for special adaptations in career education programs for such youth.

The second study was designed to measure the amount of occupational information possessed by different samples of ninth grade boys and to examine whether this aspect of vocational maturity has any relationship to choice of senior high school curriculum (Krasnow, pp. 275–80). For purposes of this study, boys who had chosen an academic college preparatory curriculum were contrasted with boys who had chosen the vocational education curriculum. Results indicated that those who had chosen the college preparatory curriculum possessed more occupational information than those who had chosen the vocational education curriculum. At first glance, this may appear odd to those who recognize that by committing themselves to a vocational education curriculum, students who had done so were apparently more "locked into" vocational choices than those picking the college preparatory curriculum, and thus should have had more occupational information on which to base their decisions. However, when the data reported in this study are examined carefully, the very large differences in mean verbal ability scores between academic (73.4) and vocational (36.3) students make one wonder how the vocational students could have done so well — relatively speaking.

The Evans and Galloway study shows clearly that verbal ability and parental socioeconomic level are closely associated with both curriculum choice and knowledge of occupations. Few students of high socioeconomic status and high verbal ability choose the vocational curriculum, and few students of low socioeconomic status or verbal ability score high on paper and pencil tests of knowledge of the labor market (pp. 24–36).

CONCLUDING STATEMENT

In this chapter, we have attempted to summarize research generalizations in career development and to provide specific examples of research carried out with middle and junior high school age students that have contributed to such generalizations. It seems appropriate to conclude the chapter with a set of summary statements that represent, in our opinion, what research tells us about the expected career development status of middle and junior high school age youth.

1. These youth are in the process of attaining vocational maturity, but on the whole, can best be described as vocationally immature.

2. Considerable individual differences in vocational maturity can be expected to be found among middle and junior high school youth. One of the major factors (although not the sole factor) contributing to such differences is parental socioeconomic status. A positive relationship (but perhaps not a cause and effect condition) exists between parents' socioeconomic status and vocational maturity of middle and junior high school age youth.

3. Middle and junior high school age youth are not, by and large, ready for specific vocational or occupational decision making. *Career* exploration is more appropriate to emphasize than *occupational* decision making.

4. Middle and junior high school age youth arrive at their schools with occupational stereotypes very similar to those of adults in our culture. In the past, the elementary school has been one source of such stereotypes, which include both prestige and sex biases.

5. Work values of middle and junior high school age students do not differ greatly between boys and girls.

6. Occupational aspirations of middle and junior high school people are more influenced by sex of the student and less by I.Q. and socioeconomic status than can be expected when these students become adults. There is some evidence that the influence of sex stereotyping of occupational plans can be reduced through systematic intervention of career development programs.

7. Middle and junior high school age youth arrive at their schools with work values which, in the absence of intervention, are likely to remain remarkably stable through the twelfth grade.

8. For more than 70 percent of the students specific vocational choices expressed by middle and junior high school people can be expected to change before they reach the twelfth grade.

9. Most middle and junior high school students have attained a sufficient degree of career maturation to justify their

making curriculum decisions of a broad nature regarding their programs in the senior high school.

10. The vocational maturity of middle and junior high school students can be enhanced through systematic exposure to the world of occupations, sound counseling and guidance, and experience with work.

11. Abilities and aptitudes, while demonstrably important in vocational decisions made by adults, are not fully developed within most middle and junior high school age students.

12. Abilities, aptitudes, values, and attributes related to work, to occupations, and to careers are in process of development during the middle/junior high school years and may be affected markedly by career education programs.

The contents of this chapter must make very confused reading to those persons who have no previous acquaintanceship with the field of career development. However, despite the obvious areas of confusion, understanding is sufficient to lay the groundwork for a different view of career development as part of a comprehensive career education program.

We have seen that those persons considered to be leaders in the field emphasize that career development is a lifelong process, not a single event in a given period of time. This process, as seen through the research examples presented in this chapter, is complex, uneven, and quite different in nature for different individuals and for differing subcultures in our society. One's career development is obviously shaped by a combination of factors both within and outside the individual.

Career development as a process is indeed seen by almost all persons in this field to extend beyond the problems and processes of occupational decision making. It must seem strange to persons outside the field to observe how much of the literature of career development seems to have been devoted to problems of occupational choice. If there is any one thing that is eminently clear from what is known about this field, it is the futility of trying to provide directional vocational guidance to youth. It would be futile enough if only individual differences in career development were to be considered. When one adds consideration of the rapidity of societal change — including occupational change — the task of providing directional vocational guidance to middle school youth in these times seems insurmountable.

Thus it would seem that it is time for us to hear Super's pleas, first made more than twenty years ago, that we consider "careers" rather than "occupations." If a true "careers" emphasis is placed on the literature of career development, it is our feeling that the place of career development, in comprehensive career education programs, will become much clearer and more definitive.

REFERENCES

Asbury, Frank. "Vocational Development of Rural Disadvantaged Eighth Grade Boys." *Vocational Guidance Quarterly* (1968), vol. 17.

Astin, Helen. "Stability and Change in the Career Plans of Ninth Grade Girls." *Personnel and Guidance Journal* (1968), vol. 46.

Borow, Henry. "Research in Vocational Development: Implications for the Vocational Aspects of Counselor Education." *Vocational Aspects of Counselor Education.* Carl McDaniels, Editor. Washington, D.C.: George Washington University, 1966.

Droege, Robert C. "GATB Aptitude Intercorrelations of Ninth and Twelfth Graders: A Study in Organization of Mental Abilities." *Personnel and Guidance Journal* (1968), vol. 46.

———. "GATB Longitudinal Maturation Study." *Personnel and Guidance Journal* (1966), vol. 44.

Evans, Rupert V.; and Galloway, Joel. "Verbal Ability and Socioeconomic Status of 9th and 12th Grade College Preparatory, General, and Vocational Students." *Journal of Human Resources* (Winter 1973), vol. 8, no. 1.

Flores, T.; and Olsen, L. "Stability and Realism of Occupational Aspiration in Eighth and Twelfth Grade Males." *Vocational Guidance Quarterly* (1967), vol. 16.

Gribbons, Warren D. "Changes in Readiness for Vocational Planning from the Eighth to the Tenth Grade." *Personnel and Guidance Journal* (1964), vol. 42.

——————; and Lohnes, P. "Eighth Grade Vocational Maturity in Relation to Nine Year Career Patterns." *Journal of Counseling Psychology* (1969), vol. 16.

——————; and Lohnes, P. *Emerging Careers*. New York: Teachers College Press, Columbia University, 1968.

——————; and Lohnes, P. "Shifts in Adolescents' Vocational Values." *Personnel and Guidance Journal* (1965), vol. 44.

Hales, L.; and Fenner, B. "Work Values of 5th, 8th and 11th Grade Students." *Vocational Guidance Quarterly* (1972), vol. 20.

Herr, Edwin L. *Review and Synthesis of Foundations for Career Education*. Washington, D.C.: U.S. Government Printing Office, 1972.

——————. "Unifying an Entire System of Education around a Career Development Theme." Paper presented at the National Conference on Exemplary Programs and Projects — Amendments to the Vocational Education Act. Atlanta, Georgia, March 1969.

Hollender, John. "Development of Vocational Decisions during Adolescence." *Journal of Counseling Psychology* (1971), vol. 18.

Krasnow, Bernard. "Occupational Information as a Factor in the High School Curriculum Chosen by Ninth Grade Boys." *The School Counselor* (1968), vol. 15.

Krippner, Stanley. "Junior High School Students' Vocational Preferences and Their Parents' Occupational Levels." *Personnel and Guidance Journal* (1963), vol. 41.

Lee, Billie; and King, P. "Vocational Choices of Ninth Grade Girls and Their Parents' Occupational Levels." *Vocational Guidance Quarterly* (1964), vol. 12.

Montesano, N.; and Geist, H. "Differences in Occupational Choice between Ninth and Twelfth Grade Boys." *Personnel and Guidance Journal* (1964), vol. 43.

Osipow, Samuel H. "Implications for Career Education of Research and Theory on Career Development." Paper prepared for the National Conference on Career Education for Deans of Colleges of Education. Columbus, Ohio: Center for Vocational and Technical Education, Ohio State University, 1972.

_____. "What Do We *Really* Know about Career Development?" *Career Guidance, Counseling and Placement.* Proceedings, National Conference on Guidance, Counseling and Placement in Career Development and Educational-Occupational Decision Making. Columbia, Missouri: University of Missouri, 1970.

Perrone, Phillip. "Stability of Values of Junior High School Pupils and Their Parents over Two Years." *Personnel and Guidance Journal* (1967), vol. 46.

Simons, Dale D. "Children's Rankings of Occupational Prestige." *Personnel and Guidance Journal* (1962), vol. 41.

Steinke, B.; and Kaczkowski. "Parents' Influence on the Occupational Choice of Ninth Grade Girls." *Vocational Guidance Quarterly* (1961), vol. 9.

Super, Donald E. "Vocational Development Theory: Persons, Positions, and Processes." *The Counseling Psychologist* (1969), vol. 1.

_____; and Overstreet, P. *The Vocational Maturity of Ninth-Grade Boys.* New York: Teachers College Press, Columbia University, 1960.

Tennyson, W.; and Monnens, L. "The World of Work through Elementary Readers." *Vocational Guidance Quarterly* (1964), vol. 12.

Career Development Practices at the Middle/Junior High School Level

Educators have been writing about and practicing career development for some time — long before the term "career education" came into being. Thus when attempting to describe reported "career development," one often finds no clear distinction between this and the other components of career education. Rather than try to dissect reported practices to make the distinctions obvious, in this chapter we will simply report practices which have been given the "career development" label by others.

Those familiar with the literature in the counseling and guidance area are well aware that many of today's *career education* concepts are only restatements of earlier recommendations made in the name of *career development*. For example, a study was reported by Peters and Farwell fifteen years ago (pp. 99–101) wherein they asked 35 junior high school teachers the following questions:

(1) What do you believe junior high school students think about in terms of their career choices and vocational development?

(2) What have you done during the past year to provide a vocational guidance emphasis in your daily work?

(3) What would you like to do in the coming year with the material now available to you in the area of vocational guidance?

Peters and Farwell found that these 35 junior high school teachers arrived at a consensus which reveals:

(1) Students seem to follow their parents' wishes with respect to their vocational plans, rather than thinking independently for themselves.

(2) As teachers, they had little other than accidental kinds of activities that they could specifically recount and in which they could incorporate career implications of their subject matter into their teaching.

(3) The teachers enthusiastically supported a proposal that *someone* help them integrate career implications of their subject matter into their regular instructional materials.

The foregoing questions and answers serve as a clear example that there is little new about proposals for career development as part of career education at the middle or junior high school level. Despite this, we find many middle/junior high school personnel asking questions pertaining to the kinds of things they might appropriately do in their career development program; ergo, this chapter.

In our attempt to provide answers by describing recommendations and practices of others, we have divided the chapter into three parts: The first is devoted to descriptions of programs and recommendations found in the professional journals. These are readily available references that can be studied (in far more depth than recorded here) by members of any middle or junior high school faculty who want to become involved in career development activities in their schools. The second contains examples of career development practices that have been integrated into career education programs since 1969. Since some of these articles and books have not yet appeared in the professional literature, they may be difficult to obtain (at this printing) as complete reports. However, readers are encouraged to contact the school systems or government agencies (referenced at the end of this chapter) and request copies of these new materials. The third part of this chapter is a brief summary of the recommendations and practices extant which can be applied to all middle/junior high school curricula to help students in their exploration of the world of work.

I. Recommendations and Suggested Practices in Career Development at the Middle and Junior High School Levels as Reported in Professional Journals

Of the many articles recommending career development practices, two stand out because they place the middle and junior high school career development practices in the context of a kindergarten through adult career education program. Both are highly recommended for careful reading and study by all concerned with career development at the middle or junior high school level.

The first is an article by Bottoms and O'Kelley (pp. 21–24). While concentrating on the problem of an integrated structure for vocational education (thus ignoring the broader problems of career development for *all* students), this article is an excellent illustration of ways in which provisions of the Vocational Education Act of 1968 have influenced the developing nature of career education programs. The article outlines an integrated structure for kindergarten through adult years in which the career development function at the middle school level can be clearly seen as part of a much broader program. In addition, this article, if studied carefully, will provide the reader with many insights regarding the rationale behind the U.S. Office of Education's emphasis on the fifteen career clusters.

At the junior high school level (grades seven through nine), the article presents a brief outline of Georgia's program of education and career exploration. At the seventh grade level, the program calls for students to receive orientation to a view of the world of work organized around occupational clusters plus *observation* of workers and work processes. In the eighth grade, students elect to explore several clusters through *mini-courses*, six to nine weeks in length, where simple work tasks are performed in a *simulated* work environment. In the ninth grade, students choose one occupational cluster for in-depth exploration. At all three grade levels, students are encouraged to think about themselves, about the kinds of decisions they would have to make if they were to enter a particular area, and about the kinds of educational preparation that would be required. There is no emphasis on *specific* vocational decision making during the junior high school years. Many of the programmatic ideas proposed by others are combined in intriguing ways in Georgia's program for junior high school students.

The second article recommended for study was written by Hansen. In a very few pages (243–50), she describes eight basic strategies for a kindergarten through twelfth grade career development program that are fully consistent with Super's general orientation to career development described in Chapter 2. With each strategy, she suggests a number of activities based on the work of others, each of which has good bibliographic entries. From this article and the references contained in the bibliography, a school faculty, completely lacking in background in career development, could formulate an excellent in-service education program for itself.

Of the eight strategies Hansen proposes, three involve career development activities at the junior high school level. Her Strategy 2 is called "Vocational Self-Exploration Experiences" and is recommended for middle school years (grades six through eight) specifically. Here, she recommends emphasizing the following:

(1) Recognition of personal strengths, emerging values, and goals

(2) Awareness of individual potential

(3) Awareness of the influence of others on the student's emerging goals

(4) Awareness of emerging personal styles for the student

(5) Exploration of the worlds of education, occupations, and work, with an overriding emphasis on an *activity-oriented* program

Specific activities proposed here include:

(1) *Strength groups* (weekly meetings in which students discuss what they can do best)

(2) *Career resource utilization* (including career resource centers, field trips, and speakers)

(3) Emphasis on *broadening career role models*, with particular emphasis on helping students see men and women in nontraditional careers

(4) *Tentative career hypothesis*, with an emphasis on opening up broader career horizons rather than narrowing the scope of one's possible career choices

Hansen's Strategy 3 is recommended for use with eighth and ninth graders and is called the "Career Exploration Module." Here, she recommends an emphasis on helping students by:

(1) Teaching decision-making skills

(2) Providing work simulation experiences

(3) Teaching manpower and economic trends

(4) Encouraging career development "contracts" in which students make definite career (not *occupational*) development plans

She calls her Strategy 8 "Career Development Subject Teams." These are recommended for the junior and senior high school level. In implementing the strategy, schools are urged to identify ways in which school subjects could be related more closely to careers and to the world of work. Here, Hansen proposes that teams consisting of a teacher from a given subject area, a counselor, a community volunteer, a parent, a worker in a field related to the subject matter area, and two or more students come together to attack the problem. For those school systems where teachers are wondering how they can possibly become acquainted with the career implications of their subject matter, this suggestion by Hansen may prove both practical and helpful.

Recommendations for Specific Activities

Based on their own experiences and the study of research and demonstration efforts by others, several authors have made rather specific recommendations for one or more particular practices in career development at the middle and junior high school levels. We have selected a few as examples because we consider them quality suggestions, and because the articles in which they appear contain many references supporting the recommendations they make.

Gambino, while emphasizing that there is no one best approach to career development, makes a particularly strong case for consideration of the concept of a career resource center at the junior high school level. He also advocates manning the center with two specialists, one an audio/video media coordinator, and the other a coordinator for school/industry cooperation. Those interested in this concept will find an intriguing outline of staff duties for each of these two specialists in this article. Gambino recommends using the concept of the career resource center as a vehicle for implementing and coordinating a wide variety of career exploration activities at the junior high school level. He argues for the broad concept of career exploration (rather than specific decision making) at this level when he says:

> ...But what makes career exploration more exciting to the seventh, eighth, and ninth grader is the realization that he has the potential to manipulate certain aspects of his environment — that, by choosing a certain course, he can expect to gain a certain end, and that, eventually, the decision will be his to make (p. 57).

Richard Johnson supports the use of *work simulation* as a career exploration activity at the junior high school level. His article is highly recommended for two reasons: First, it reviews the research of several others on the efficacy of work simulation approaches where positive results have been obtained. Second, Johnson gives practicable suggestions for ways in which the local school can establish its own work simulation center. In his suggestions, he sees good problem-solving tasks as the key to success. He suggests selecting problems that:

(1)   Reflect occupations where the employment picture (locally and nationally) looks good

(2) Can be worded at a reading level low enough so that 95 percent of the students can be expected to read it

(3) Are presented in ways that are of intrinsic interest to the students

(4) Do not require most students more than fifty minutes to solve

(5) Have been endorsed by specialists in a given occupation as representative of real tasks that are performed in one or more occupations

He makes the point that, while work simulation may at first glance appear to be encouraging students to limit their vocational preferences, the goal is actually to help students explore career areas that they have overlooked and thus increase alternatives available to them. The topic of "work simulation" in the middle/junior high school is discussed in greater detail in chapter 6.

The use of "life career games" as a middle school career exploratory activity was evaluated in a study reported by Johnson and Euler. The study was aimed at comparing the effectiveness of the Boocock life career game with a traditional approach to teaching occupational information to junior high school students. In an experiment involving 39 ninth graders, the students were given an educational and occupational information exam three times: once before the start of the experiment, once at its conclusion, and again four weeks afterward. The experimental group used the life career game, while the control group was taught occupational information in a traditional manner.

Results indicate that the students in the experimental group found the life career game not too interesting. Moreover, these students learned less educational and occupational information than the control group, who had been taught by a regular classroom teacher. However, in a follow-up a month later, Johnson and Euler found that the experimental group retained more occupational information than the control group (pp. 155–59). Since the latter group had less knowledge of life careers at the end of the experiment, this study would seem to point toward the advisability of using some form of life career game as part of a career exploration program.

An attempt to secure parent involvement in a junior high school career exploration program was interestingly reported by Cuony (pp. 227–29). The article is especially engaging because it emphasizes and recommends including post-high school educational planning in middle school career exploration programs. Cuony describes a program at a junior high school in Geneva, New York, that involved group counseling sessions for parents, where topics discussed included a wide variety of subjects relating to post-high school educational planning — particularly planning for college and university attendance. While no research evaluation is reported in the article, Cuony does point out that parents were sufficiently enthusiastic about this approach to request continuance of the meetings. We recommend it for reading, not only because of its contents, but also because of the intriguing possibilities that come to mind if one considers extending the idea to include all forms of post-high school educational opportunities. Perhaps if this were done, educators might be able to help parents avoid pushing their students only toward college attendance.

An examination of the feasibility of "work experience" as a tool for career exploration at the junior high school level was reported by Krippner (pp. 167–70). A total of 189 boys and 162 girls from middle-class, suburban backgrounds, at the seventh and eighth grade levels, was involved in this study. Krippner was interested in studying relationships that existed between the part-time jobs the students held and their expressed vocational preferences. He found that 53 percent of the boys and 36 percent of the girls had some work experience. He reported that while fewer of the girls had worked, relatively more had worked at jobs related to their stated vocational goals. Based on his results, Krippner concluded that even at the upper end of the social class scale, the cultural milieu does not provide junior high school boys with enough opportunity to attain first-hand information about the tentative career selections through actual work experience. Krippner also points out that it was feasible to arrange work experiences related to expressed vocational preferences, even though it did not seem to be occurring.

If what we know about the total career development process is considered, there would seem to be little point lamenting the fact that student work experiences do not correspond highly to the vocational preferences they state at the junior high school level. The challenge, it would seem, is to capitalize on work experience inside and outside the walls of the school as part of the total career education program.

Two examples exist which involve the evaluation of the use of particular printed materials as part of the junior high school career exploration programs. The first is described in an article by Vetter (pp. 28–30), and is specifically concerned with career exploration for girls at the junior high school level. This article represents one that is recommended not only for the specific suggestions it contains, but also for its excellent review of the literature and its fine bibliography. Vetter clearly points to the need to provide better career guidance and to broaden the career aspirations of girls who are predicted, in very large numbers, to combine the roles of homemaker and "breadwinner" when they become adults. After reviewing the literature on this subject, Vetter describes a curriculum unit especially designed for junior high school girls which is called "Planning Ahead for the World of Work." This unit, requiring eight to ten class hours to teach, was used with girls at the seventh, ninth, and eleventh grade levels in Ohio and Tennessee.

After collecting data from the 326 girls involved in the study, Vetter was able to demonstrate that this unit did allow students to acquire a broader understanding of the world of work, and particularly about the present and projected role of women in the labor force. She found that after the unit was ended, girls who participated in the project did see themselves more clearly as prospective members of the work force. Follow-up of these students showed that while they rather quickly lost some of the specific occupational information they had learned, they retained their attitudinal changes with respect to both the desirability and probability that they will someday be part of the labor force. Vetter concludes that while this unit can be used at all three grade levels, it seems particularly appropriate for use at grade nine.

A second study of the effectiveness of printed materials was reported by Wurtz and Jalkanen (pp. 73–75). It was aimed at evaluating the effects of Science Research Associates' occupational exploration kit. The kit was applied to 86 ninth graders as an "add on" to the regular social studies class in their junior high school. The results indicate that use of the kit did indeed serve to suggest additional occupational areas to these students over and above those they indicated they had considered before using the kit. The authors then discuss their suggestions for optimizing the construction of such a kit, and conclude that it can be a helpful tool in career exploration if used in conjunction with a definite plan.

At McTigue Junior High School in Toledo, Ohio, the idea of a "career week" is used as a basis for the junior high school exploration program. This experiment is chronicled by Roman and Doenges (pp. 62–63). Rather than encourage all teachers to incorporate career implications of their subject on a regular and continuing basis throughout the school year, McTigue has adopted a plan that calls for systematically using two weeks at each of their three 12-week trimesters for planned career exploration activities on the part of all teachers and all students. The first of these two weeks is spent in planning for career week itself by having both teachers and students research ideas for use during the actual career week. During career week, each class is dedicated to illustrating to students career implications of subject matter, rather than attempting to impart any more subject matter per se. By utilizing resource persons from the community (including parents and persons employed in various occupations), McTigue has found it possible to combine field trips, team teaching, individualized instruction, flexible scheduling, and a host of other educational innovations into these career week efforts without, in any way, disrupting regular teaching activities at other times during the school year. They report enthusiastic endorsement of their program by all concerned, that through this program, teachers are made much more aware of the career implications of their subject matter, and that junior high school students, as a result of the program, set more realistic goals and course objectives than did students in earlier classes.

The McTigue idea may prove appealing to a number of other junior high schools who, when faced with a rather rigid regular school schedule and a situation that finds most teachers unaware of the career implications of their subject matter, simply don't know how to get started on a school-wide career exploration effort. This, while not what we would want to see as an eventual continuing pattern, certainly does appear to be one workable way of getting started.

Olson Junior High School in Minneapolis has a different approach to career exploration at the junior high school level (Rachel Leonard, pp. 221–22). In this school, at the seventh grade level, students concentrate on learning more about specific occupations included in their community. Under guidance of social studies teachers, students write letters soliciting resource persons as volunteers, set up speaker visits to the classroom, and view filmstrips depicting various occupations. During the eighth grade, the students explore community agencies, with an emphasis on job "families" rather than on specific occupations. Working again through social studies teachers, they have an opportunity to explore seven job families, to engage in research designed to acquaint them with the nature of each job family, and to take a number of field trips to settings where they can see people in these job families actually at work.

During the ninth grade, students participate in four different "career days," each concentrating on educational opportunities at the post-high school level in one of four of the following kinds of settings: military, college, large company training school, or trade school. With each, students are encouraged to identify specific job opportunities toward which such training would lead. The career days themselves are set up with one featured speaker, along with a number of small group sessions, on a schedule that allows each student to attend two small group sessions (a total of eight sessions during the year).

While not highly emphasized in Leonard's report, this same program at Olson Junior High School is described in terms of "student involvement" in an article by Knox (pp. 202–04), who emphasizes the extensive work done by the student leadership club in arranging for speakers, field trips, and resource activities that are a part of the junior high school's career exploration program. The potential of student involvement has not received sufficient emphasis in career education to date, and Knox's contribution is much needed.

Examples of Counselor Involvement in Career Exploration Programs

Counselors were deeply involved in the career exploration program at both the McTigue and Olson junior high schools. In the following discussion, we describe several other career exploration programs that either have been initiated by counselors or have seen counselors play a crucial role.

An approach designed as an alternative to the traditional "testing-telling-interpreting" approach of vocational guidance has been reported from Metcalf Junior High School in Burnsville, Minnesota (Braland and Sweeney, pp. 260–61). The authors (both of whom are counselors in the system) approached the problem of how the junior high school student can be provided with a model of the decision-making process that will enable her or him to cope with the ever-changing world of work. The prime emphasis was one of *simulation*. At grade seven, students were placed in a unit in social studies designed to challenge the child's fantasy world. Here, they were confronted with requirements of specific occupations in a very "hard-nosed" manner. As part of the unit, students were presented with an imaginary position and faced with the problem of making a decision to either accept or reject it, based on all they know about themselves.

In grade eight, students were given information about a "typical student" and then asked to plan his or her future (including post-high school planning). A number of "change cards" were used, and students were told to select one at random (to gain an understanding of how one's situational changes can affect his or her future life). In the ninth grade, students were given specific training in decision making and practiced those skills in planning their high school programs. While reporting no data on evaluation, the authors do report that the program was enthusiastically accepted by students — particularly the eighth grade simulation experience.

A study involving junior high school students in Muskegon, Michigan, was aimed at testing the effects of supplementary counseling on the educational-vocational planning and academic achievement of junior high school students (Engle *et al.*, pp. 50–55). Initially involving 721 seventh grade students, the study ran three years. A control group was exposed to previous guidance procedures (e.g., testing, individual conferences, and parent conferences on request). The experimental group participated in:

(1) Home visits by counselors

(2) Use of the publication "Planning for Our World of Work"

(3) Supplemental phone calls to parents

(4) Group meetings with parents

(5) Discussion of study skills with students

(6) Twice as many individual counselor contacts with students as were available to those in the control group

The single most significant result was the increase in subject matter achievement found for students in the experimental, as opposed to the control, group. In addition, statistically significant increases in student satisfaction with guidance services, using the Ohio "student inventory of guidance awareness," were observed. There were no significant differences in parental opinions (the Illinois "inventory of parent opinion" was used for this). The most important findings were those related to student achievement. It is significant that career exploration was the vehicle used in this study as a rationale for these increased counselor contacts.

Anderson and Heimann conducted a study designed to determine the effects of short-term vocational counseling on the career development and career maturation of junior high school girls (pp. 191–95). Subjects were 60 eighth grade girls from two junior high schools in Phoenix, with half randomly assigned to an experimental and half to a control group. Members of the experimental group were given six individual counseling sessions, 35 minutes long, focusing on:

(1) Expressing interests as related to their vocational future

(2) Exploring assets and relating them to work potential

(3) Clarifying factors to consider in career decision making

(4) Working on a form called the "occupational work sheet"

When school started again in the fall, the students were given a "vocational maturity scale," an "occupational information test," and a "self-estimate" measure. Statistically significant differences in favor of the experimental group were found on the vocational maturity scale, with no such differences on the other two.

Based on these findings, the authors concluded that:

> Among the implications of this finding is that girls at the eighth grade level are developmentally ready for preliminary career planning activities. Given the opportunity to sit down with a counselor at regular intervals and think about and discuss themselves, the world of work, and their perceptions of their vocational future, they will benefit significantly by becoming more vocationally mature as reflected by their increased scores on the [vocational maturity scale].

Again, we see an example showing that concentrated counselor involvement produces positive results indicative of success in the career exploration process.

Several authors, while not citing examples of practice in particular schools, have commented extensively on the changing role of the school counselor in career development. One of these is Gaymer, who wrote about career counseling as "teaching the art of career planning" (pp. 18–25). In her article, she asserts that the art of career planning is a more important part of career counseling than hastening students toward career decisions. This is a good example of an article stressing the clear differences between "career" as a dynamic, creative state of changing from one state to another and the kinds of static connotations inherent in terms such as "vocation," "job," or "position." The major emphasis in this article is on the rapidity of change students face in these times and their great need to be flexible and adaptable to changing conditions. She concludes by asserting that counselors must know:

(1) How this complicated world fits together

(2) How one job can lead to another

(3) How one job can act as preparation for another (or for many others)

(4) How occupations are interrelated and how jobs can vary in different environments

The emphasis that Gaymer places on changing *external* conditions that are sure to face the student in the future is a healthy one for counselors to understand.

McDaniels wrote an article in 1968 that should be required reading for all middle school counselors concerned about their responsibilities in career development as part of a comprehensive career education program (pp. 242–49). Though at first glance, the article may appear to be an attempt to refute Super's research findings (see Chapter 2) that youth at the junior high school level are too young to be exposed to specific, directional vocational guidance, McDaniels makes some cogent points when he refers to the fact that, with the senior high schools moving increasingly toward serving all youth (not just those who contemplate college attendance), youth *must* make some choices with reference to high school curricular subjects. Further, such curricular choices have definite career implications. Finally, McDaniels points to the equally obvious fact that youth *are* making choices now, with increasing numbers being in the labor market on a part- or full-time basis. Perhaps the most significant point McDaniels makes is that the myraid of studies indicating youth's lack of readiness for vocational planning may be untrustworthy for one reason: Their observations on career development of youth have been made, by and large, in situations were systematic, professional assistance was absent. Given such support to the youth, the findings might have been quite different. McDaniels, after quoting several research studies indicating positive results, concludes by pleading for a developmental career guidance emphasis on kindergarten through fourteenth grade that recognizes specific vocational decision making as only a wide variety of vocational decisions that are made in the maturational process of career development.

Contrasted with McDaniels' article is one written by Peterson (pp. 152–58) which is concerned with the counselor role at the junior high school level. She argues strongly in favor of a broad emphasis on personal growth and assistance in "planfulness" on a far broader basis than career development concerns.

In so doing, she seems to feel that career development is but a part of personal development, and broader phases of personal development are proper to emphasize at the junior high school level. The following summarizes Peterson's point of view:

> Counseling in the junior high school should help students grow toward increasing planfulness and competence in decision-making, but its primary focus should be on the personal and developmental tasks of early adolescence. The school counselor can help this age group move toward a clearer perception of their own identities and of their own relationships with other people. This growth provides the soundest possible foundation for success in the later developmental tasks of vocational choice and development.

Of these two contrasting points of view, it is our feeling that McDaniels comes much closer to being right than Peterson. In addition to contrasting Peterson's point of view with McDaniels', readers are urged to study an article written in 1963 that perhaps can be considered a compromise between the two (Caplan *et al.*, pp. 129–35). That article need not be reviewed here.

Of broader interest is an article directed toward the general problem of vocational counseling (not specifically at the junior high school) written by Morrill and Forrest in 1970 (pp. 299–306). They outline four types of vocational counseling well worth thinking about. These include:

(1) Counseling which aids the individual with a specific decision by providing information and clarification of the issues

(2) Counseling which aids the client with a specific decision by focusing on decision-making skills rather than only on the decision at hand

(3) Counseling which views career as a process rather than an end-point, and so focuses changes to the process of making a continual series of choices

(4) Counseling which focuses on creating in the individual the ability to achieve self-determined objectives and to influence the nature of future choices, rather than merely adapting to external pressures

The authors refer to this last type as "process counseling," and while not saying so directly, obviously prefer this point of view. While in our view these are not "types" of counseling, they do provide the practicing counselor with a framework for determining his own professional goals, objectives, and values in vocational counseling. It is an article deserving of careful study.

An earlier article by Ivey and Morrill further clarifies what is meant by "process counseling":

> How can satisfaction with career process be bestowed? Our answer is abolish vocational choice. Let the individual be himself. Don't push him to select an occupation. Don't teach him about occupations. Let him learn himself. Don't lecture him, don't elevate or denigrate him. Help him to examine himself. Let him decide how and in what ways he can benefit from career process. Most of all, help him to become aware of his own ability to make decisions and to solve problems (pp. 644–49).

Our point of view is quite the opposite of that expressed in the above quote. In our opinion, the counselor has neither the right nor the power to "abolish vocational choice," and does not effectively serve his clients when he attempts to do so.

Three general articles commenting specifically on the counselor's role in career education are recent additions to the literature. While these are not aimed directly at counselors in the middle school, each does have implications for counselors working at this level. For that reason, it seems appropriate to review them briefly here.

In 1973 the Arizona State Department of Education published a document titled *Career Education: Leadership in Learning.* As part of this document, there appears a statement on the counselor role in career education by Delbert Jerome, in which he states that the counselors' role will *increasingly* become defined as:

(1) Consultants to teachers and administrators

(2) Coordinators of group guidance activities

(3) Counselors to teachers and parents

(4) Coordinators of community resources

(5)   Consultants for curriculum development

(6)   Coordinators of placement activities

(7)   Coordinators of special student needs

In his contribution to the book Jerome says: "This role of the counselor as a resource person and as an activist will grow in importance as the career education movement increases in range and depth."

An article was recently published on the same subject, wherein Meyer specified four roles for the counselor in career education:

(1)   To provide assistance in initiating, developing, and implementing career education into the regular curriculum

(2)   To provide up-to-date and relevant career education information for pupils and faculty

(3)   To provide appropriate group guidance activities

(4)   To provide counseling services for individual pupils

Near the end of his article, he makes the following statement:

> After pupils have had the benefits of a comprehensive career education program, the counselor can assist them in exercising their freedom of choice by helping them fit all the pieces together and place them in proper perspective. Finally, the counselor can help individual pupils make the transition from school to their next step, whether that be immediate employment or further education.

A third view of the counselor's role in career education can be seen in the Hoyt article of the *SRA Guidance Newsletter.* In that issue, the role of the counselor in career education is discussed under the following outline of role statements:

(1)   Helping classroom teachers emphasize career implications of subject matter

(a) Participating in policy decisions regarding the way(s) in which the general nature of the occupational world is to be pictured

(b) Helping teachers become familiar with the career implications of their subject matter

(c) Helping teachers develop understanding of and commitment to the goals and objectives of the career education movement

(2) Helping to emphasize vocational skills training in formal education

(a) Serving as an influencer of curriculum change designed to broaden the variety, appropriateness, and opportunity to choose vocational education courses at the junior and senior high school levels

(b) Studying the vocational education opportunities available to students at the senior high and post-high school levels as different *kinds* of educational opportunities from which students might choose

(c) Helping "academic" teachers understand that they too are engaged in vocational skills training

(3) Helping the business-industry-labor community engage in career education

(a) Serving as liaison between the school system and the business-industry-labor community

(b) Building positive relationships with the business-industry-labor community through actively participating in observational, work experience, and work-study activities designed to increase counselor understanding of that community

(c) Participating in the job placement program

(d) Helping students make a successful transition from school to work

(4) Helping the home and family participate in career education by helping parents change their attitudes toward education and work

(5) Providing leadership in the career development program by helping to correct misconceptions currently existing regarding the meaning of work, of career, of

the dynamics involved in the changing nature of work values, the process of occupational decision making, and the importance of professional counseling in career education

These three articles, while varying somewhat in content and specific recommendations, seem to be in general agreement that the career education movement does call for change in the counselor's role. Among the kinds of changes that are implied as needed, we find the following:

(1) A change toward serving as a more active agent of curriculum change

(2) A change toward serving as an active *collaborator* (not simply as a consultant) to classroom teachers in career education activities and projects in the area of career development

(3) A change toward becoming more actively involved with the business-industry-labor community

(4) A change toward becoming more actively involved in the placement function (whether educational or occupational in nature)

(5) A change toward becoming more involved in career guidance functions

It seems to us particularly important that professional counselors at all levels, including the middle and junior high school levels, be especially cognizant of their responsibilities for making sure the career education program in their school is consistent with the best thinking and research that exists with reference to the career development process.

II. CAREER DEVELOPMENT PRACTICES IN ONGOING CAREER EDUCATION PROGRAMS IN MIDDLE AND JUNIOR HIGH SCHOOL SETTINGS

When one goes beyond the literature published in professional journals, it is difficult to provide the reader with many accurate referrals to specific practices. Much of the activity conducted in the realm of career development as part of comprehensive career education programs is still unpublished or appears in informal publications produced by those school systems in which the career education programs operate. The best that can be done here is to describe the source of information referred to as accurately as possible. There can be no guarantee that if readers write to that source, they will be supplied with the publications we refer to in this portion.

An attempt has been made to catalog and briefly describe some of the practices that have emerged since 1969. The first part of this section will be devoted to a listing and brief description of such resources. Following this, we describe some career development materials and practices (called to our attention) that have been accomplished on the local level.

Summaries of Career Development Practices in Career Education

The materials referred to here are limited neither to career development nor to the middle or junior high school level. Instead, they concern themselves with the broader topic of career education and typically cover a kindergarten through adult span. Despite this broader coverage, there are specific references to career development activities at the middle and junior high school levels in each of these publications.

One of the best sources of summary data for exemplary projects supported under Section 142(c) of Part D of the Vocational Education Amendments of 1968 is *Abstracts of Exemplary Projects in Vocational Education.* Information relative to ways in which this document can be obtained will best be found by writing to the U.S. Office of Education's Division of Vocational Education Research. This document provides short abstracts of career education programs funded under the U.S. Commissioner's discretionary funds provided by the Act. In addition to an abstract of the complete project, there is also provided the name and address of the project director. Those studying these abstracts will note that all provide a short summary of efforts in career guidance, counseling, and placement, and almost all provide a short description of career education programs included at the middle or junior high school level. Readers will discover many similarities in these abstracts, but will also find several which outline some new and exciting approaches to career education at the middle school level. With this document in hand, the reader will be in a position to write individual project directors and request additional information on activities in which they have particular interest. Some difficulty in obtaining replies can be anticipated.

Another valuable document prepared under the direction of Dr. Sidney C. High, Jr., and available from the same source is *Bibliography on Career Education.* This bibliography, in addition to listing specific sources by which the reader can keep up to date on the career education literature, also provides selected references on career education thought to be pertinent to those in the field. Section III lists such references under a number of topical headings. Those headings that might be of particular interest to those interested in career development include "Career Guidance and Counseling," "Computer-Based Guidance Systems," "Career Information," "Placement and Follow-up," and "Women in the World of Work." Each of these contains a wide variety of references from the published literature that school systems interested in developing local programs may wish to study.

Still another publication coming from Dr. High's office is *State Administered Exemplary Projects in Vocational Education.* This publication, while providing no actual descriptions of programs, lists career education projects supported by each state under this Act. For each state, the title of the project and the name of the school district in which it was conducted are shown in the references at the end of this chapter. Interested readers will find many projects that directly pertain to career development activities at the middle or junior high school level. It is to be hoped that inquiries sent to project directors will find them in a position to reply or send samples of materials they have developed.

A very comprehensive publication bearing directly on the topic of career development has been published by the Oklahoma State Department of Education. The 1973 revision of this document is referenced as *A Guide for Developmental Vocational Guidance, K–12.* Divided into four major sections by grade level, the third section covers grades seven through nine. This section, "Exploring Occupations and Careers in the

World of Work," is largely organized around career development goals. For each goal, the reader is provided with an outline of what the student needs to know, suggested activities, and instructional materials and resources. Separate sections are provided for each subject matter area typically found at the middle and junior high school levels. We regard this as a document that can be immediately helpful to the middle or junior high school that desires to initiate a program of career education with a strong career development component.

Another good resource, similar in nature to the Oklahoma *Guide*, is that of the North Dakota State Board of Vocational Education: *Career Development K–12: Guideline of Career Development Activities*. This publication, again divided by goals and by grade levels, provides illustrated examples of career development and career education activities developed in cooperation with the Bismarck Public Schools by Dr. Larry Selland and his staff in the North Dakota State Department of Public Instruction. Middle and junior high school personnel will find sections of this publication addressed specifically to them.

The North Carolina Department of Public Instruction has published, as an outgrowth of a middle grades career exploration institute for teachers of children with exceptional ability, a fascinating workbook — *Hands-On: Career Exploration for Bright Students*. Teachers in this workshop concentrated on developing career education, teaching units based on six of the U.S. Office of Education's fifteen clusters. This publication outlines 43 teaching units developed during the workshop. While directed toward bright students, these units — a cursory inspection leads us to believe — are generally applicable to all students. An especially interesting feature of this workbook is an instrument called "work temperature," which lists a wide variety of work that is commonly performed, either paid or unpaid in nature, by middle school age boys and girls. Students use it as an indicator of interest in these various kinds of work activities, as well as a log indicating those that they have tried. It is an especially intriguing idea.

In 1971, the California State Department of Education published *Career Guidance: A California Model for Career Development K–Adult*, a handbook on career guidance. This publication will be of interest to those concerned with development of career guidance models. Objectives, with behavioral outcomes, are listed in a systematic manner.

Also in 1971, the Wisconsin State Department of Public Instruction developed a kindergarten through adult guide for integrating career development into local curricula. Apparently, in order to meet demands for this publication, a decision was made to allow it to be published commercially. Written by Drier and others, it is referenced as *K-12 Guide for Integrating Career Development into Local Curriculum.* The first 55 pages present Wisconsin's rationale for career development, the sixteen career development concepts developed through this state department's effort, and a fairly comprehensive list of career development objectives that accompany the "concepts." The "objectives," to many persons, will be viewed as better "concepts" than the sixteen Wisconsin career development concepts that have been widely publicized. The objectives alone make it worth obtaining. The remainder of this publication is devoted to a listing of career development resources.

Drier has recently updated and expanded this list in a new publication, *Career Development Resources: A Guide to Audiovisual and Printed Materials for Grades K-12.* Pages 127 through 194 of the revised version are devoted to career development resources (both printed and audio-visual in nature) that have been specifically designed for use at grades seven, eight, and nine. It is a comprehensive resource guide indeed, and will be useful for those middle and junior high schools that want to order career development materials.

A manual specifically concerned with career orientation programs in grades seven and eight has been produced by the Ohio Department of Education for its Career Continuum Program and is called *Career Orientation Program, Grades 7-8.* This manual presents a rationale for career orientation at the junior high school level and is oriented around six career development "concepts": (1) the individual and the environment, (2) world of work, (3) education and training, (4) economics, (5) employability and work adjustment skills, and (6) decision making. With this broad focus of the meaning of "career orientation," the booklet then presents two sets of suggested career orientation activities. One set is organized around ten industrial clusters, while the other is organized around traditional subject matter of the junior high school. An illustrated example of a career orientation activity is presented around each subheading in this organizational structure.

Those readers who study the six aforementioned state publications may find themselves wondering whether *career development* is a term that can be used as if it were synonymous with *career education*. In our opinion, it is unfortunate that those producing such materials did not try more carefully to make distinctions between these two terms. In our view, as expressed in other parts of this book, career development is but one part of career education. This can in fact be seen in these publications when one notes in them the absence of a large concentration of content on vocational skills training, on the business-industry-labor community, and on the home and family. These publications have been included here, not to add confusion to the controversy, but simply because each represents a good example of solid career development suggestions and materials which can contribute to a complete program of career education.

A state department of education publication specifically aimed at helping schools identify learning resources for career education at the junior high school level was produced by New Jersey: *Grades 7, 8 and 9 Learning Resources for Career Education*. This booklet is in itself a kind of annotated bibliography prepared especially for use by persons working in career education at the junior high school level. It should be of practicable benefit to many school systems.

During the 1971–72 school year, North Carolina State University's Center for Occupational Education (under a U.S. Office of Education contract) studied 41 exemplary programs of career education located in various parts of the United States. In 1973, it published fairly comprehensive descriptions — edited by Morgan and others — of fifteen of these 41 programs: *An Anthology of 15 Career Education Programs*. Each of these 15 career education programs is described as kindergarten through twelfth grade efforts. Those readers interested in career guidance, career development, or career education in the middle school will find sections of each program description that include discussions of these topics. It is interesting to see how, almost without exception, these fifteen programs describe the middle school years as devoted primarily to "career exploration." There seems to be a wide degree of agreement on this subject.

Career Development/Career Education Practices in Specific Middle or Junior High Schools

The career development/career education practices to be reported here are those which we have either observed in person or from which we have received information from the school in which the practice is used. It is unlikely that many of the schools whose practices are to be described here have sufficient resources to make complete reports of their programs available to interested persons. Here, we will try to describe practices in terms of ideas that we believe might work for other schools.

In the first section of this chapter, we reported examples of career development practices at McTigue, Olson, and Metcalf junior high schools, each of which represented some compromise between the practical, operational problems facing those schools and the ideal career development program that involves all teachers, counselors, and students throughout the school. The first examples to be presented here will extend this notion of "compromise with reality" to other junior high school settings.

In a publication of the Texas Education Agency in 1967, we find a description of a "careers of the month" program carried out at Mann Junior High School, Abilene, that appears to have some fascinating potential. The central idea is that during each month of the school year, one or more disciplines are picked as those that will emphasize career implications of their subject matter during the month. When faced with the call for use of outside resource persons, field trips, and a wide variety of similar kinds of student activities, the school counselor, by concentrating on only a few of the disciplines each month, may find himself of concrete assistance to teachers in ways that would not be possible were he to try to serve all teachers throughout the entire school year. Perhaps, by beginning in this way, teachers would have less need for consultative assistance by the second year, and such a program might evolve into the kind of continuing infusion into all subject matter areas that we would hope for in an ideal career education program.

At School No. 72 in Baltimore, a special kind of career education effort was launched for 21 boys and girls described as "high risk potential dropouts." This is a euphemistic way of describing that small minority of students found in most junior high schools who are over-age for their grade, whose level of achievement is far below that of their classmates, and who apparently are just waiting for the time when they can drop out of school. A career development approach, built around work experience, was taken with these students. Part-time paid jobs were found for them in the afternoon, and a special teacher was assigned to teach them basic subject matter in the mornings. The program has apparently worked well in terms of both student satisfaction and improved student academic performance, motivation, and school attendance. If work experience seemed to provide a valuable way for these students to see themselves as worthwhile and worthy persons, the question logically arises as to whether it might not also be considered worthwhile for students who are not yet in difficulty in their school progress.

In Perry Hall Junior High School, Maryland, a special career education effort has been launched for students who, during the seventh and eighth grades, were underachievers and exhibited disciplinary or attendance problems. For these students, a career development team of teachers is used. This team has sufficient members so that the teacher-pupil ratio is lower than for other parts of the school. Team members work together in planning a number of joint activity projects that cut across subject matter lines and involve a great deal of cooperative planning and action on the part of all members of the teaching team. When this program is observed in action, it seems to be working very well for these previously disruptive students. We cannot help but object to seeing a school that, in effect, rewards disruptive behavior by providing for such students the kinds of flexibility and exciting activity approach to teaching that career education asks for all students. This is certainly not the fault of the staff at this school, for they too would like to expand their program for all students. Funding limitations prevent them from doing so.

In yet another Maryland middle school (Bel Air), we observed a situation where, during the 1972–73 school year, subjects which had formerly been "electives" for eighth and ninth graders — including typing, industrial arts, home economics, art and music — were converted to career exploration units under arrangements where each student spent part of the school year in each of the areas. While there, the student was exposed to career implications of the subject area, given introductory basic skills and an opportunity to assess his or her ability to master the kinds of skills taught in the area, and to think about whether this area represented a possible career choice for him or her. At the same time, other teachers were assigning students career education projects as part of their regular classes but not to the same degree as these former "elective" courses. Here, we see a situation where no new facility had to be built, or any new teacher employed, in order to initiate a career education emphasis. Most of the students and teachers seem to prefer this arrangement over what has existed in a traditional sense.

Teachers in the Lawrence Cook Junior High School, Santa Rosa, California, used the services of paraprofessionals called "career education specialists" to contact community workers willing to come to class and discuss the kinds of life-styles they are leading in their work. By careful planning, teachers were able to construct career education learning experiences, having direct relationships to their specific subject matter areas, which cut across subject matter areas. For example, when a forest ranger came to school, his work and the work of others in the area were related to history (historical guide), geography (location of state and national forests), and art (restoration of artifacts). When bank representatives appeared, they were able to relate mathematics to the economic necessity for banks in a community (social studies) and communication in the banking industry (English) to students. Thus each representative was able to relate careers in his industry to a number of subject matter areas while discussing his or her life-style and those he saw in his customers (e.g., a discussion of customers in an organic food shop brought about discussion of a wide variety of life-styles). The important points to be observed here are:

(1) Contacts with industry representatives were made, typically, through assistance of a paraprofessional from the career guidance center.

(2) Visitations concentrated on careers and life-styles rather than the details of specific occupations.

In the Apex school system, Wake County, North Carolina, career education in the middle school grades (five through eight) are coordinated by a counselor-coordinator. An interim report of this project covering the period January to March 1973 provides several examples of career development/career education activities that resulted. These included:

(1) Mini-courses for the dental hygienist and secretarial-receptionist areas to fifth graders

(2) Projects cutting across several subject matter areas for eighth graders, including a communications system with module telegraph poles and building an electric map of the United States

(2) Exploratory courses for eighth graders in the construction trades and health occupations, and a modern sewing class

In addition, this middle school counselor-coordinator reported increased counseling contacts with parents and students, increased involvement with a social services counselor from the court systems, and use of the county health department. This description is included here to illustrate the great variation from traditional roles played by middle school counselors when a career education emphasis comes to a school system.

An extensive developmental career guidance project has been going on in Detroit since 1964. This project, directed by Dr. George E. Leonard, Wayne State University, published a report in 1972 called *The Developmental Career Guidance Project*. A portion of this excellent report is devoted to a description of career guidance activities at the Burroughs Junior High School, where — using a career guidance consultant — a wide variety of developmental career guidance activities was conducted. In addition to those commonly seen in other places, the following unique features at this junior high school seem worthy of note. First, weekly parent meetings were held on Wednesday mornings where parents were informed of various educational and job opportunities, given contact with speakers from industry, and encouraged to participate in field trips. Second, a developmental career guidance committee of teachers was established. In addition to other activities, the committee participated in monthly Saturday meetings devoted to in-service education in career guidance. Third, a weekly bulletin on career guidance was prepared for and distributed to teachers so all would know the variety of career guidance activities that had transpired and those that were planned. These kinds of ideas are well worth consideration by other schools.

In May 1972, representative teachers from thirteen Maryland middle and junior high schools, who had participated in a career exploration workshop during the summer of 1971, met to report on the kinds of activities in which they had engaged during the 1971–72 school year. While the complete list of activities reported by these thirteen schools is far too long to be included here, the following activities, each of which had some unique aspect, may be those that will give other middle or junior high schools ideas of how they might incorporate a career development emphasis in their total career education program:

(1) In one middle school, seventh graders were made *aware* of the world of work through spending a day with their parents on the job. While done for all students, this activity was a direct outgrowth of a family living unit in home economics.

(2) In another middle school, *work values* were emphasized, using the vehicle of line production in industrial arts that included forming competing corporations, selling stock, simulating assembly-line production, marketing products, and distributing dividends to stockholders.

(3) Again to emphasize *work values*, another middle school had students clip newspaper articles depicting what they regarded as "success" or "failure" among workers in various occupations. By discussing the meaning of these terms, they felt they became deeply involved in work values.

(4) A fourth middle school initiated a project with the acronym CAN (Commmunity Action Now) that concentrated on changes they would like to see in their community. By using this single school-wide project, it involved all teachers and students in a study of a wide variety of existing careers. The report is that this project was especially useful in helping students comprehend the economic, sociological, and psychological needs for work. Another middle school used essentially this approach, but called its school-wide project "Patriots against Pollution," which actually involved students in community projects as volunteer workers.

(5) Ninth grade activities in these schools almost uniformly culminated in some kind of activity designed to help students choose senior high school courses. Sometimes this involved visits to area vocational schools, clipping help-wanted ads from newspapers, and discussing education required for job vacancies. In other schools, concentrated attempts were made to study educational requirements for various occupations included in each of the U.S. Office of Education's fifteen occupational clusters.

In general, trends among the thirteen middle and junior high schools reporting at this conference indicated that grade seven was being used primarily for "occupational awareness," grade eight for "work values," and grade nine for "career exploration." While this is not ideally a theoretical comprehensive career education program that begins in kindergarten, it represents the general kind of solution these schools used under circumstances wherein, prior to the junior high school years, students had not had a systematic career education emphasis in the elementary school. There are many middle and junior high schools across the land that will be faced with similar situations. This is one of the many kinds of solutions they may wish to consider.

Among school systems funded as exemplary programs of career education under provisions of Part D of the Vocational Education Amendments of 1968, one of the most active, in terms of publishing a variety of high-quality career education materials, has been that of the Knox County Department of Public Instruction in Knoxville, where William L. Neal is project director. Among the materials produced is a document called "Curriculum Guide: Middle Grades." This publication (237 pages in length) contains a wide variety of truly exciting and innovative "homemade" materials developed for providing a career development emphasis to students at the middle and junior high school levels. Included are many games, activities, and projects in which students at this level could engage. Those schools who are successful in obtaining a copy of this publication will find hundreds of practicable ideas and suggestions for their career development programs.

Several junior high and middle schools are making use of "free" time available to their students at area vocational schools in their communities; for example, in Indianapolis, Indiana, in Norfolk, Virginia, and in Hagerstown, Maryland. The central idea is that since the area vocational schools are often empty of students during late afternoon hours during the regular school year and for many periods of time during the summer, they could be used to provide junior high school students with vocational exploratory experiences, through mini-courses, to explore what the various kinds of training opportunities offered in the area vocational school would be like, and the kinds of careers toward which such training would likely lead. We have seen examples of this, during the regular school day, where junior high school students visit area vocational schools and are given some "hands-on" exposure to various shops, using students enrolled in such schools as tutors.

In Pittsburgh, junior high school students are exposed to various course offerings available in senior high school vocational education through exploratory activities conducted in special facilities located in various parts of the city. There, students can move from one vocational area to another with much instruction carried on in an individualized education format. An added feature of Pittsburgh's system is that classroom teachers, from various junior high schools, are assigned, on a rotating basis, to these career exploratory centers. This has been reported as valuable for helping such teachers learn more about the career implications of the regular courses they teach at the junior high school level.

Semester or full academic year courses called "introduction to vocations" (or some similar title) have been taught for several years now at the junior high school level. This practice appears to be particularly common in New Jersey and North Carolina, where state departments of education have made curriculum guides for use in such classes. As we see career exploration programs developing across the land, we do not see a trend toward increasing the number of separate classes. On the contrary, the trend would seem to be away from such separate classes and toward integrating a career exploration emphasis in every classroom.

III. Summary

In this chapter, we have tried to put together a number of general recommendations, resource references, and selected examples of actual practice with reference to career development at the middle and junior high school levels. The most obvious impression the reader should gain from this effort is that as career development practices have expanded beyond merely the activities of the school counselor, they have moved increasingly in ways that have served to integrate the area of career development into the total career education concept. Rather than being diminished in importance, this integration has resulted in an increased emphasis on the vital importance of career development as a pervasive and influential part of career education. More importantly, with its integration into career education, the career development concept today holds greater potential for serving as a helpful source in career decisions made by youth than ever before in its history.

Those who have studied the contents of this chapter will have seen the almost universal agreement that exists on viewing the middle and junior high school years as concentrating on career exploration activities. If there are persons still advocating a concentration on specific vocational decision making at this level, they do not appear to be putting their recommendations into the literature. Perhaps more significantly, we have not seen such an emphasis in the practices that have come to our attention. This is not to say that some pupils may not be engaged in the making of specific vocational decisions even prior to reaching the middle school level. Of course, some do. When this happens, they have every right to do so, and the school has an inherent obligation to help them examine such choices carefully without pretending, or implying, that they have made a mistake. We are simply trying to point out that, so far as we have been able to determine, the middle school years appear to be well accepted as appropriate for career exploration on the part of most students.

While refraining from concentrated efforts to help middle school age youth make specific vocational decisions, we have also seen, particularly in our review of actual practices, that many middle and junior high schools are still including a strong emphasis on career *awareness*, as well as on career *exploration*, for members of their student body. This does not seem to have been done because of any desire to take the career awareness role away from the elementary school. Rather, it seems to be merely a function of the fact that, in many elementary schools, that role has not yet been effectively assumed. Interestingly, the examples contained in this chapter find middle and junior high schools emphasizing career awareness primarily through exposing their students to a wide variety of occupations. The emphasis on occupations, rather than careers, as a career *awareness* activity (but not as a career exploration), seems justified both on theoretical and on practical grounds.

It is hoped that the recommendations and examples presented in this chapter will enable many middle and junior high schools to answer some of the operational problems many now face in implementing a career exploration program in their school. We have presented here no examples of what we would consider theoretically ideal, middle school, career exploration programs because we have found none that fit our ideals in an exact manner. This neither surprises nor discourages us. We do not expect to find, nor should anyone demand, perfection in a movement as new as this one. Instead, we have found many schools that, while keeping the ideal clearly in mind, have been willing to settle for less when that is the best they can do, given the operational restrictions in opportunity for change that most schools face. Thus we are in no way disappointed with the practices reported here, nor do we feel they deserve criticism because of their imperfect nature. On the contrary, it is our feeling that middle and junior high schools are facing up to the challenges for change called for by career education in a realistic and positive fashion.

In this chapter, we have identified 34 specific recommendations for career exploration programs at the middle and junior high levels, most of which are represented in the actual examples of practices we have used. Rather than simply list all of these changes, we believe it might be more helpful if we try to summarize them by using these recommendations as possible answers to a number of practical questions middle and junior high schools face in mounting and operating programs of career exploration. Thus we have organized this summary around a number of such questions. We hope this arrangement will be helpful to the reader.

1: How can a school move toward attainment of the goal of providing career exploration experiences for all pupils in all classrooms in situations where such an emphasis does not now exist? Possible answers to this question based on contents of this chapter would include the following:

(1) Rather than trying to reorganize the entire school schedule, that schedule might be altered in such a way that several periods of time throughout the school year are reserved for career exploration activities.

(2) If career exploration cannot be provided for all students at this time, perhaps it could be provided at

least for those who appear least likely to finish high school.

(3)   If classroom teachers resist adopting a career exploration emphasis in teaching, a special career exploration class can be formed and made available to students as a separate offering.

(4)   If existing facilities and staff must be utilized, electives can be rearranged so that all students are exposed to each on a mini-course career exploration basis.

(5)   If all classroom teachers do not find it possible to incorporate a career exploration emphasis, perhaps one or more can be discovered who will be willing to make special provisions for career exploration as a regular part of their instructional activities.

2: What kinds of career exploration activities seem to work with middle and junior high school students? Our general answer to this question is that we have found no suggested career exploration practice that does not seem to be working in those situations where it is endorsed and accepted by teachers and counselors. While we know that for a wide variety of reasons, all possible career exploration activities will not work in all schools, the following are those that are working somewhere and are recommended by those using them:

(1)   Systematic instruction with reference to the nature of the fifteen occupational clusters recommended by the U.S. Office of Education

(2)   Field trips, including individual and group observation of work

(3)   Use of representatives of the business-industry-labor community as career resource persons in the classroom

(4)   Career resource centers containing much locally produced (by students wherever possible) materials devoted to occupations and careers in the community, as well as published materials and audio-visual aids

(5) Work experience programs (involving both paid and unpaid work) for students in the community

(6) Work simulation activities conducted within the school where students can experience the economic, sociological, and psychological necessity for work

(7) Mini-courses in a wide variety of career areas in which students can obtain some "hands-on" exposure to basic vocational skills required in the area, along with general information concerning their nature and outlook

(8) Community action projects in which students work as volunteers on a community improvement project that is meaningful to them

(9) Career games, puzzles, and projects which are fun for students to do and which also increase their awareness of possible career options open to them

(10) Use of former students as role models who can demonstrate to today's students how they "made it" and the kinds of life-styles they now lead

(11) Helping students assess their own work values through encouraging them to think about the kind of life they (or a hypothetical person) would have if they were to choose a particular career

(12) Allowing junior high school students to gain some hands-on basic vocational skills during the late afternoon or the summer months at local area vocational schools

(13) Conducting "strength sessions" for students where they can recount and consider their many previous accomplishments and the implications such accomplishments hold for their future work

(14) Teaching study habits to students as a special demonstration of good work habits

(15) Encouraging middle and junior high school students to think about a wide variety of possible post-high school educational opportunities that might be available to them and the career implications of each

There are still more examples in this chapter, but these few may suffice to demonstrate that there exist many kinds of possible activities.

3: How can parents become involved in a career explora-tion program? Examples found in this chapter include the following as representative of possible answers to this question:

(1) Parents can take their own children to work with them to let them see the parents at work.

(2) Parents can donate equipment and materials used by the school in its career exploration programs.

(3) Parents can serve as career resource consultants to teachers and to pupils.

(4) Parents can serve as volunteers on student trips.

(5) Parents can teach work values and work habits in the home.

(6) Parents can be given training designed to broaden their perspective and understanding of educational and career options available to their children.

(7) Parents can become involved as part of a citizen's advisory committee for the school's career exploration program.

(8) Parents can serve to effectively open up opportunities in the community for student field trips and other kinds of career exploratory experiences.

4: How can teachers be aided in increasing their knowledge with respect to career implications of their subject matter? Examples found in this chapter include:

(1) Using career advisory committees composed of par-ents, persons from the business-industry-labor com-munity, and students to help teachers discover career implications

(2) Using career resource persons in the classroom who come from the business-industry-labor community

(3) Using a career resource center as a source of materials, both printed and audio-visual in nature, that can be used in career exploration programs

(4) Participating in weekend or summer in-service training programs designed to upgrade their skills in the career exploration process

(5) Going with students on field trips to the business-insutry-labor community

(6) Devising career exploration learning packages of their own

(7) Obtaining work experience in the business-industry-labor community during the summer months

These are but a few of the many ways for the classroom teacher to gain knowledge in the career exploration process. Few of them are expensive, and some are without cost.

5: How can counselors at the middle school and junior high school levels become more actively involved in career exploration programs? Examples of the kinds of answers found in this chapter include:

(1) Counselors can work, in a collaborative fashion, with classroom teachers in provoding them with information concerning careers and the process of career exploration.

(2) Counselors can teach students decision-making skills.

(3) Counselors can become more active in group counseling with students.

(4) Counselors can serve as coordinators of relationships between school personnel and personnel from the business-industry-labor community.

(5) Counselors can establish career resource centers for use by teachers and students.

(6) Counselors can supervise the work of paraprofessionals employed to work in the school's career exploration programs.

(7) Counselors can arrange for representatives of a variety of kinds of post-high school educational institutions and programs to meet with their students.

(8) Counselors can collect and disseminate knowledge with respect to the career development process, work values, economic and labor market trends, and follow-up results of former students to teachers and to middle school students in clear and accurate form.

(9) Counselors can make career guidance a high-priority item in their statements of role and function.

Perhaps these five questions, along with the examples of possible answers to each, will serve to illustrate our feeling that helpful career exploration programs can be mounted and implemented in any middle or junior high school. While we have seen no "ideal" programs, neither have we seen any school where career exploration appears to be impossible. The career education movement holds great potential for making both the need for and the worth of the junior high school counselor clear to teachers, parents, students, and the general community. It is up to counselors to see that this happens.

REFERENCES

Part I

Anderson, Dale; and Heimann, R. "Vocational Maturity of Junior High School Girls." *Vocational Guidance Quarterly* (1967), vol. 15.

Arizona State Department of Education. *Career Education: Leadership in Learning.* Phoenix: Arizona State Department of Education, 1973.

Boocock, S. "The Life Career Game." *Personnel and Guidance Journal* (1967), vol. 46.

Bottoms, Gene; and O'Kelley, G. "Vocational Education as a Developmental Process." *American Vocational Journal* (1971), vol. 46.

Braland, Ross; and Sweeney, W. "A Different Approach to Vocational Counseling in Junior High." *The School Counselor* (1970), vol. 17.

Caplan, S.; Ruble, R.; and Segel, D. "A Theory of Educational and Vocational Choice in Junior High School." *Personnel and Guidance Journal* (1963), vol. 42.

Cuony, Edward. "Post-Secondary Counseling in Junior High School." *The School Counselor* (1968), vol. 15.

Engle, K.; Williams, R.; and Mazer, G. "Supplemental Counseling and Educational-Vocational Planning." *Vocational Guidance Quarterly* (1970), vol. 19.

Gambino, Thomas. "Junior High: The Exploratory Years." *American Vocational Journal* (1971), vol. 47.

Gaymer, Rosemary. "Career Counseling — Teaching the Art of Career Planning." *Vocational Guidance Quarterly* (1972), vol. 21.

Hansen, L. Sunny. "A Model for Career Development through Curriculum." *Personnel and Guidance Journal* (1972), vol. 51.

Hoyt, Kenneth. "The Counselor and Career Education." *SRA Guidance Newsletter* (November-December 1972). Chicago: Science Research Associates.

Ivey, A.; and Morrill, W. "Career Process: A New Concept for Vocational Behavior." *Personnel and Guidance Journal* (1968), vol. 46.

Johnson, Richard. "Simulation Techniques in Career Development." *American Vocational Journal* (1970), vol. 45.

——————; and Euler, D. "Effect of the Life Career Game on Learning and Retention of Educational-Occupational Information." *The School Counselor* (1972), vol. 19.

Knox, Kenneth. "Student Involvement in an Expanded Vocational Guidance Program." *The School Counselor* (1969), vol. 16.

Krippner, Stanley. "The Occupational Experiences and Vocational Preferences of 351 Upper Middle Class Junior High School Pupils." *Vocational Guidance Quarterly* (1962), vol. 10.

Leonard, Rachel. "Vocational Guidance in Junior High: One School's Answer." *Vocational Guidance Quarterly* (1969), vol. 17.

McDaniels, Carl. "Youth: Too Young to Choose?" *Vocational Guidance Quarterly* (1968), vol. 16.

Meyer, Robert S. "Career Education: An Opportunity for Counselors and Teachers to Work Together." *Guidelines for Pupil Services,* vol. 11, no. 3. Madison: Wisconsin State Department of Public Instruction, May 1973.

Morrill, W.; and Forrest, D. "Dimensions of Counseling for Career Development." *Personnel and Guidance Journal* (1970), vol. 49.

Peters, Herman; and Farwell, G. "Junior High School Vocational Guidance: A New Frontier." *Vocational Guidance Quarterly* (1959), vol. 7.

Peterson, Barbara. "The Distinctive Role of Counseling in the Junior High School." *The School Counselor* (1966), vol. 13.

Roman, Robert; and Doenges, J. "Career Week at McTigue Junior High." *American Vocational Journal* (1971), vol. 46.

Vetter, Louise, "Planning Ahead for the World of Work: Women's Career Patterns and Their Implications." *American Vocational Journal* (1970), vol. 45.

Wurtz, Robert; and Jalkanen, A. "Use of the Occupational Exploration Kit in a Ninth Grade." *The School Counselor* (1963), vol. 11.

Part II

California State Department of Education, Bureau of Pupil Personnel Services. *Career Guidance: A California Model for Career Development K–Adult.* Sacramento: California State Department of Education, 1971.

Drier, Harry N., Jr. (Editor). *Career Development Resources: A Guide to Audiovisual and Printed Materials for Grades K–12.* Worthington, Ohio: Charles A. Jones Publishing Company, 1973.

_____; et al. *K–12 Guide for Integrating Career Development into Local Curriculum.* Worthington, Ohio: Charles A. Jones Publishing Company, 1972.

High, Sidney C., Jr. *Bibliography on Career Education.* Washington, D.C.: U.S. Government Printing Office, May 1973.

Leonard, George E. *The Developmental Career Guidance Project, 1965–1970.* Detroit: Wayne State University, 1973.

Morgan, R. L.; Shook, M.; and Dane, J. (Editors). *An Anthology of 15 Career Education Programs.* Raleigh: Center for Occupational Education, North Carolina State University, 1973.

New Jersey State Department of Education. *Grades 7, 8 and 9 Learning Resources for Career Education.* Edison: New Jersey Occupational Resources Center, 1973.

North Carolina State Department of Public Instruction, Division of Exceptional Children. *Hands-On: Career Exploration for Bright Students.* Raleigh: North Carolina State Department of Public Instruction, 1972.

North Dakota State Board for Vocational Education. *Career Development K–12: Guideline of Career Development Activities.* Bismarck: North Dakota State Board for Vocational Education, 1971.

Ohio State Department of Education. *Career Orientation Program, Grades 7–8.* Columbus: Instructional Materials Laboratory, Ohio State University, 1972.

Oklahoma State Department of Education, Guidance, Counseling, and Testing Section. *A Guide for Developmental Vocational Guidance, K–12.* Edmond: Oklahoma State Department of Education, 1973 (revised).

U.S. Office of Education. *Abstracts of Exemplary Projects in Vocational Education.* Washington, D.C.: U.S. Government Printing Office, June 1973.

_____, Division of Vocational Education Research. *State Administered Exemplary Projects in Vocational Education.* Washington, D.C.: U.S. Government Printing Office.

Career Education in the Basic Academic Classroom

The first component emphasized for career education is the obligation of the classroom teacher to incorporate into academic subject matter an understanding of the relevance that knowledge and skills gained in the classroom have for the students' future work and careers. Among the key concepts involved are:

(1) Education's primary goal is to prepare students for life, including their working lives, with no necessary conflict between preparing for work and preparing for citizenship, culture, or any other of the numerous aspects of life to which education attempts to contribute.

(2) Knowledge, and the analytical capability, understanding, and skills to apply it, is the school's essential product. There is far more subject matter to be taught than can be included in any curriculum, and priorities in selection are necessary. The best test for inclusion is the question: What contribution will this subject matter make to the person this student wants to, and should, become?

111

(3) There is no subject matter currently included in school curricula which does not contribute in some way to the career potential of some students.

(4) Pointing up the career relevance of subject matter can provide double reinforcement:

(a) Motivation through demonstration of usefulness in contributing to an objective the student can relate to and endorse

(b) Clarification in providing illustrations within the student's range of experience and understanding

In the middle and junior high schools, the student is usually exposed for the first time to education organized around subject matter disciplines taught by teachers who are specialists in their particular field. There are of course advantages and disadvantages in every useful way of organizing the teaching/learning process. The one teacher, one classroom setting (even with supporting specialists, learning resource centers, and so forth) treats the student as a whole and facilitates integrating all subject matter into projects which can be related directly to the student's needs. Teachers cannot be specialists in every subject, but such expertise is not so important as other concerns at that time in the child's life. In the elementary school, teachers of the same grade level can coordinate, consult with, and assist each other, but they rarely have experience with the same students over whom to consult.

The middle/junior high school tends to move the focus from the student to the subject matter, no longer treating him or his expanding knowledge as an integrated whole. However, the quality of knowledge tends to improve as teacher specialization by subject matter becomes possible. The middle/junior high tends to be compartmentalized in contrast with the departmentalization of the high school. That is, there are subject matter specialists; but as a rule, the subjects and the teachers are too few to be segmented into departments — as high schools often do in mimicry of college — which is a consequence of intensive specialization in highly technical disciplines. Junior high teachers teach different subjects but the same students; and organized by grade level, they have the opportunity (if it is institutionalized) to integrate their efforts in fulfillment of student needs.

In our most advanced middle or junior high schools, team teaching, open classrooms, and flexible use of nonclassroom facilities and learning resource centers all work together to reduce the tyranny of architecture and encourage projects which cross the boundaries of limited subject matter specialties. Whether subject oriented or project oriented, subject matter content usually includes a required curriculum of science, math, English, social studies, and health and physical education... accompanied by a varied offering (sometimes elective, sometimes required) of music, art, languages, home economics, and industrial arts.

In this chapter, we advocate and illustrate the integration of career education into the five basic academic subject matter areas, either on a subject-by-subject basis or through integrated projects guided by cooperating teachers from a number of subject matter disciplines. Chapter 5 deals with the fine and practical arts. Since both chapters provide examples of career education activities in this variety of disciplines, it should be useful here to give teachers an approach and format for developing career education learning experiences.

DEVELOPING CAREER EDUCATION LEARNING EXPERIENCES

In chapter 7 we list forty career education concepts with which teachers might seek to familiarize their students. These are but a few of the nearly endless lists of possible concepts that teachers might want to incorporate into their teaching as they introduce career education into the academic subject matter courses. Having once decided what the concept is to which students should be introduced, the teacher is faced with the challenge of emphasizing these concepts in ways that will help students learn more subject matter.

The following suggested approach is adapted from *Career Education and the Elementary School Teacher*. The career education learning experience is the vehicle for putting over the concept within its academic setting. There are three essential ingredients involved: (a) the subject matter, (b) the career education concept, and (c) the activities to be included in the career education learning experience. Teachers will be most successful if they are encouraged to build this learning experience in ways that leave them free to begin with any one of the three essential ingredients. It matters little whether the teacher begins with a concern for subject matter or for a career education concept, or with an interest in a particular kind of prepared student activity. Conversely, it matters greatly that all three ingredients are clearly present in the completed career education learning experience.

Doubtless the most unfamiliar ingredient to the typical middle/junior high school teacher is the career education concept and all it entails. Therefore it is essential that such a concept be adopted and developed by teachers in ways that are meaningful to them. For most schools, this will require an in-service education effort such as described in chapter 6 of *Career Education and the Elementary School Teacher*. Once the major concepts to be incorporated into the curriculum are known to and understood by those teachers who will be building the career education learning experiences, it is not at all unusual to find teachers proposing many subconcepts that are meaningful and important to them. This is a most desirable practice. Career education concepts are not automatically meaningful to teachers. Yet it is essential that they become so if the teacher is to develop a good learning experience for the students.

There is a natural inclination for teachers, when looking at a particular set of career education concepts, to think that either (a) all of the concepts should be covered at each grade level, or (b) the concepts should be divided so that some are taught at each of the grade levels. In general, it is not initially productive to opt for either of these approaches. Instead, each teacher should pick a concept the teacher considers important for pupils to understand. As time goes on and more and more learning experiences are developed, the staff will find that all of the concepts are covered — and sometimes several times — at each grade level. It is much more important for teachers to develop learning experiences that are personally meaningful and important to them than to worry about whether all are covered when the program begins.

An additional difference between a career education learning experience and many other teacher-devised activity projects lies in the extent to which the business-labor-industry community is used in project activities. This important topic is discussed in chapter 4 of *Career Education and the Elementary School Teacher.*

The career education learning experience concept approach can be applied within a single academic course by a single teacher, or it can support a project activity approach involving more than one academic area. Of course, it is of central importance that the specific academic knowledge to be developed in each area be clearly identified as part of the written learning experience. One major weakness of many efforts to develop such experiences is the tendency of some teachers to ignore, underemphasize, or fail to capitalize fully upon opportunities to incorporate academic skills from several subject matter areas into their learning experiences. This seems to occur very often when teachers begin with an idea for a project activity that they think will be interesting for their pupils to follow and that may have direct career implications.

To build a career education learning experience without paying careful attention to the academic skills to be mastered during the project is to defeat one of the most important reasons for the entire career education movement. Two basic principles must be constantly kept in mind: (a) not taking time from imparting subject matter, and (b) using increases in student achievement as one criterion for evaluating the effectiveness of the career education program.

It cannot be too strongly emphasized that the most effective way to help students see the career implications of their subject matter is to let each teacher develop his or her own set of learning experiences. The reasons for emphasizing this point are numerous and include:

(1) The individual teacher is the operational expert best qualified to know where students are at any particular time in terms of academic skills development and then to determine both the nature and level of skills to be built into the career education learning experience.

(2) Opportunities to use careers and kinds of workers in a particular learning experience vary immensely from school to school. That which is appropriate in one school might not be so in another.

(3) The activities that form the central planning core of the career education learning experience are enthusiastically endorsed most by the teacher who invented them.

Students will gain more if each teacher uses personal learning experiences as his or her own "invention." Granted, teachers develop many ideas for building these learning experiences from looking at those which others have developed; but a truly dynamic program cannot be developed by trying to take what a different teacher in a different neighborhood — with a different class of students — found ideal, and assume that it is "transportable" across the country.

There are many ways of writing a guideline or profile for a career education learning experience for middle/junior high school students. The essentials are these:

(1) The goal to be accomplished and the performance objective with which to measure that accomplishment must be explicitly stated.

(2) Educational activities to be undertaken should be described.

(3) The media, the resources, and the personnel needs should be inventoried.

(4) Career implications and learning outcomes must be identified.

(5) Evaluation procedures ought to be supplied.

CAREER EDUCATION IN SCIENCE TEACHING

The objective of incorporating career education concepts into the teaching of middle/junior high school science courses should be to demonstrate:

(1) Seemingly abstract concepts (as well as laboratory demonstrations) of the various sciences have "real

world" applications that are meaningful to students in:

(a) Their effect on the environment in which the student lives

(b) The many careers which incorporate that type of knowledge

(2) Occupations within the career area range across the spectrum of educational requirements from those available to individuals not completing high school to those receiving Ph.D.s

Typical of each of the required academic core subjects is the fact that they encompass a broad range of subject matter relevant to many occupations but fill the specific requirements of none; i.e., no student will likely be employed merely as a "scientist." Further specialization in a particular science is necessary (mathematics to some degree is an exception), but that specialization is based upon subject matter found within the introductory science (or other) course. Later, instruction will be subdivided into still broader but more specialized categories, such as biological and physical sciences, and ultimately into narrower and narrower technical specialties within them. Crossing this vertical specialization will be horizontal divisions into occupational levels, perhaps ranging from paraprofessional to technician to a renowned research scientist. However, it is often overlooked that career ladders to which beginning science ultimately may contribute include a broad variety of occupations at all levels. Automobile mechanics, cosmetologists, engineers, and executives of science-related industries are all influenced by and dependent upon some degree of scientific knowledge. But the basic justification for teaching science to pre-adolescents is found simply in the fact that they will spend their lives in a science-permeated world. Thus courses in general science, though they may be designed primarily to purvey subject matter, can offer exploration into *What am I like? What is my world like? Who and what am I going to be?*

Career cluster materials, designed to support career awareness and exploration, also offer insight into life-styles, the nature of society, and the usefulness of subject matter. Every

subject matter specialist and in turn every professional association which serves each subject matter area should be anxious
to include career education material because it can motivate
and clarify for better classroom achievement, and it can interest a student and encourage him or her to seek further study,
and even choose a career within that subject matter area.

Regrettably, a review of professional journals, as well as
journals directed toward secondary school teachers in subject
matter specialties, shows that only science among the academic
subjects has explored extensively the possible contributions
of career education to its discipline. It may be too early in the
career education movement for others to follow this lead, but
it is gratifying to find that this one discipline is abreast of the
concept, though it is disappointing to find that it stands alone.

Perhaps it was the widespread unemployment among scientists and engineers consequent to a cutback of federal research and development expenditures, especially in the space
program. Perhaps it was the fact that such an unprecedented
loss of jobs in a highly esteemed professional field coincided
with a business recession. Perhaps it was the overreaction to
the consequent, mostly temporary, reductions in demand for
such manpower. Whichever cause or causes motivated them
to do so, science education journals are unique in supplying
data to secondary and other schools on the long-range outlook for employment in scientific occupations (*Science Education News*, April 1973, and Berglund, pp. 42–43). These journals
are also leaders in relating scientific training to specific occupational and career areas and in suggesting approaches to
career education within science courses (Radang, pp. 273–75).

Science teaching in elementary and secondary schools
generally follows a sequence complementary to career education; i.e., exploratory general science courses are taught in the
sixth and seventh grades of the middle/junior high school, with
more in-depth treatments of physical and biological sciences in
the ninth and tenth grades, and specialization by discipline
(chemistry, physics, and so on) in the eleventh and twelfth
grades. Unfortunately, however, these courses suffer too often
from an excess of textbook teaching, limited student involvement, and an obvious omission of applied science, engineering,
and technology.

An almost universal assumption that every student is being prepared for college contributes to neglect of those aspects of science which are related to daily life or needed in occupations below the college-degree level. Also, because of teacher and course specialization, there is a tendency to neglect the necessary linkages between science and mathematics. A career education approach could help remedy these errors by involving students in laboratory work, field trips, and simulated work experience with scientific techniques and tasks.

Even as knowledge and careers in the sciences are changing rapidly, so are the methods of teaching science. The progressive science teacher today is more likely to act as guide and director of learning, as the students discover scientific concepts and individual study, than as a traditional lecturer, laboratory demonstrator, and enforcer of memorization. The corollary with career education is obvious. Students can discover scientific principles not only in the classroom and laboratory, but also by visiting industry, tearing down and reassembling an automobile engine, repairing an electric motor, listening to visitors who not only have the scientific knowledge but carry with them evidence of the career applications, and in any of hundreds of additional ways. Career education units should include materials on scientific careers as well as scientific concepts, but students can be led to discover both. Junior high school science rarely attempts to introduce students to the scientific method of reasoning and research, but its applicability to the decision-making skills appropriate for career choice is another point of commonality between career education and science teaching.

In *The Science Teacher*, we read:

> An integrated approach to the primary curriculum cuts across subject boundaries in providing meaningful work for the children. It is an approach which, by basing the child's work as far as possible upon first-hand experiences of the world in which he lives, enables him to acquire knowledge, understanding, skills, values, attitudes in such a way that he can perceive relationships more easily than if he were made to master isolated skills or particular components of knowledge and left to make his own syntheses, a re-

quirement which is contrary to all we know about the psychological development of young children (Chrisman, pp. 20-21).

Though individual differences are wide, it is generally about the ages of eleven or twelve that students are assumed to be developing the power of formal reasoning. Yet that occurs just as they are leaving the integrated and comprehensive elementary school to be fragmentized into the separate disciplines of the subject matter-oriented secondary schools. The student is anxious to come to an understanding of himself through exploration of his relationship to the world around him. He and that world are integrated wholes, and the subject matter disciplines seem alien to that concept and need. Yet the complexity of the knowledge to be imparted suggests the need for teachers who are specialized in the subject matter. Team teaching and other approaches for integration of diverse subject matter through a variety of project approaches offer the advantages of both the depth of specialized knowledge and the breadth of "real world" interrelationships.

Career education has the advantage that it can be used in either the subject matter orientation or the integrated core curriculum and can also provide a vehicle for that integration.

Examples of projects which could integrate career education exploration into the teaching of middle/junior high school science classes are almost endless. For instance, a project for a class in botany — to learn various tree-grafting techniques and investigate the growth capabilities and final outcome of tree grafts — can be related to the careers of tree surgeon, forest ranger, fruit farmer, and so forth (*Handbook for Implementation*, p. 49).

When planning approaches to incorporate the career education concepts into the established curriculum content of a science class, the teacher should have a clear idea of why science is being taught to the middle/junior high school students. To quote *The Science Teacher* again:

> ...While the major purpose of science instruction is to help students discover knowledge and learn of the processes by which knowledge can be discovered, an additional purpose would be to understand how sci-

entists use these capabilities in the world of work (April 1973).

Northern Illinois University has a program called "Project ABLE" wherein suggestions for the middle/junior high school give the following relationships among academic learning, occupations, and hands-on experiences:

Immediate Task	*Possible Career*	*Classroom Project*
To classify animals into groups	Zoo or museum worker	Organize a make-believe zoo.
To classify plants into groups	Gardener, agronomist	Convert school grounds into a botanical garden.
To demonstate how chemical changes produce new materials	Artist, chemist	Make plaster of paris sculpture, or make fire extinguishers. Display products and report process.
To discuss basic water cycle, rain, evaporation, and clouds	Weather reporter on radio or television	Set up model weather station.
To plan an electric circuit	Electrician	Experiment with batteries, bells, bulbs, buzzers, and beepers.

One science class resolved to undertake mock court trials to simulate the process of bringing suit against persons or organizations guilty of polluting the air or water. Students interviewed a wide range of citizens in the community and identified instances of air and water pollution. In conducting the mock court, they invited working scientists to the classroom as expert witnesses and quizzed them about their jobs as well as their ecological knowledge. In the process, the students became more aware of social issues and legal system, along with increased knowledge of the application of science and the consequent career opportunities (Berglund, p. 58).

A biology class simulated a seaside town to explore its environmental problems. As the students became interested in the town's problems, excitement built. They identified and studied 22 occupations necessary to environmental management. So long as the philosophy is clear and the teachers understand the planning format, the committed teacher can develop the projects and provide the needed career exploration without endangering the teaching of science.

A clear statement of the science teacher's role in career education was formulated during a discussion session at the National Science Teachers Association convention:

> The career education concept, in contrast to traditional vocational education, presents a real challenge to all teachers at a time when public education is under serious indictment for failure to establish and maintain a viable and purposeful level of interest for students of all types.... While the major purpose of science instruction is to help students discover knowledge and learn the processes by which knowledge can be discovered, an additional purpose would be to understand how scientists use these capabilities in the world of work.... Career education is partly, then, a problem of relating a conceptual science to the working conditions of a career (*The Science Teacher*, pp. 28–33).

Part of the genius of the career education approach is its adaptability to the needs and interests of the student and teacher. The familiarity of example and the realism of its career potential *for him or her* will determine the motivating ability of any student's career education learning experience. The extent of involvement in the development of that career education learning experience will determine the teacher's enthusiasm for it and the effectiveness in using it. Therefore, the examples which follow in this and other chapters are profiles of what other teachers have done — but any teacher *could* do. They are not recommended activities per se. The profiles illustrate both the content and the format of career education learning experiences that a number of states have used to integrate career education into the established curriculum in the middle/junior high school.

SCIENCE PROFILES

We have drawn from the experience of three states for suggested activities for the science classroom. Though each was developed differently, all three show a similarity of purpose: to coordinate and unify concepts to the world of work. It will also be noticed that the examples tend to follow the objectives-activities-resources-outcomes-evaluation sequence advocated earlier in the chapter for construction of career education learning experiences.

Ohio

A science example devised in Ohio focused on the career of conservationist. First, the stated rationale was a public concern for ecology and student involvement in saving the environment. Second, the developmental objectives of the project were:

(1) To understand the importance of conservation for the future of society

(2) To learn of the variety of careers related to the area of conservation

(3) To consider possible positive and negative aspects of the career of a conservationist

Under the third category, the school listed the following questions and activities which were planned to help seek the answers:

A. Why are conservationists needed in society?

1. Students bring to class newspaper or magazine articles which deal with current conservation problems; e.g.:

a. Forest fires

b. Pollution of lakes and rivers

2. Students discuss possible solutions to the conservation problems discussed in the articles.

3. If interested, students can explore the possibilities of making a class contribution toward conservation; e.g.:

a. Students contact a local industry known for its concern in ecology and volunteer the services of the class for a short period of time.

b. Students set up school display of types of pollution prevention in which each person could actively take part; e.g., buying of returnable soda containers rather than cans.

B. What careers are available in the area of conservation?

1. Students discuss various jobs with which they are familiar in the area of conservation; e.g.:

a. Forest ranger

b. Sanitation specialist

2. Students discuss the double role of each — occupation and needed service to society.

3. Students discuss the frustrations of serving people who ignore the importance of conservation; e.g.:

a. Careless campers

b. Highway litterbugs

C. What are the possible positive and negative aspects of the occupation of a conservationist?

1. Students discuss possible advantages of conservation work; e.g.:

a. Service to society

b. Primarily out-of-doors work

2. Students discuss possible disadvantages of conservation work; e.g.:

a. Frustration of "fighting a losing battle"

b. Often have little contact with other people; e.g., forest ranger often lives within the park in which he works

3. Students evaluate for themselves their interest in learning more about the career of a conservationist.

New York

Electricity was the focus of science activities developed in New York State. As source material, the students used pamphlets and booklets published by well-known manufacturers of electrical appliances, gadgets, and so forth. Its project followed a threefold outline: showing the course content, explaining the career concepts as they applied to each segment, and giving techniques whereby the two can be integrated.

A. Of all forms of energy, electricity is most useful to man. Almost every phase of daily living has been heavily influenced by man's use of electrical energy.

   Concept: Occupations involving electricity are usually highly technical — math- and science-oriented jobs, or practical jobs involving manipulative skills in conjunction with general knowledge of properties of electricity.

   Technique: Using a Van deGraffe generator, leyden jar, or both, demonstrate the strength of large static charges. (If this equipment is not available, or as a supplement to using it, discuss the destructive force of lightning.) Discuss the relationship between static electricity and job safety. In what situations are large charges likely to accumulate? In what settings would small discharges be disastrous? How are static charges dissipated in industrial settings?

B. Electricity can best be understood in terms of scientific models and mathematical relationships.

   Concept: Large static charges or high-power electric current may pose serious shock hazards to workers.

   Technique: Discuss the differences and similarities in skills, aptitudes, interests, training time, pay, work environment, and prestige between an electrical engineer and an electrician.

C. The electrical engineer is responsible for designing devices which depend upon electricity as their source of energy.

   Concept: Since all of us come into contact with electrical devices, some knowledge of safety procedures related to electricity is important.

   Technique: Discuss the question: How has electricity affected your life? Use this discussion to lead into a lesson on industrial processes which would be impossible without electricity.

D. The electrician is responsible for installing, maintaining, and repairing many of the devices created by electrical engineers.

   Concepts: (1) Electrical devices have made man's work easier; (2) many industrial processes would be impossible without electricity.

Missouri

For the seventh through ninth grades, Missouri educators outlined a science/career education activity that was open-ended in that it was designed for students to identify skills required in occupations of interest to them, connecting the skills with those that can be acquired in school. The two goals of the project were: (a) for the individual to understand the relationship between what goes on in school and out of school, and (b) for the individual to understand how participation in school activities can relate to selected occupational areas. The stated outcome was: Given a list of basic scientific skills — i.e., a systematic approach to problem solving — the individual will select an occupational area of interest to him and explain how people in this occupation make use of these skills. The resources were listed as: measuring equipment, classroom teacher, carpet layer, and the film "Andromeda Strain." Three major activities were presented:

A. Students will measure an area of the classroom to be carpeted. A carpet layer will be invited into the classroom to describe the methods and tools he uses in measuring a room to be carpeted and remeasure the classroom. He will emphasize the importance of a systematic method as well as precision in measurement, noting the difference in cost that inaccuracy could produce.

B. Show the film, having the students identify in writing the steps taken in the systematic solution of the mystery. The class can follow up this film with a discussion of a solution, replicating the logic and emphasizing the realism of the film.

C. The class will be broken into groups of three, four, or five students. Each group will be given a statement to "prove" true or false (teacher may use any "known" theories, or make up fictitious statements). In "proving" the statement true or false, the important point will be the systematic method used in coming to a group conclusion. Groups will then share and compare methods, suggesting alternate procedures if possible. A possible example might be the statement: "You're a doctor involved in medical research. You believe that people in sedentary (mainly sitting down and low level of activity) occupations have more heart attacks than people in more physically active occupations." Design an experiment (systematic problem-solving method) to either prove or disprove your hypothesis. The rightness or wrongness of your hypothesis is not as important as your method.

MATHEMATICS PROFILES

There are few better evidences of the faith that children and youth place in their adult counselors and guidance personnel than their willingness to submit to the discipline of mathematical abstractions. Especially since Sputnik, some exposure in high school to levels of mathematics previously reserved for college students is an almost universal requirement. The arithmetic concepts formerly taught in grades six through eight (but now completed in elementary school) were rarely exciting, but their applicability to daily life was beyond doubt. The "new math" emphasizes the derivation of the concepts rather than their application. It may enhance the analytical skills of the college-bound, but it does little to motivate the potential school leaver. The algebra, trigonometry, and geometry usually required and the trigonometry and calculus now often taught in junior high schools are so far beyond adolescent experience that it is difficult for a youth to conceive of an application for them other than college entrance requirements. That is not to say that the applicability does not exist. They are clearly applicable to a career as mathematician, physicist, or engineer. But that is not apparent to youth of limited experience.

It is useful to ask: Why teach math? Is its purpose, beyond simple arithmetic, to prepare for math-using vocations or to use in daily living? Is it for love of its abstractions, because it supposedly exercises the mind, or because it is required for college entrance? If one accepts the philosophy that the role of the school is to aid each youth to become the kind of adult he seeks to emulate, it is clear that some mathematics are necessary for everyone as part of preparation for life, but the level and nature of that need vary widely. Sputnik proved the need for science-oriented math and locked it into the curriculum. Emphasis on preparation for college has supported that orientation, even though the math needs of college-trained students vary as greatly as that of the rest of the population. An integration of career education into the math curriculum can provide proof of the subject's relevance, examples useful in its teaching, and a measure of the math requirements of various occupations.

Too many students describe math as generally taught as boring, timewasting, dull, and uninteresting. Teaching of it ranges from highly abstract theory to mundane applications in shop math. The choice should be not those but what will help the child become what he wants to be.

From the career education viewpoint, the teaching of math seems to be deteriorating. The problem is two tiered. In some places the titles of business and other applied math have simply gone through a rechristening to become career education math. The "new" math can lead in the opposite direction. Its stress on deriving the concepts may strengthen analytical skills (a clear gain for career education as well as for everything else), but it offers little as a vehicle for insights into the usefulness of math in occupational settings other than mathematics itself, or in other applied settings. That need not be so. New math programs emphasize discovery learning. But the "discovery" of abstract mathematical relationships may not be exciting to all. Why not discovery of career applications as well? Examples of applicability can be supplied, including those involving careers, without giving up the analytical approach.

A balance is needed between the theoretical and practical in math. Students should learn to discover, analyze, and generalize, as well as acquire manipulative skills. Theoretical mathematics may aid the development of analytical skills and give experience in logical thinking. The practical application provides the motivation of usefulness and demonstrated contribution to a goal prized by the student. Career education applications are as important in the teaching of the advanced math required for many of the college bound as in the math designed for noncollege students. Career education can therefore serve as the necessary balancing factor between the theoretical and the practical in the teaching of math.

Teaching math in a career education context can also put its importance in context, since it requires the teacher to identify not only those occupations in which math is an important component but also those in which it is not. At the middle/junior high school level,. all should have the same exposure to math as they explore to discover their future career directions. However, as choices begin to be made and implemented, it becomes apparent that some will have great need and some limited need for knowledge of more advanced mathematics.

All too often the elementary and secondary schools' math requirements are but a reflection of college entrance requirements. Not only is such dictation a burden upon the noncollege bound, it is also an imposition upon many aiming at college study in nontechnical fields. Why should those with interest and talent for drama, the humanities, languages, music, and so forth, be required to absorb the same mathematical preparation as those seeking engineering careers? Some knowledge of mathematics is vital in a science-permeated world, but how much of what kind for whom is a question too infrequently asked.

There appears to be some tendency in the middle/junior high school, as well as in elementary and secondary school math in general, to move away from the practical uses and toward emphasis on abstract concepts. *Why Johnny Can't Add* with its criticism of the new math and other recent approaches may represent a beginning backswing of the pendulum. The need for relevance for the teaching of math is well illustrated in *How to Survive in Your Native Land*, which presents the example of the youth who, working in a bowling alley, could keep in his head and calculate the interrelationships among bowling scores for five teams simultaneously, but could not achieve a passing grade in his math classes.

Math lends itself particularly well to the integration of the theoretical and the practical — of the abstract and the concrete. Its usefulness can be demonstrated for almost every level of occupation, and occupational illustrations are available to aid the teaching of almost every concept. Cash registers, office machines, calculators, and computers are all teaching devices and examples of practical uses. Geometry can be shown to be a tool of the architect, the mechanical or civil engineer, the industrial designer, the draftsman, and the operating engineer rigging a crane. Surveying for a highway or cutting a rafter are functions of trigonometry. Statistics can be shown to be a necessity for the politician, the social scientist, the demographer, the business manager, to name only a few.

Again, a few examples from various states illustrate approaches which are emerging and the formats within which they are derived.

California

The Sonoma County Office of Education devised a planned career education experience for seventh grade students which taught them the formalities and consequences of banking. Though the activity was confined to writing and cashing checks and to saving money, the program held other ramifications of the banking business. In short, the project was as follows:

A. Preparation required:

1. Students were taught about the importance of accuracy and competence in cashing checks (incorporating this into math experience).

2. A bank representative visited the classroom and told the students of the different occupations in the bank. He explained the codes to be found on checks and the routing of the check if it should "bounce."

3. An investigating team of students was formed, and the class elected an interviewer, a photographer, a reporter, and a director (to coordinate the entire experience). These students gathered information and relayed it to their classmates.

4. A slide-tape presentation was developed by the elected committee, with a follow-up by the teacher to obtain the necessary photos and to help the students synchronize the taped interview and the slides.

B. Objectives:

1. To develop the necessary math skills to complete the exercise

2. To organize the presentation in a logical fashion

3. To be aware of decision making and career opportunities in a bank

4. To be able to work together with classmates

5. To relate making a check and its purpose with the responsibility entailed in having an account

6. At a later date, students to be able to enact (in play form) the different occupations in a bank, portraying a typical situation between client and employee

7. To be able to write a check, balance a checkbook after writing several checks, and follow the route that an unpaid check takes

C. Resource people used:

1. The instructor prepared the class before the activity started.

2. A career education specialist worked with the class compiling questions for the interviewer to ask and later issuing equipment and accompanying the students who were working on the project.

3. A vice president of a nearby bank prepared a presentation for the class and later took five students on an investigative tour of the bank.

D. What curriculum areas were incorporated into the project, and how?

1. The ability to work with one another

2. English skills, reading aptitudes (used in nearly every job in the bank)

3. History, socioeconomic values due to the economy, and how it affects bank policies and rates (e.g., veterans loans have increased)

4. Skills of organization — the play to be shown in the English class

5. Skills in mathematics — writing checks as well as percentiles in loans

E. Evaluation in terms of students' enthusiasm, success, or failure (the percentage of objectives that were met by the students)

1. Students in one particular class were lauded by their teacher for their excellent preparation of questions for the resource banker, and were congratulated for the rapid progress of their play.

2. This same teacher reported that students were "amazed" by the diverse skills needed (80 percent in the project and 90 percent in the play), but that their photo skills needed to be "brushed up on." He planned a follow-up on the photos.

F. What concepts were incorporated into the experience? Career planning should be a privilege and responsibility of the individual. The goal is for the student to actively engage in his own career development process. He increases his self-knowledge and his knowledge of the world of work and the society that affects it. He accepts responsibility for a series of choices that carry him along the career development continuum.

North Dakota

The general objective of the North Dakota experience was to broaden sixth grade students' interests that would open up an expanded basis for vocational choice. The concept was to expand their understanding of the fact that mathematics helps people in their work, thus making math more meaningful to the students. The specific behavioral objective was that students would be able to name one way in which each worker studied used fractions in his or her occupation.

Resource materials were: math textbooks, worksheets and packets of fractional parts, blueprints and instructions, industrial arts patterns, filmstrips, building trades books, and magazines that emphasize mechanics. The outline gave the following suggestions:

Activity: Have students measure things around the classroom to have them become aware of fractional parts of an inch. Relate fractions to the world of work by having students find how workers use the following fractions in their work: carpenter, housewife, seamstress, painter, mechanic, and wallpaper hanger. Draw to scale what you are to use. Make a blueprint. Build birdhouses, doghouses, or rabbit hutches of cardboard or plywood. Also build needed equipment for the classroom.

Techniques: Develop awareness that some people have talent for building, designing, and handling tools, while others must learn proper procedures and safety. Discuss the importance of the carpenter and his need for understanding measurements (such as fractions). How can this be correlated with different geometric designs? Review the fractional parts of an inch on a ruler or yardstick. Assign specific places for specific small groups to measure. Have each group measure the area exactly. Discuss the student's findings. Have volunteer students demonstrate how each of the workers use fractions. Ask students if they know any other workers who use fractions in their work.

To add to this experience, the teachers were asked to evaluate the activity by answering the following questions:

(1) Did this activity apply to the suggested subject area?

(2) Are the criteria for student performance (the specific behavioral objective) too high, too low, or satisfactory?

They were then asked to comment regarding:

(1) What additions or deletions could you suggest in the activity and technique realm?

(2) Could you suggest additional resource materials for this activity?

Missouri

As before, the Missouri experience was aimed at seventh through ninth graders. The two goals were the same as those stated for the science activity. The stated outcome was: Given a list of occupations in the index in the "chronicle guidance kit," the individual will select the three occupations that most interest him and describe what areas of math, and which specific mathematical skills, are most important in performance of the duties of those occupations. The resources were listed as: counselor to provide resource persons, surveyor, computer programmer, parents, and students.

> *Activity:* Invite a surveyor to visit the class and bring the equipment he uses in his occupation. After explaining the use of his equipment, he will aid the students in surveying the school grounds. Take the class on a field trip to a computer center to see what sorts of occupations are found there. A computer programmer would explain to the students the need for accuracy and a systematic approach in writing a program. The students will interview their mother or father (observe each on the job if possible) about how math is used in his or her occupation. They will then report their findings to the class. Special notation might be made where students report different uses of math for individuals in similar jobs. Students will share with the class how they have made use of mathematical skills in part-time or summer jobs they have held.

Minnesota

Ninth grade students in Minnesota were given a math project that had as its objectives:

(1) Helping the student explore interrelationships and interdependence between jobs

(2) Helping the student evaluate the relevance of his own aptitudes and abilities for broad occupational areas

(3) Helping the student relate his or her value concepts to a variety of job choices

(4) Helping the student examine occupations in terms of his or her current life-style, considering such factors as personal and parental aspiration, family background, and personal values

(5) Helping the student identify the personal compromises he may have to make in order to attain a chosen occupation

The specific concepts of the activity were manifold, including: role, association, interdependence, services, socialization, self, scarcity, resource, distribution, money and credit, culture, environment, incentives, competition, institutions, models, status, and labor. Materials needed were: information of the metric system, community resource people, and "planning a house" resource sheet, which included such typical occupations and math relationships as "lumber dealer — board feet, area," "electrician — ampere hours, watts, ohms, measurement," "bricklayer — ratio, measurement angles," and "plumber — psi, distance, measurement."

The activities outlined for the teachers and students were as follows:

A. *Planning a house: a study of the construction career cluster.*
Because of the number of jobs involved in the construction industry, this activity illustrates well the interdependence between various segments of a job cluster. In addition, it is economically significant not only to those employed in the field, but to virtually all members of society. An integral part of this activity is the developing awareness and listing of the occupations involved in each step of construction. Included with this listing, the student should provide examples of the mathematical problems involved in each occupation. For the use of the teacher during this activity and for the students at the end of the activity, a number of construction jobs and possible related math problem areas are listed on the resource sheet. The teacher will provide for each student a lot plan similar in configuration and size to those common in the local community. Using this lot plan, the student will design to scale a complete floor plan for single-family dwelling in accordance with

local building requirements (such as 1,000 square-foot, one floor minimum, set back, and sewage disposal). The steps involved in the process of the planning of the home will be:

1. Design the home

2. Acquire financing

3. Locate the building on the lot and excavate

4. Construct footings and basement

5. Do capping and rough framing

6. Enclose the structure

7. Begin electrical, plumbing, and heating construction

8. Do the interior walls

9. Finish interior construction

10. Finish mechanical construction (electric, plumbing, heat)

11. Have utilities hooked up

12. Do the basic decorating (paint, stain, varnish)

13. Complete the final interior decorating (drapes, carpet, shades)

14. Do the final grading and landscaping

As a part of this activity, students could profit greatly from · visits by speakers involved in the construction industry and ventures into the community to talk to resource people.

B. *Metric measurement in occupations.* This activity should culminate the study of metric measurement and conversion. At this time the students should realize the great importance of metric conversion in industry. From all indications, the metric system will eventually become a universally accepted system of measurement. Presently the United States and the United Kingdom are the only countries which do not use the metric system entirely. In this activity, the student will investigate the aspects of a job involving metric measurement. The job under investigation will be selected by chance (drawing from the hat).

Sample occupations could be: race driver, garage mechanic, secretary, lawyer, homemaker, doctor, pharmacist, heavy equipment operator, map maker, carpenter, dressmaker, surveyor, teacher, landscaper, chemist, nurse, clerk, and tool and die maker. Regardless of what occupation the student selects, the investigation should include different ways that metric measurements would be used in that job. The activity should show to the student the importance of mastering the metric system for occupational competence.

LANGUAGE ARTS PROFILES

The goal of English as taught to the pre- and early adolescents is to help them communicate more effectively and to develop more understanding and perception of literature and language opportunities. There should be little argument with this statement, but how to accomplish the goal is less easily agreed upon.

The ability to read is crucial — but how is it best taught? By reading Shakespeare, Chaucer, Melville, or Twain? Or by reading topics of interest to the students from such popular sources as *Hot Rod* magazine (see *English Journal*, p. 118), as the recent study *Hooked on Books* deftly argues? There is much of value in the classics or they would not have survived to attain that status. But these may also be less of value than those steeped in them suppose, and — more importantly — they are of no value to the "turned off" student whose interest is not aroused.

The same applies to writing. One learns to write by writing, and a student is more likely to write about what interests him. Spelling seems more important if the words have meaning and can be equated to happenings in the student's life.

Career education is one but not the *only* means of making reading a book seem worthwhile to an otherwise unmotivated student. Experiences and interests including work and careers are more effective written assignments for many than less personal matters. Words related to careers may help motivate the learning of spelling. There is no reason why a wide range of topics in reading, writing, and spelling would offer a less useful learning experience than a narrow and rigid one.

Communications underlie all human relations, and it can be demonstrated that the quality of speech and writing is a major determinant of where an individual will come to rest in the occupation and income scale. Recognition of this fact can provide motivation and illustration.

English courses are threatened from two sides: (1) They may carry a burden from the teacher's past training — a conviction that all that is worth reading and writing about occurred centuries or decades ago or in noncontemporary worlds far from the student's experience; or (2) they may become catchalls for extraneous matter; e.g., how to watch television, how to write letters of invitation, facing teenage problems, and so forth. Career education may be a useful vessel for navigating between those opposing shoals.

An experienced English teacher writing in the *English Journal* attacks traditional methods for failing to motivate students and advocates vocationally related English, not as "watered down" content but as a vehicle through which as much can be taught and learned with greater enthusiasm:

> Citizenry suffers because of poor communication skills; yet we often waste the opportunities we have with our students' time in many English classes.... The reason students do not respond is not that they are less intelligent; it is that their interests and motivations lie in other fields.... The emphasis in the vocational English classes is on using English on the job, in the community, and in the student's personal life. The stress is on the immediate, practical use of English to improve their vocational success, and on their immediate and future need of English to be better citizens and to have more profitable and enjoyable personal lives (pp. 116–20).

The author reports success in English classes which emphasize communications on the job, in the community, and in the student's personal life. Stress on immediate practical uses of English to improve career success, develop better citizenship, and experience more profitable and enjoyable lives should be as effective for the college bound as for others. With no texts available for that approach, the use of contemporary books, magazines, audio-visual materials, technical and trade journals, research into careers, learning to fill out job applications all provide fresher material than a textbook can offer. Students were demonstrated to increase their self-confidence, intensify and broaden their reading habits, and even register for non-required English courses upon learning that English had something to offer for them. To quote again:

> Though our students may not study Bacon, Shakespeare, Milton, or even Dickens in our vocational English classes, we feel they learn attitudes and skills immeasurably more useful. And perhaps of most importance, our students like English. They find out that reading is fun and that they can speak and write. We believe they grow in self-reliance and initiative. They become more aware of the importance of communication.... The greatest problem is not that the students or administrative officers approve the course, but that teachers do.... Most English teachers trained thoroughly in American and English literature, have neither the inclination nor the background for this approach. It takes a very special teacher of more than average understanding, imagination, initiative, flexibility, and optimism (*English Journal*).

However, the mistake must not be made of limiting career education approaches in English teaching to the noncollege bound. Potential college students too have yearnings toward their careers and can find needed motivation in the reciprocal relations between study of the language arts and career pursuits. The following examples illustrate contents and techniques used by four states.

Oklahoma

Some provocative word games were devised by educators in Oklahoma (see Figures 2 through 4). The ultimate objective of this unit of instruction was that the students be able to demonstrate:

(1) The ability to form words

(2) The ability to decode scrambled letters to make a word related to the student's vocational area

Words in Carpentry

See if you can find fifty or more words using the letters in the word *carpentry*. Your words must contain three letters or more. No proper nouns, abbreviations, or foreign words should be used.

1. _____   18. _____   35. _____

2. _____   19. _____   36. _____

3. _____   20. _____   37. _____

4. _____   21. _____   38. _____

5. _____   22. _____   39. _____

6. _____   23. _____   40. _____

7. _____   24. _____   41. _____

8. _____   25. _____   42. _____

9. _____   26. _____   43. _____

10. _____   27. _____   44. _____

11. _____   28. _____   45. _____

12. _____   29. _____   46. _____

13. _____   30. _____   47. _____

14. _____   31. _____   48. _____

15. _____   32. _____   49. _____

16. _____   33. _____   50. _____

17. _____   34. _____

Figure 2. Carpentry Word Game

Scrambled Words for the Construction Industry

Below are some scrambled words associated with the construction industry. Unscramble the letters to form words that apply to that industry; for example, the first, "mehmar," rearranged spells "hammer."

1. mehmar   hammer
2. evis   _____
3. earcb   _____
4. gesuar   _____
5. velel   _____
6. ibt   _____
7. wsa   _____
8. lnai   _____
9. wescr redvir   _____
10. sliper   _____
11. fahl htachte   _____
12. hups lridl   _____
13. slandoiga   _____
14. eiwhn   _____
15. cetrecsn   _____
16. rameer   _____
17. lina tse   _____
18. kcalh niel   _____
19. blump bbo   _____
20. tirsnat   _____
21. sichel   _____
22. leur   _____

FIGURE 3. Anagrams for the Construction Industry

Word Game for Construction Industry Terms

The words listed below are hidden in this puzzle. Find and circle each one. They may be forward, backward, or diagonal. One has been located for you. Some letters are in more than one word.

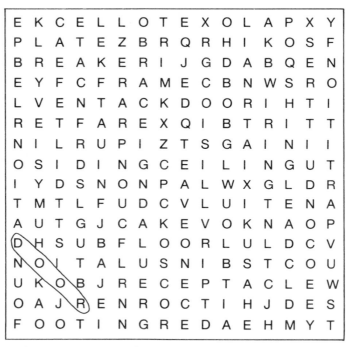

```
E  K  C  E  L  L  O  T  E  X  O  L  A  P  X  Y
P  L  A  T  E  Z  B  R  Q  R  H  I  K  O  S  F
B  R  E  A  K  E  R  I  J  G  D  A  B  Q  E  N
E  Y  F  C  F  R  A  M  E  C  B  N  W  S  R  O
L  V  E  N  T  A  C  K  D  O  O  R  I  H  T  I
R  E  T  F  A  R  E  X  Q  I  B  T  R  I  T  T
N  I  L  R  U  P  I  Z  T  S  G  A  I  N  I  I
O  S  I  D  I  N  G  C  E  I  L  I  N  G  U  T
I  Y  D  S  N  O  N  P  A  L  W  X  G  L  D  R
T  M  T  L  F  U  D  C  V  L  U  I  T  E  N  A
A  U  T  G  J  C  A  K  E  V  O  K  N  A  O  P
D  H  S  U  B  F  L  O  O  R  L  U  L  D  C  V
N  O  I  T  A  L  U  S  N  I  B  S  T  C  O  U
U  K  O  B  J  R  E  C  E  P  T  A  C  L  E  W
O  A  J  R  E  N  R  O  C  T  I  H  J  D  E  S
F  O  O  T  I  N  G  R  E  D  A  E  H  M  Y  T
```

1. brace	12. frame	22. receptacle
2. breaker	13. header	23. shingle
3. ceiling	14. insulation	24. siding
4. cellotex	15. joist	25. sill
5. conduit	16. junction box	26. stud
6. corner	17. nail	27. subfloor
7. door	18. partition	28. tack
8. eave	19. plate	29. trim
9. electrical outlet	20. purlin	30. window
10. footing	21. rafter	31. wiring
11. foundation		

FIGURE 4. Word Puzzle Terms in the Construction Industry

(3) The ability to write as many words as possible, which may be found within a word related to the student's vocational area

(4) The ability to select words hidden within scrambled letters

The teachers were asked to provide students with assignment sheets on which the various word games were printed, and to discuss the objectives listed in (1) through (4) above.

North Carolina

The following example in the language arts field is one of many used in a publication from North Carolina State University's Center for Occupational Education for middle/junior high schools (Scherer and Clary). Teachers could opt to choose among several related occupations such as advertising, theater arts, communications, and so forth. Resource materials were books, articles in journals, and filmstrips. One example is the following profile of occupations in television:

A. Purpose: The television industry is relatively young and expanding. Many jobs will be created by this industry which affects all of us. Television can provide interplanetary communication as well as programs originating on our own planet.

B. Objectives:

1. To learn the variety of types of jobs in television related to communicative skills

2. To recognize the oral and visual communicative aspects of the medium

3. To discover the need for teamwork when putting together a station broadcast that lasts approximately twenty hours a day

4. To explore three occupations within broadcasting that emphasize the need for and uses of communications: writing and news reporting, sales, and programming

C. Activities:

1. In discussing news writing and reporting, the class will be most concerned with news writing.

    a. Have each student write one or two minutes of news copy (e.g., have some outsider break into the room and create a disturbance for students to write about).

    b. Have each student present his news item and record his presentation on a tape recorder.

    c. Have the class or a small group of students listen to the news for the inclusion of:

        (1) Who, what, where, when, why, and how

        (2) Interest level of the material presented

        (3) The vocal interest of the reading

2. Class project concerning television sales:

    a. Assign three students to contact each of the local television stations, asking for the sales department, to request a schedule of time-prices for advertising time periods (e.g., prime time from 7:30 to 11:00 p.m. is more expensive than morning or afternoon time).

    b. Have these students form a panel presentation for the class, covering:

        (1) Who purchases advertising time on local stations?

        (2) Who sells time for each station?

        (3) How much does advertising time (prime time) cost in relation to other time blocks?

        (4) Who ultimately pays for television programs?

        (5) Whatever else the panel members feel they have learned about the operation of a sales department.

3. The class project concerning programming is especially good for the new fall series.

    a. Have each student keep a diary on three new television programs, beginning with the introduction of the series.

b. Contents of the diary should include a discussion of the following:

(1) Plot of the program

(2) Characters on the program

(3) Degree of quality (What was good about the show and what was bad about it?)

(4) Type of program: drama, situation comedy, variety show, adventure, detective, and so forth

(5) Recommendations for future viewing

c. Each student should then try to find a professional review of the programs he has selected.

North Dakota

The broad objectives of the North Dakota assignment were to show students the various occupations involved in the publishing of a book, together with the interdependency of workers. After the teacher presented the "people pyramid" (Figure 5), each student was to demonstrate a knowledge of such interdependency by listing at least 70 percent of the occupations covered in the pyramid.

The resource materials involved encyclopedia, books on publishing, and films. The teachers were asked to evaluate the exercise by answering the following questions:

(1) Did this activity apply to the suggested subject area? Grade level?

(2) Are the criteria for student performance (specific behavioral objective) too high, too low, or satisfactory?

In addition, they were requested to comment on: (a) What additions or deletions could you suggest in the activity and techniques? (b) Could you suggest additional resource materials for this activity?

A. Activity: Use a people pyramid to illustrate the various levels, processes, and related vocations involved in the ultimate publication of a book. (This will illustrate the

Book

Salesperson   Truck driver

Printer   Proofreader   Bookbinder

Writer   Artist   Editor   Inkmaker

Tree | Lumber | Machine | Paper | Paper
planter | jack | operator | maker | cutter

FIGURE 5. People Pyramid in the Publishing Field

division of labor plus the interdependency of workers, and can be adapted to any product.)

B. Suggested techniques:

1. On the chalkboard, list as many occupations as possible that are involved in publishing a book.

2. Construct a people pyramid that illustrates how these jobs lead to the final product.

3. Emphasize how these workers are interdependent.

4. Go through each of the jobs listed, discussing the kinds of work these people do.

5. Have students construct other people pyramids depicting other products if desired.

Missouri

The exercise for seventh through ninth grade students in Missouri was to give the students an understanding of the relationships between learning activities in school and career activities outside school, and an understanding of how participation in school activities can relate to selected occupational areas. The student was to identify skills required in occupations of interest to him or her and to determine where these skills can be acquired in school. The outcome was stated as: Given a list of basic communication skills, the individual will select one of them to use in a simulated performance as it would be used in an occupation of his or her choice. Resource materials were: counselor to provide the "chronicle guidance kit," want ads, stamps and envelopes, and the school personnel director. The activities were as follows:

A. Each student will be given a want ad section of a newspaper or an occupational brief from the chronicle guidance kit. He will then select a name and address of a firm which encompasses an occupation of interest to him. He will then write a business letter to be mailed to that source in search of occupational information.

B. After receiving the occupational information, the class will share the information they have acquired.

C. Given a local, state, or national issue, students will debate the issue on the basis of available research.

D. Each student will list three occupations of interest to him or her that require debating skills, and will share these with the class.

E. The school personnel director will visit the classroom and demonstrate with the help of a student how he interviews someone for a job in the school district. Each student will then make a list of desirable interviewing questions and behaviors, and will role-play the interviewing situation.

SOCIAL STUDIES PROFILES

The primary goal of social studies in the middle/junior high school is to describe man in society and to develop good citizenship. Too often, however, social studies courses neglect study of what man does with a major portion of his time in society; that is, work. Also too infrequently stressed is inclusion of the principle that good citizenship requires being a contributing member of society through self-support, production of goods and services, payment of taxes, and volunteer work, as well as through voting and participating in the political process. The typical social studies sequence in the middle/junior high school begins with study of the world that students are aware of (immediately around them), then moves to wider and wider explorations leading to specialization that starts in high school. However, the lack of integration between the late elementary years and junior high school often violates this principle. A typical social studies sequence experienced in early adolescence is history of the United States in the fifth grade, history and geography of the world in the sixth grade, history of the relevant state in the seventh grade, and back to history of the United States in the eighth grade. Boredom with repetition is a common student complaint.

A well-recognized study of school practice for this age group identifies the following objectives for social studies:

> ... [It should] help the child comprehend his experiences and find meaning in life. This should be interpreted to include opportunities for the student to

analyze some aspects of the environment and his reactions to it and the forces operating in society that tend to make people what they are.... Each child must be prepared to participate effectively in the dynamic life of his society. Correspondingly, his society needs active, aware, and loyal citizens who will work devotedly for its improvement.... Each person needs to acquire an understanding of analytical processes and other problem-solving tools that are developed by scholars in the social sciences. With increasing maturity the students should learn to ask fruitful questions and examine critical data in social situations.... To achieve these goals, it is necessary that junior high school students become acquainted with the world and society of today, become educated for citizenship, and learn and maintain the values of democracy (Howard and Stoumbis, p. 148).

One of the more difficult tasks for social studies teachers is deciding upon the area, content, and material to cover. Everything appropriate to social studies cannot be covered; thus selection is inevitable. Sometimes a thematic approach is followed — subject matter is formed around themes such as war, social history, and so forth — but the subject matter approach — history, economics, and so on — is more common. Social studies is especially vulnerable to the charge that the middle/junior high school's major fault is the aping of high school practices. Too often it tends to be text oriented and fact centered. Most teaching depends too much on lecture, reading, and memorizing, with critical issues and social problems ignored.

Career education can make a significant contribution to social studies teaching for this age group. For instance, the repetition between the fifth and eighth grades can be handled by emphasizing the role of careers in history. Following career education lines, a career unit or frequent referral to career implications can emphasize career awareness in the fifth grade and exploration and decision making in grade eight, with in-depth study of job content coming later in high school. Economics is too little taught, primarily because of the failure of teacher training institutions to prepare elementary and secondary school teachers in this area. Yet no social science

has more to offer the future citizen, breadwinner, and consumer; and studies of the job market are an ideal place to learn
of the nature and role of employment in individual and family
life and in society.

The present social studies curricula were developed decades
ago. Reform attempts during the 1960s urged the teaching of
concepts rather than chronological fact. Career education can
fit well into this structure, personalizing the meaning of both
fact and concept. Career education's message is not only the
inclusion of career information, but the principle that all
teaching will be more effective if its relevance to the student's
present and future lives is made apparent. Consumer education
can play the same role in study of the economy. Whenever
explicit instruction in separate classes of career education or
exploration of the world of work is undertaken, the social
studies teacher is generally an obvious person for the assignment. The message is a simple one: To be effective, teachers
should ask why they use the subject matter techniques and
materials they do. How can social studies (and other topics) be
made challenging and meaningful? Again career education
concepts are not the only way, but they are a useful way, as the
following examples illustrate.

Wisconsin

The following profile of a project in Wisconsin gives as an
overview: to communicate to students that there is a direct
correlation between the world of work and the entire range of
human relations both on and off the job. The ten objectives
listed would fit easily into most units of a general social studies
or civics course.

Three periods in history were pinpointed to bring out their
interrelationships with the world of work: the Colonial period
— establishment of the Protestant work ethic; the Jacksonian
period — the social and political rise of the common man and
its influence on his economic aspirations and endeavors; and
sectionalism, slavery, and the Civil War — socioeconomic
effects on the nation as a result of regionalism, sectionalism,
and the institution of slavery, and the eventual resolution of
sociopolitical differences allowing for a blending of diversified

economic endeavors. Resources for this unit were books and films. The following activities, concepts, and objectives were prescribed:

A. Activities — methods:

1. The teacher may use resource people to discuss common reasons for losing a job, emphasizing interpersonal relationships (concepts 1, 3, 5, 11, 14, 15).

2. Students may listen to and discuss tapes about certain words that "get you fired" (concepts 5, 7, 9, 12, 15, 16).

3. Students may view and discuss filmstrips depicting trouble on the job and getting and keeping the first job (concepts 5, 7, 9, 12, 16).

4. Students may research the work ethic, minority groups, and the job market (concepts 1 through 4, 8, 11, 16).

5. A counselor or clergyman may discuss family problems relating to the work environment (concepts 1 through 3, 10).

6. Students may conduct a survey regarding work and leisure time (concepts 1, 2, 5, 7, 11).

7. Students may study the Protestant work ethic and compare it to today's work ethics (concepts 1 through 3, 6, 7, 10, 15).

8. Students may examine various job levels and investigate the percentage of minority groups employed at each level (concepts 1 through 4, 10, 11).

9. Students may participate in role-playing activities involving employee-customer relationships (concepts 1, 2, 5, 7, 10, 16).

10. Students may debate: "Resolved: Working Mothers Are Detrimental to a Healthy Family Structure" (concepts 3 through 5).

B. Concepts:

1. An understanding and acceptance of self is important throughout life.

2. Persons need to be recognized as having dignity and worth.

3. Occupations exist for a purpose.

4. There is a wide variety of occupations which may be classified in several ways.

5. Work means different things to different people.

6. Education and work are interrelated.

7. Individuals differ in their abilities, attitudes, and values.

8. Occupational supply and demand have an impact on career planning.

9. Job specialization creates interdependency.

10. Environment and individual potential interact to influence career development.

11. Occupations and life-styles are interrelated.

12. Individuals can learn to perform adequately in a variety of occupations.

13. Career development requires a continuous and sequential series of choices.

14. Various groups and institutions influence the nature and structure of work.

15. Individuals are responsible for their career planning.

16. Job characteristics and individuals must be flexible in a changing society.

C. Objectives — The student should:

1. Appreciate the idea that keeping a job can be more difficult than obtaining a job

2. Realize that jobs may have an important effect on family relations

3. Be aware of how parents (or other people in the community) got their jobs, what they do, and what they like and dislike about their jobs

4. Understand the meaning of the societal work ethic

5. Be able to analyze the job market relative to minority groups

6. Be able to list factors necessary for job satisfaction

7. Develop an awareness that the choice of an occupation can have an effect on family relationships and on relationships with other people

Utah

Two profiles chosen to demonstrate Utah's program of integrating career education into an eighth grade classes' social studies curriculum are but two examples from an extensive junior high school career education program undertaken by one local school district in that state. All the examples are similar in structure, but diverse in nature. "Geography Affects Career Choice" used an almanac as its source material and focused on "the United States today."

A. Behavioral objective: The student will demonstrate his understarding that the amount of income and the availability of his career choice may vary with geographical area by compiling a list of five selected career choices and the mean income in five geographical areas.

B. Learning activities:

1. Actual observation or experience:

a. Make a list of average incomes in the following careers located in the following cities: accounting clerks (man), draftsmen, messenger, office girl, carpenter, painter, truck driver (local); Bethlehem (Pennsylvania), Worcester (Massachusetts), Atlanta (Georgia), Los Angeles (California), Milwaukee (Wisconsin), and Albuquerque (New Mexico).

b. What accounts for the differences in income?

c. Which area averages the highest? The lowest?

2. Follow-up activities (students and teacher to develop).

A second exercise, "City Planning," sent the students to the city planning offices for their resource materials and to invite a representative from that office to visit the school and speak to the students. Its focus was "settlement of the West."

A. Behavioral objective: Given the assignment of constructing a model city, students will perform their assigned tasks. They will also be able to list two reasons for acceptance of the master plan. This plan must be ratified by two-thirds of the class members. They will also, at the end of the class discussion, list at least five careers associated with city planning.

B. Learning activities (actual observation or experience): The class will systematically select a geographic location for a model city. They will then draw up a plan for it. The students will be divided into groups. Each group shall have different responsibilities, such as transportation, industrial or business facilities, recreational, educational, housing, city services, and cultural facilities. Group leaders should consult freely with other group leaders in making a master plan. Two-thirds of the class must approve the master plan before it can be accepted.

California

The seventh grade classes of a junior high school in Sonoma County were given an exercise in career education/geography. In preparation for the project, the teacher obtained a film applicable to the subject and led the students into a discussion of modern-day explorers (especially petroleum). The remainder of the project was as outlined below.

A. Objectives (student to be able to):

1. List as many jobs as he can that relate to petroleum exploration

2. List two outside leisure-time activities that appeal to him

3. List the jobs that would best fit this leisure-time activity

B. Describe the experience:

1. Film and class discussion on students' reaction to the film.

2. Students wrote comments about the film (as though they were film critics).

C. What curriculum areas were incorporated into the project? How?

1. Social sciences — need to understand environmental implication

2. Science — geologist, mathematician, chemist

3. Technical skills areas:

    a. Welding

    b. Drilling

    c. Ship operating

D. Evaluate experience in terms of students' enthusiasm — success or failure. In other words: What percentage of students met the objectives?

1. Students showed a good deal of interest in technical occupations.

2. Comments generally were: "Good film. I learned a lot about looking for oil."

3. Follow-up exercise — discussion on which job found requires what type of education.

4. (The teacher enclosed the classroom set of papers so that the administrators could review the overall reaction.)

E. What concept or concepts were incorporated into the experience?

1. Individuals must be adaptable in a changing society.

2. Career planning should be a privilege and responsibility of the individual.

3. Education, work, and leisure alternatives.

4. There is a relationship between the commitment to education and work and the availability and use of leisure time.

New Hampshire

New Hampshire administrators created a versatile pattern that all teachers could use to construct a career "display" in their classrooms (Figure 6). Materials needed were simply listed as: bulletin board, construction paper, thumb tacks, magic marker, colored yarn, and spotlight. The following description — printed verbatim — gives definitive explanations while still leaving wide latitude for teachers and students to be artistic.

> *Description:* Seven circles with words "Careers in Social Sciences" in center circle with yarn connecting from center out to six circles in which are printed occupational titles for six social sciences. Related occupations are connected to major occupational areas. Cut-out object representing tools for the various occupations will be located at base of display. These are to be placed in appropriate occupational circle by students observing the board. At bottom of bulletin board will be indication that for additional information students should refer to Social Sciences Career box [another innovation created by this school].

PHYSICAL EDUCATION AND HEALTH PROFILES

Too often physical education in junior high school is a preliminary training ground and a weeding out stage for the interscholastic sports program of the high school. It can, and at best does much more. It can teach the importance of team-work in work relationships and of sticking to the end of the game (or day or job). It can help develop healthy bodies and minds, an obvious contribution to career success. It can also provide skills for recreation and use of leisure.

If teachers were to carefully examine and justify their objectives, they would probably put more emphasis on individual sports interests and activities likely to continue over a lifetime, and less on team sports, body contact, and competition. There should be more emphasis on intramural activities and less on interschool rivalries. With enjoyment and health as the objectives, swimming, track, tennis, volleyball,

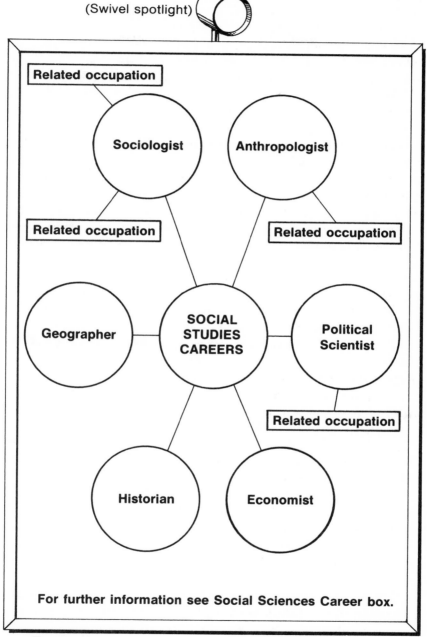

FIGURE 6. Spotlight on Careers in the Social Sciences

ping pong, golf, softball, bowling, dancing, and soccer all may be found to equal football and basketball.

These are also the areas where the relationship between physical capability and employability should be explored. There has been too much said about the decline of physical requirements of jobs and the increase of mental requirements. A stenographer at a typewriter, a teacher before a classroom, an executive with a sixty-hour workweek have different but no less physical requirements than the farmer, the construction worker, and the assembly line worker, even those of the past. Students should learn to appraise their own health, physical abilities, handicaps, and interests and relate to them in the variety of possible careers. Compatability between aspiration and capability can then be achieved either by adapting aspirations to realistic expectation or by improving physical capabilities. The growing emphasis on job safety under the new Occupational Safety and Health Act is another obvious interface between career education and physical education and health.

More specific than these general relationships is exploration of the many and growing number of health-related occupations and careers. Recreation personnel, coaching staffs, physical therapists, health inspectors, along with all of the medical occupations are only a few such careers.

Programs of exploration into the health cluster of occupations are fairly numerous in middle/junior high schools throughout the country, and there is a substantial body of materials. Exploration of the general interrelationships between health and employment are few but are growing in number. For this reason, only one example (Utah's) is provided of the many medically oriented career exploration projects available, while New York City's and Wisconsin's are included to illustrate the general approach.

New York City

Four examples of the New York City approach to career education in the physical education and health disciplines are outlined below. The first is a general association of sports and careers.

A. Activities of a scientific and technical nature:

   1. In the world of work:

      a. Automobile mechanic

      b. Plumber

      c. Electrician

      d. Medical profession

   2. In physical education and athletics:

      a. Team sports in general

      b. Individual sports in general

B. Illustrations:

   1. Numerous occupations require that the workers have a knowledge of a scientific or technical nature. As an example, the automobile mechanic must be thoroughly familiar with the theories in combustibles, electricity, physics, and so forth, as they apply to the functioning of an internal combustion engine.

   2. Even as the mechanic knows about an engine, the diver or gymnast knows or should know how the body moves. He must have a working knowledge of physiology and kinesiology in order to understand how to efficiently execute movements.

   3. Examples in team sports where the participants are involved in technical matters are the understanding and developing of specific plays and game strategies such as in football, soccer, hockey, and so forth.

The second example deals specifically with "temperaments."

A. Activities involving the evaluation (arriving at generalizations, judgments, or decisions) of information against sensory or judgmental criteria:

   1. In the world of work:

      a. Airline pilot

      b. Truck driver

      c. Carpenter

2. In physical education and athletics:

    a. Baseball and softball

    b. Rhythms and dance

    c. Tennis

    d. Basketball

    e. Officiating

    f. Other

B. Illustrations:

1. In order to hit or catch a ball (in any activity), an individual must rely on the rapid evaluation of sensory information and criteria. Many factors are considered before an evaluation and response can be made — wind, speed, height, spin, angle of flight, distance, and so forth. The task (hitting, catching) depends on the successful evaluation of these criteria (and a successful response!).

2. Successful completion of dance forms relies on perception, evaluation, and response to sensory stimuli.

3. Officiating demands evaluation and decision making, based almost solely on sensory and judgment criteria. Students should be encouraged to participate in activities of an officiating nature.

Although the third example was not given a title, it is obvious that it traverses the spectrum of physical endeavor from least to most; in other words, strength.

A. There are five degrees of physical demand: sedentary, light, medium, heavy, and very heavy work, such as carrying, lifting, pushing, pulling.

1. In the world of work:

    a. Accountant

    b. Typesetter

    c. Service salesperson

    d. Farm supervisor

    e. Logger

2. In physical education and athletics:

   a. Softball

   b. Soccer

   c. Football

   d. Calisthenics

   e. Gymnastics

   f. Wrestling

B. Illustrations:

1. The degrees of strength required in different physical education activities vary widely. Although there are extremely few activities which could be described as "sedentary," there are activities which cover the other four degrees.

2. Softball requires very little "strength" as such, and does not involve a certain amount of standing.

3. Soccer requires very little lifting, carrying, pushing, or pulling, but does require a high degree of activity (since running is a major factor).

4. Calisthenics may require speed, endurance, agility, or strength, and in varying degrees.

5. Gymnastics and wrestling could be classified as very heavy work in that strength is a prime factor for success.

The final example concerning "motor coordination" gives us these exercises:

A. Reaching, handling, fingering, or feeling:

1. In the world of work:

   a. Carpenter

   b. Truck loader

   c. Fruit picker

   d. Physician

2. In physical education and athletics:

   a. Basketball

   b. Wrestling

   c. Softball

   d. Football

B. Illustrations:

   1. In basketball, softball, and football, reaching and handling are involved in catching and throwing. To some extent, fingering is involved in shooting a basket, pitching a softball, or passing a football.

   2. In wrestling, there is a great deal of seizing, holding, grasping, and turning, which is considered as "handling."

Wisconsin

There are two concepts in the first exercise of a Wisconsin profile for career education in the seventh through ninth grade physical education classroom: (1) occupations exist for a purpose, and (2) persons need to be recognized as having dignity and worth. The resources were stated as: (1) student recommendations as to what responsibilities the job should entail, and (2) checklist prepared by the instructor as to job responsibility. When the exercise was completed, the students were asked to write their evaluations and recommendations of job responsibility. The outline below gives the manner in which this exercise was conducted:

A. Objectives — The student should:

   1. Realize that occupations exist for a purpose, and all occupations are important in the world of work.

   2. Understand that dignity, worth, and responsibility accompany each person and every occupation.

B. Activity — The student may:

   1. Assume various responsibilities in the physical education and athletic area

   2. Have the experience of assuming responsibility for one of the following jobs:

   a. Equipment manager

    b. Assistant athletic trainer

    c. Locker-room towel duty

    d. Develop playfield or athletic field

    e. Instruct lesser skilled students

C. Outcome — The student will:

    1. Understand that work is essential for all activity, and if the total individual is to be developed, good workmanship must be achieved.

    2. Acquire pride in achievement and a sense of accomplishment in any occupational endeavor, regardless of how menial the job is.

A second exercise, also for seventh through ninth grades, used film strips as source material. The concepts were: (1) individuals differ in their interests, abilities, attitudes, and values, and (2) occupations and life-style are interrelated. As an evaluation procedure, they were asked to take a skills test in three chosen activities.

A. Objectives — The student should:

    1. Acquire experience in activities that will provide pleasant recreational leisure-time pursuits

    2. Become aware of the increased amount of leisure time that will be available and the importance of creating worthwhile and relaxing activities during this leisure time

B. Activity — The student may participate in many of the following team and individual sports:

1. Archery	8. Paddleball
2. Boating	9. Skiing
3. Bowling	10. Softball
4. Canoeing	11. Swimming
5. Fishing	12. Tennis
6. Golf	13. Water skiing
7. Horseshoes	

C. Outcome — The student will:

1. Realize the fact that increased leisure time is a part of the immediate future and must have plans as to how to use the time in a worthwhile manner in a wholesome pursuit.

2. Acquire experience in many individual sports to the degree that he can perform with a reasonable degree of proficiency in three of the listed activities. At least one activity should be a winter and one a summer sport.

Utah

A Utah example for eighth graders is called "Exploring Jobs in a Hospital." A specific unit on careers in health, the exercise was designed to give the students the behavioral objective of being able to "list fifteen occupations or jobs involved" in running and operating a hospital." In preparation for the experience, the teacher invited a school nurse to attend the class and show a film concerning hospital life, with the students taking notes on the film and her discussion of it.

When the film had been viewed, the students, teacher, and nurse held a "rap" session on what had been depicted. The students came up with a list of subjects they wanted to discuss with the nurse concerning the following: nurses (male and female), "candy stripers," licensed practical nurses, registered nurses, nurses' aides, "pink ladies," doctors, various specialists, and housekeeping staff. They also wanted to know about such jobs as bookkeeping, insurance, in- and out-patient care, food services, groundskeeping, and the dispensary. Follow-up activities included a field trip to the hospital, collecting magazine articles about hospital jobs, and making a pamphlet on a hospital job.

PROFILES OF INTERDISCIPLINARY APPROACHES

Most instruction in middle/junior high schools occurs within separate classes in subject matter-oriented curricula. Although it is convenient for purposes of faculty study and training and for school administration to construct curricula in this fashion, they clash with the realities of the world in which the student does and will live. Except for those few hired as pure mathematicians, math does not exist in the job world separate from science, engineering, marketing, or some other practical application. Hence these subjects cannot contribute in the job world without heavy math inputs. The same can be said for other topics.

Though career education can and does make a major contribution as it is incorporated into individual subject matter courses, its inherent bias is toward project approaches; i.e., since the real world is not segmented into separate disciplines, a reality-oriented approach tends to use examples which interrelate the same variety of disciplines as the labor market. However, separate subject matter specialties among faculty need not impede an interdisciplinary approach both to career education and to its academic contributions. The fundamental requirement is leadership and initiative from at least one teacher or staff member, cooperation from the essential teachers, and a bit of imagination. The following are examples where these ingredients have been applied.

Delaware

The career development learning unit in a Delaware experience consisted of 35 sixth grade students (and five teachers) who were investigating the career clusters of (a) business and office, (b) marketing and distribution, and (c) manufacturing. The time required for the unit was five hours per week for five weeks. The outline is as follows:

A. Objectives:

1. The student will participate as a productive member of the group.

2. The group will manufacture and distribute a product.

3. The student will be able to list at least three factors to consider when organizing and operating a manufacturing business.

4. Several students will become leaders and assist the teachers directly in the planning and operation of the production.

5. Each student will assume at least three occupational roles associated with this business enterprise during the course of the activity. The occupations to be studied are:

   a. Business and office:

      (1) Accountant

      (2) Bookkeeper

      (3) Secretary

   b. Manufacturing:

      (1) Custodian

      (2) Foreman

      (3) Production manager

      (4) Inspector

      (5) Assembly line worker

   c. Marketing and distribution:

      (1) Market surveyor

      (2) Cashier

      (3) Sales manager

      (4) Salesperson

      (5) Messenger

      (6) Advertising technician

      (7) Stock boy

B. Activities sequence:

   1. Teaching team meets with four select students — approaching them with the idea of manufacturing and selling a kite to the other students in the school.

   2. Student group is divided into teams to conduct research in building and testing kites.

   3. Prototype kites are built and tested with the final model being decided upon.

4. The board of directors selects a production manager, an accounting manager, and a sales manager.

5. Students are divided into working groups for each stage of the production, and production is started.

6. Workers are rotated so that everyone can get a chance to participate in phases of the production.

7. Accountants receive the bills, and accumulate and record them on ledger sheets.

8. The accounting group determines the selling price per kite.

9. Conduct an advertising and sales campaign. This includes the making of posters and the sales talk to sixth grade classrooms. Orders for kites are taken.

10. At the conclusion of the kite sales, a profit and loss statement is prepared.

C. Correlation with other disciplines:

1. Language arts:

a. Business letter writing to kite manufacturers, retailers, and American Kiteflyer's Association.

b. Report writing and advertising copy are included.

2. Social studies — Corporation structure, cost and profit, production, and sales are studied.

3. Reading:

a. Books about kites, flight, and business are read.

b. Several groups of students write comic books on the building and flying of their kites. Vocabulary and spelling skills are practiced during all phases of the project.

4. Science and mathematics:

a. Design, measurement, and drawing are involved in constructing the prototype.

b. Principles of flight and elementary bookkeeping also stress science and mathematics.

D. Evaluation — A written test to determine increase in career awareness is administered. It tests for knowledge of titles, tools, terms, and environment associated with the project. Individual subject area teachers test for outcomes in their areas of interest.

Maryland

An interdisciplinary approach to career exploration was developed in Maryland to establish such an approach at the junior high school level "to the process of self-realization, broad occupational exploration, and a realistic orientation" to the world of work. The goal was to provide a "broad range of experiences and exposures from which implications can be made to the world of work." The assignment was broken down into two segments, one for teachers and the other for students.

A. Staff objectives:

1. To create a positive attitude among staff members toward career exploration at the junior high school level

2. To acquaint staff members with career trends and opportunities

3. To stimulate the teacher to examine and relate to the students' career implications relevant to the teacher's discipline

4. To encourage the teachers to create situations wherein students must employ the decision-making process

5. To inform the parents and community of the structure and contents of career exploration

6. To involve teachers in planning activities both in their own area and in an interdisciplinary manner

B. Staff activities (to be evaluated):

1. First objective:

a. Present members of the career exploration workshop team will take their information back to their own discipline areas at the start of the school year.

b. Reserve a faculty meeting and introduce a speaker from the career exploration workshop.

2. Second objective:

a. During the in-service day, present a fact-finding game to acquaint teachers with knowledge and limitations of career opportunities.

b. Set up a display area illustrating job opportunities.

c. Provide U.S. Department of Labor brochures and local opportunity pamphlets in professional library and teachers' lounge.

3. Third objective:

a. Invite teachers to observe working team members and then interaction with students.

b. Send a survey sheet to all teachers (participation voluntary), asking them to list their familiarity with careers within their own disciplines.

4. Fourth objective:

a. Form a task force, and verbally encourage this activity.

b. This will hopefully be a natural outcome after the presentation of the preceding three objectives.

5. Fifth objective:

a. Present a program (or programs) at parent-student-teacher meetings orienting those in attendance to career exploration.

b. Provide information concerning the program in the school newsletter.

c. Because of school activities, parents and community should become aware of career exploration.

d. Place descriptive annotations showing progress on the "schools" page of the local newspaper.

e. Provide evidence of career exploration at the back-to-school night.

6. Sixth objective:

    a. Have ongoing meetings (starting with the present task force) and subsequent natural expansion.

    b. Discuss progress and plans.

Student goals and objectives were then listed, with suggested activities and strategies tied in with these goals.

A. Objectives:

1. The student will recognize the dignity of all work.

    a. Acquaint the student with people in the community and the roles they play; and enable the students to list essential contributions each makes to the community.

    b. When responding to job preferences within each occupational group, the student will reply to his or her interests and capabilities, rather than the "status" the job carries.

2. The student will realistically evaluate his or her capabilities, perceived limitations, and attitudes.

    a. Through analysis of her or his characteristics — e.g., personality, habits, abilities, interests, limitations, and so forth — the student will list those jobs in which she or he could be successfully employed and those in which she or he could not be successfully employed.

    b. The student will speak with the counselor about the purpose, meaning of results, and implications for his or her own future of the evaluative tests given by the guidance department.

3. The student will be exposed to the general process of decision making. He or she will follow systematic steps in decision making by:

    a. Definition and application of inductive and deductive reasoning, given specific situations

    b. Solving a problem and, in retrospect, identifying the values he or she used in forming the decision

4. The student will broaden his or her knowledge in the spectrum of the world of work.

a. The student will identify the needs of society in general and the community in particular.

b. Given the nine occupational areas, the student will name three additional occupations within each area by means of pre- and postevaluations.

c. Each student will prepare correctly:

(1) Work permits

(2) Social Security applications

(3) Job applications

(4) A résumé

(5) Job descriptions

(6) Payroll deduction sheets

d. The student will identify the proper channels to follow in obtaining job information.

B. Activities and strategies:

1. In one of the all-student-encompassing disciplines, the student will poll various job offerings:

a. Poll family members

b. Poll teachers

c. Poll community resources (government, industry, private)

d. Suggested format:

(1) Occupational title

(2) Education or training

(3) Working conditions

(4) Salary

(5) Job description, benefits, disadvantages

(6) Potential for advancement

(7) Possible media: tapes, slides, interviews, field trips, guest speakers, films, brochures, job fairs

e. Follow-up: Catalog this activity and make information available to the library.

2. During the job opportunity fair, the junior high will sponsor a parallel activity at the school depicting the information gathered during the school year. (See activities 1 and 8 for suggestions.)

3. Students being given hands-on experiences are to save the material to present as a personal career folder for all classes.

   a. English:

      (1) Construct a job résumé

      (2) Write letters of inquiry

      (3) Write biographical sketch

      (4) Fill out job applications

      (5) File for a work permit

   b. Social studies:

      (1) Establish channels in business, industry, trades, governmental job information

      (2) Relate jobs to total integration of the community

      (3) Labor management relations

   c. Math:

      (1) Write payroll deduction sheets

      (2) Construct personal budgets

      (3) Study insurance rates in relation to jobs

      (4) Relate need for mathematics to specific trades

      (5) Inductive-deductive reasoning

   d. Industrial arts:

      (1) Line production — birdhouses

      (2) Exposure to specific vocational occupations: a) welding, b) carpentry, c) metal work, d) drafting, e) interior design

   e. Home economics:

      (1) Demonstrations — cake decorating

      (2) Field trips — meat market

      (3) Films — interior decorating

      (4) Guest speaker — meat cutting

      (5) Line production — centerpieces

  f. Science:

      (1) Projects related to career areas: a) wind tunnel construction, b) slides of polluted water, c) relate careers in music to sound

      (2) Field trips

  g. Personal development:

      (1) Personal relationships

      (2) Public relationships

      (3) Value realization

      (4) Grooming for a job

  h. Art:

      (1) Psychology of advertising

      (2) Draw, shade, render, and so forth, a modern, labor-saving device

  i. Physical education: Have student construct a personal ability chart.

4. Interdisciplinary project — line production and sale of framed samplers:

  a. Art — Design and print samplers; design frame; make posters and so forth.

  b. Math — Keep all records, cash and supply, pricing, sales, profit and loss sheet, state of the company; make stock certificates.

  c. Home economics — Buy materials and thread; do handwork; press (ready for frame).

  d. Industrial arts — Build frames; finish frames; cut out backing; attach method of hanging.

e. Personal development — Sales work, hiring, personal relationships, grooming for employability.

f. Guidance — Coordinate endeavor.

g. English — For advertising, write ads and news articles.

h. Make tags for the history of the samplers where they are appropriate; sell stock in company.

5. Interdisciplinary project — opening a recyling center in the community:

   a. Shop — Design and produce a binding device for use on newspapers and a can crusher.

   b. Math — Establish necessary money to balance cost of transportation; keep a record of costs.

   c. Social studies — Investigate resources in community (junk companies, trucking, collection sites, and so forth); take proposal to city; call personnel on school newsletter or public newspaper to get publicity on endeavor.

   d. Physical education — Stress the proper use of muscles in the activities of the job.

   e. English — Write a proposal to the city council that they ask the city to adopt the model; write articles for the school newsletter or public newspapers.

   f. Science — Investigate what can be done with recycled materials.

   g. Art — Display visual advertising (such as posters) in school and public places [with permission, of course].

   i. Personal development — Assess the attitudes of the community (public relations).

6. After administration of the guidance tests, individual counseling of students and group career sessions (related occupations) will be held:

   a. Biographical sketch prepared:

      (1) Previous work experience

      (2) Family data

    (3) Personal data

    (4) Likes and dislikes

    (5) Interests

    (6) Skills

    (7) Goals

  b. Orientation (to sources of occupational literature)

  c. Maintenance of individual career folders

7. Have a day of mini-courses:

  a. Each teacher teaches a specialty not necessarily related to his or her subject area (e.g., yoga, antiquing, and so forth).

  b. Students sign up for course (know which materials to bring).

  c. Mini-course is related to occupations.

8. Collage of occupation activities and objectives:

  a. Relate art and social studies.

  b. Social studies — Investigate careers behind pictures; group according to training items from a help-wanted column.

  c. Art — Display artwork.

9. Have student go into the community to find one high school dropout, one high school graduate, one college graduate, and one retired person.

  a. Get job description from each.

  b. Try to get at least one of the above to accompany him or her to the classroom to speak to the other students.

10. Request students from community college to "take a student to school" for a day.

  a. On a one-to-one basis, selected eighth graders will go to the nearest community college.

  b. A list containing the college students' names and schools will be posted.

    c. Student will make a report (oral, written, slides, tapes, and so forth, as he or she chooses) to bring back to the class.

The following points were listed after the exercise so that this career exploration experience could be evaluated:

(1) Each participating teacher will be encouraged to keep a personal log of any activities aimed toward student goals.

(2) Each participating teacher will report to a central person as to his or her activities.

(3) Pictures of significant activities will be kept by a student photography club.

(4) Participating teachers will be asked to evaluate their project and to make suggestions at the end of the school year.

(5) Nonparticipating teachers will be asked to comment on their observations of the program.

(6) Students will be asked to evaluate specific activities.

New Mexico

A New Mexico example incorporates the disciplines of English, home economics, physical education, social studies, language arts, and science, and is built around the health careers cluster. Materials used in the project were first-aid kits, "job opportunity kits," a mouth-to-mouth resuscitation kit, and a model of the human torso. Teachers were asked to make the following preparations:

(1) Line up field trips to visit hospitals, day-care centers, health center (clinics), and rehabilitation centers that focused on drug addiction, alcoholism, the mentally retarded, handicapped children, and juvenile homes and orphanages.

(2) Provide films applicable to the subject areas.

(3) Contact such resource people as school (or public) nurses, directors of health centers, students in training, and case workers.

The career education/health careers curriculum was then outlined as follows:

A. Objective — At the end of this unit, the student will be able to demonstrate his or her knowledge and comprehension by:

1. Responding effectively to different career opportunities in health to be measured by listing all the possible careers open to them in this area upon graduation from high school

2. Dramatizing successfully how to use different first-aid procedures as a class

3. Role-playing successfully the training, proper use of tools, and skills needed in health careers

4. Discussing intelligently a movie on alcohol and the human body

5. Discussing with understanding alcohol and drug rehabilitation programs and careers open in these fields

6. Discussing different communicable diseases, how they are transmitted to others, possible cures, symptoms of diseases, and possible job opportunities in this area.

7. Responding favorably to class discussions after a field trip, viewing a movie, or listening to a guest speaker

8. Writing an essay on a health career of their choice

B. Content:

1. Doctors:

a. Surgeons

b. Specialists (eye, nose, heart, ears, kidney, or other organs)

c. Interns studying to become a doctor

2. Hospital directors

a. Chief of staff

b. Assistant directors

c. Area supervisors

3. Nurses and their assigned duties:

   a. Registered nurses (aid doctors)

   b. Licensed practical nurses (change linens, feed patients, and so forth)

   c. Nurses' aides (give shots, take pulse, and so forth)

   d. Candy stripers and other volunteers

4. Maintenance personnel and their duties:

   a. Custodians (clean, and keep supplies stocked)

   b. Cleaning ladies or men (keep hospitals sanitary)

5. Food services:

   a. Dieticians (plan menus)

   b. Cooks (prepare food)

   c. Servers (deliver meals to patients)

   d. Busboys and dishwasher (clean lunchroom and kitchen)

6. Secretarial work:

   a. Typists

   b. Bookkeepers (keeping hospital records)

   c. Accountants (financing)

   d. Receptionists (incoming-outgoing desk)

7. First aid:

   a. Life guard

   b. Ambulance drivers

   c. Drivers' assistants (watching patients while they are being transported by ambulance)

8. Psychologists (recommend treatment)

9. Psychiatrist

10. Case workers (to keep records of family situations)

11. Therapists (help patients recuperate from disabilities)

12. Dental care:

   a. Dentists (fix teeth)

   b. Dental hygienists (clean teeth and teach people, young and old alike, to care for their teeth at home)

   c. Dental assistants (help the dentist, but do not work on the patients' mouths)

   d. Receptionists (answer phones, set up appointments, do paperwork)

13. Eye care:

   a. Optometrist (checks eyes and prescribes glasses)

   b. Optician (grinds lenses and assembles eyeglasses)

   c. Oculist (specializes in medical and surgical treatment of the eye)

   d. Orthoptist (eye therapist) (treats defective visual habits, muscular imbalance, and so forth)

   e. Ophthalmologist (treats defects and diseases of the eye)

   f. Receptionist (answers phones and does paperwork)

14. Foot care:

   a. Podiatrist (foot specialist) (removes corns, callouses, and so forth; also fits shoe pads or inlays for children with handicaps in legs or feet)

   b. Chiropodist (same as podiatrist)

   c. Receptionist (answers phones and does paperwork)

C. Activities:

   1. Field trips

   2. Essay writing (on chosen health career)

   3. Dramatization of first-aid procedures:

   a. Mouth-to-mouth resuscitation

   b. Artificial respiration

   c. How to stop bleeding

    d. Care of: a) shock; b) epileptic seizures; c) bruises, cuts, and burns; d) broken bones

    e. Moving an injured person

4. Dramatizing roles in health careers

5. Discussing intelligently a movie on alcohol's effect on the human body; communicable diseases and how they are transmitted (also possible cures); drug addiction and its ramifications; and job opportunities in these fields

6. Listing career opportunities in the health field

7. Discussing (possible quiz) topics presented by guest speakers

Wisconsin

An interdisciplinary program set up by the Wisconsin educators involved industrial arts, social studies, English, history, and art. Resource people included lawyers, representatives from unions and management, librarians, individuals from community resources, and local governmental workers (such as city hall or courthouse employees). The concept was to expose the students to various groups and institutions that influence the nature and structure of work. The objective was that the student understand the influences exerted upon the nature and structure of work by laws, labor and management, professionals, and society, and that he or she would thoroughly understand licensing procedures. The learning outcome was stated as: "The student should understand the influence exerted on the structure of work." The following activities were prescribed:

A. Listen to representatives of labor and management.

B. Have representatives from several professions explain licensing requirements.

C. Symposium by students on each segment of the objective.

D. Develop a cartoon series on influences of the structure of work, using aforementioned objective.

E. Time line on laws affecting the structure of work.

F. Field trip to learn about licensing.

Minnesota

The broad objective of a Minnesota program was to develop the student's positive attitudes toward self through an awareness of his or her developing talents, values, and interests as they relate to work roles. The performance objective was to describe work as valuable in terms of its intrinsic satisfactions. The behavioral objective: Describe how several occupations would provide ways of satisfying his or her basic needs of livelihood.

The teachers were to evaluate the program by having students describe economic requirements for various life-styles, such as salaries and fringe benefits of occupations in various job clusters. For seventh graders, the teachers were to emphasize part-time work and personal budgets, and then carry through in ninth grade with simulated family budget and occupation planning as emphasized by the life career game. As source material, they were to use various books and pamphlets concerning occupations and work, films about work, and the life career game. Interdisciplinary subjects were social studies, math (algebra *et al.*), economics, home economics, and English. Because the activities were slanted toward specific grades, these are listed here in parentheses at the end of the activity.

A. Have students study the salaries described in the want ads. Discuss the possible reasons for different salaries (seventh and eighth grades).

B. Discuss the suggested minimum budgets in the life career game. Update these budgets, based on student knowledge and current economic information (such as census data) (ninth grade).

C. Ask students to describe a preferred style of life in terms of major expenditures and purchases in the future (eighth and ninth grades).

D. Have students convert various ways of paying salaries; i.e., hourly, monthly, and yearly wages; percentage of commissions (seventh through ninth grades).

E. Have students compute the costs of future education on a yearly basis (seventh through ninth grades).

F. Have students prepare a weekly budget for their school year. Have them look at short- and long-range financial goals and plans (seventh through ninth grades).

G. Have subcommittees examine the various types of paycheck deductions (seventh through ninth grades):

1. Federal Insurance Contributions Act (F.I.C.A.)

2. U.S. withholding tax

3. Other deductions such as union dues, health insurance, and savings bonds

H. Have the class study the financial aspects of family living; e.g., life and health insurance and home ownership (eighth and ninth grades).

GETTING IT DONE: SOME SUMMARY COMMENTS

Career education is not a panacea...there is none. But it can provide motivation for many students by demonstrating the relevancy and usefulness of academic subjects. It can also enhance teaching and learning by supplying explanatory examples within the experience and understanding of the learner, and often by allowing the learner to actually experience the principle to be learned.

Middle/junior high school teachers, as well as high school teachers, sometimes fear career education for two reasons. They are concerned that it will add extra time, effort, and subject matter to an already crowded curriculum. They are also fearful that emphasis on career exploration might allow neglect of the academic subject matter they consider to be their primary assignment. It should be clear by now that career education is meant to be a process and approach to the present curriculum content, not an addition to it. Overenthusiasm could make the latter threat a reality. It should be clear that the first responsibility of the mathematics teacher, for instance, is to teach (and help the student to learn) math. Career education must be an aid, not an obstacle, to this primary objective, with the added career knowledge and decision-making skills as a welcome bonus.

If career education is to reach the full potential, it must be implemented into all subject areas. Not only guidance counselors but teachers in subject matter areas not normally associated with vocational and career development must be committed and working creatively to develop new concepts of career education to find new ways of incorporating them into their own teaching approaches. For instance, the science education statement on career education quoted early in this chapter introduced the concept of "work style," a concept not commonly found in career education literature. Such creative inputs can only emerge as energetic and creative teachers in all subject areas put their minds to developing and teaching career education concepts. Career education, in turn, should provide a route for involving students more deeply in each subject area, making it more exciting and relevant for them.

There is a variety of ways beyond those enumerated above to increase the excitement about the career relevance of academic subject matter: career assemblies and career clubs in various subject areas, service clubs which involve students in career-related service activities, articles in the school newspaper, student government recognition of the potential for politically connected careers...the list could go on and on.

The curricula of the middle/junior high school are undergoing change, and career education has a contribution to make in that process. The difference in the nature and needs of the ten- to fifteen-year-old student (as contrasted with those older and younger) must be the key to that reform. There must be incorporated into all subject areas more opportunities for exploration of self and its relationship to society. Since the five basic academic subjects discussed in this chapter are ordinarily required of the middle/junior high school student, and since these subjects are taught each year for those ages, teachers have a greater obligation to be innovative than those who teach elective subjects (where students have the choice of dropping the class or taking it only once).

The middle/junior high school curricula must also be different from and coordinated with that of the elementary and high schools if needless boring repetition is to be avoided. With all there is to be taught in this age of "knowledge explosion," repetition in science, math, and social studies — beyond that which is good pedagogy — is unconscionable. Career education offers one way to avoid repetition, for the teacher can design a curriculum unique for each school level, helping the student through awareness to exploration to specialization in each topic. The scope and sequence of every course should include career education (scope meaning the content covered, and sequence meaning the continuity). If we include career education in the scope, it can help determine the sequence.

Methods of teaching are changing. New technology and novel ways of presenting knowledge are constantly introduced. The lecture is out; discussion is in. Teacher-dominated classes are passé; student involvement is "where it's at." Career education is an effective way of encouraging student involvement — through experience as well as through study and discussion. Knowing students better is often best accomplished by seeing them outside the classroom in their natural setting. Many who show little classroom promise are leaders in the neighborhood and on the street. Better acquaintance and understanding of students is a byproduct of career education that is often overlooked. An additional advantage is that career education can start the science teacher talking with the English teacher, and both of them communicating with the social studies and the industrial arts teachers. Teachers enthusiastic about career education are excited about the possibilities of planning joint class activities, correlating topics around career-related projects, cooperating on field trips, speeches, and so forth (Antonellis and James, 1973).

But it would not do to overpromise. Career education faces many problems. Major resistance is confronted from some teachers, some administrators, and some teacher-training institutions. Where there is no resistance, there is often apathy. Yet the public — parents, school boards, and legislators — are rarely either opposed or apathetic. It all makes sense to them.

Some teachers are rightly concerned that the innovation might water down their courses. Such dilution is not only a concern to those few purists for whom subject matter is sometimes more important than students, but also to those committed to putting over the assigned subject matter as a contribution to the student's future. One answer is that career education can build bridges to professionals who were trained in the same subject areas and are now employed in business, government, and research, and all this to the advantage of teacher and student alike.

Other teachers hold back because of a genuine lack of knowledge about careers. Their reticence springs more from their fear that they cannot teach about jobs because they are knowledgeable only about teaching than from an opposition to the career education concept. Consequently, these teachers must be introduced to career education materials, to labor market data, and to practical work experience. For instance, a little study of the *Dictionary of Occupational Titles* or the *Occupational Outlook Handbook* will open new vistas for teaching, not only about careers but about the subject areas as well.

Reluctance to change is always a source of resistance. One teacher successfully experimenting with career education and demonstrating improved student interest and classroom performance can leaven resistance and start a "bandwagon" (to use a mixaphor). An effective technique used in a number of schools is called "quest." Periodically, once a week or month, a class period or a day is set aside for teachers to present something unique about themselves or their subject. Students select which class they will attend, choosing that which interests them most of course. Quests on careers — in science, in public service, in journalism, in aerospace or baseball — attract students and provide motivation for teachers not to fall behind in attracting student interest.

The teacher-training institutions can best be changed by the selectivity exercised by their customers, the schools who hire the teachers. If they demand career education training in the present competitive situation in teacher employment, the colleges of education will not lag behind. For career education to succeed, the classroom teacher must be supported by counselors, administrators, and subject specialists, but it will be the classroom teacher who will make it work or fail.

Career education can be worked into all classes, as special individualized units for fast or slow learners, for extra credit work, as special mini-courses or as a programmed learning unit. Incorporating career education into the basic academic subjects ranges from the simple to the complex. Any teacher wanting to incorporate career education can start by simply adding one new subtopic to his lesson plans — "career implications." This single addition will cause the teacher to start thinking about careers, as well as concepts and coverage. Preferably, of course, career education should permeate the entire curriculum. A reasonable approach to that end would include:

(1) When establishing course goals, include goals relating to career education and knowledge of career opportunities available, such as in related employment (both professional and nonprofessional).

(2) Write objectives for the course, the unit and the daily lesson plan, including career education objectives. As an example of such a performance objective, we submit: After reading the section in the textbook about the influence of Samuel Slater upon the development of industry in the United States, the students will list five new types of careers or jobs available to Americans at the end of the eighteenth century.

(3) Develop a plan for evaluating the objectives, including the career objectives. Include multiple-choice or essay questions that relate to the career objectives. For example: Vector analysis is a mathematical concept used often by:

(a) A truck driver

(b) A manager of a department store

(c) An airline pilot

(d) An electrician

(4) Decide upon the learning activities needed to teach the objectives. This could include a simulation where the students apply the concepts learned in class to a

real situation. For example, after a unit on news reporting, have the students make a class newspaper, assigning editors, reporters, printer, delivery personnel, and so forth.

(5) Determine what materials or resources are needed to teach the objective; for example, a film on baseball or a professional athlete as a guest speaker.

All of this can be facilitated by effective in-service teacher training. But it is not necessary for the alert teacher to wait for what is in someone else's control. Imagination is the only requirement.

REFERENCES

Antonellis, Gerard P.; and James, George B. *Cross Discipline Planning.* Salt Lake City: Olympus Publishing Company, 1973.

Berglund, Rene A. "Future Space Activities." *The Science Teacher* (March 1973), vol. 40, no. 4.

Chrisman, Dennis G. "Teaching Integrated Science." *The Science Teacher* (February 1973), vol. 40, no. 2.

"Employment Opportunities for Natural Scientists and Engineers in the 70's." *Science Education News* (April 1973).

Fader, Daniel N. *Hooked on Books: Program and Proof.* New York: Putnam, 1968.

Herndon, James. *How to Survive in Your Native Land.* New York: Simon & Schuster, 1971.

Howard, Alwin W.; and Stoumbis, George C. *The Junior High and Middle School: Issues and Practices.* Scranton, Pennsylvania: Intext Educational Publications, 1970.

"How Much Career Education in Science?" Discussion session of the National Science Teachers Association, 1972, vol. 40, no. 4. Area convention in San Diego, April 1973.

Hoyt, Kenneth B.; Pinson, Nancy M.; Laramore, Darryl; and Mangum, Garth L. *Career Education and the Elementary School Teacher*. Salt Lake City: Olympus Publishing Company, 1973.

Kline, Morris. *Why Johnny Can't Add: The Failure of the New Math*. New York: St. Martin's Press, 1973.

Olympus Research Corporation. *Career Education in the Environment*. Produced for the U.S. Office of Education, Division of Vocational and Technical Education. Washington, D.C.: U.S. Government Printing Office, 1972.

Radang, Doris H. "Advanced Biology as an Introduction to Science Careers." *American Biology Teacher* (May 1973), vol. 35.

Scherer, R. T.; and Clary, Joseph R. *Middle School Curriculum Guide*. Raleigh: North Carolina State University, Center for Occupational Education, 1973.

U.S. Department of Health, Education and Welfare, Office of Education. *Career Education: A Handbook for Implementation*. Salt Lake City: Olympus Research Corporation, 1972.

U.S. Department of Labor, Manpower Administration, Bureau of Employment Security. *Dictionary of Occupational Titles*. Washington, D.C.: U.S. Government Printing Office (any year).

"Wanted: English for Vocational Students." *English Journal* (1971).

5

The Fine and Practical Arts

An almost universal characteristic of the middle/junior high school is the availability of specialist teachers in the fine and practical arts. The most common subjects involved are art, music, home economics, and industrial arts. Business teachers, especially teachers of typing, are increasing in number, and some schools are adding specialists in agriculture, health occupations, and other practical arts subjects, as well as specialists in vocal and instrumental music and in the other arts.

All of these subjects share an emphasis on activity which offers the pre- or early adolescent student a welcome change from the heavy emphasis on classroom work which is characteristic of most other school subjects at this level. Moreover, since these fine and practical arts subjects often are required in the junior high school and not in the senior high school, there is the opportunity within them to reach every student, but also a freedom from the senior high school requiring or expecting that certain things should or must be taught in the junior high school. This relative freedom of setting and of curriculum allows unusual opportunity for teaching career education concepts. Moreover, since the subject matter is relatively new to the students (who sometimes think they already

189

know a great deal about mathematics, English, social studies, and science from their elementary school experiences), there is a high level of student motivation for learning.

All is not rosy, however. While a few schools combine many of these subjects into a unified arts program available to all students, it is very common to have rigid segregation by sex in home economics, industrial arts, and physical education. A second difficulty is that teachers in some fine and practical arts programs in the middle/junior high school have over-emphasized their uniqueness and separation from related senior high school programs and have rejected vocational and emphasized avocational goals. A principal reason for this has been that as teachers of a required subject, they have wanted to emphasize the utility of their subject for every student. They have seen that every student should have an avocation, but sometimes they have failed to see that every student needs to explore careers in relationship to exploration of self. A third problem lies in the background of middle/junior high school teachers: Few have had experience in occupations outside of education.

In spite of biases and experiences which minimize the importance of career exploration, however, it seems likely that teachers of the fine and practical arts have been among the most successful in helping students to know themselves in relationship to the real world. This appears to be due in large part to the aforementioned freedoms of curriculum and physical setting. But it is also due to the opportunity to work closely with students who are frank, curious, ready for independent work, and aware of and interested in knowing the consequences of rapid personal changes. Another major factor has been teacher willingness to deal with their load of 120 or more students each day by getting to know each student's strengths and weaknesses, attitudes and desires, not only in the cognitive, but also in the affective and psychomotor domains.

Career education in the middle/junior high school seeks not only to capitalize on this teacher knowledge of the individual student, but to aid the teacher in making it even more thorough and complete. It attempts to make a unique contribution while maintaining ties with career education in the elementary and high schools; it seeks to help the student to *learn to be* (in the sense that UNESCO uses this phrase); it provides opportunities for the student to test self against reality, to extend the student's awareness, to prepare the student for performance at many levels, and to lead to understanding of the relationships between performance and lifestyles. The following sections of this chapter discuss the career education activities of teachers in the more frequently taught practical and fine arts subjects, and then list a wide variety of activities which cross subject matter lines.

INDUSTRIAL ARTS

Far more than any other middle/junior high school field, industrial arts has been the subject of intensive curriculum development which is directly applicable in career education for paid employment. This was not, however, the original goal. Instead, these curriculum developers were concerned with analyzing and teaching salient aspects of a major portion of the world of work which has gone under the names of "industry" or "technology." As usually defined, it has included transportation, communication, power generation and transmission, manufacturing, construction, and the design and servicing of manufactured products, but usually it has excluded agriculture, mining, fishing, personal service, homemaking, health, finance, sales and marketing, office work, and careers in the fine arts. The rationale for exclusion of these major kinds of work has never been well understood, but it appears to be related to: (a) the origins of industrial arts in "manual training," "manual arts," and the "activity curriculum" (lack of a substantial content of manual activity could be used to rule out the study of work performed by most white-collar workers), (b) the need for developing an understanding of the industrial revolution (agriculture, mining, and fishing apparently were thus excluded unjustly), and (c) adequate coverage elsewhere in the junior high curriculum (thus excluding homemaking).

Industrial arts attempts to make "industry" or "technology" more intelligible. Because such understanding is needed by all students, industrial arts is rightfully a part of general education, and until recently, most of its leaders have rejected any attempts to relate it to vocational education. In practice, however, it has served a preparatory and student screening function for the trade and industrial section of the high school vocational curriculum. In addition, it has been closely related to advanced industrial arts programs in the secondary school.

In spite of its philosophy of general education service to all students, it has, in practice, been a program for males. Females rate industrial arts as the least popular course in the curriculum, although they frequently excel in industrial arts courses regardless of whether they have been designed for girls or boys. The continued exclusion of boys from most home economics and girls from most industrial arts classes can be explained (but of course, not justified) by sex biases related to occupations. Surely there must be deeper, unexplored reasons, however, since industrial arts is not usually designed for occupational preparation.

The following outline of bases for industrial arts in the middle/junior high school (adapted from Householder, 1972) illustrates some of the more important analyses which have been developed in attempts to make "industry" or "technology" more intelligible. Most of the analyses in the outline are applicable to career education, though none of them could serve as an outline of the whole of career education. One of these, however, is used much more frequently than others in career education programs in the middle/junior high school. This program is the product of the Industrial Arts Curriculum Project of Ohio State University and the University of Illinois. It consists of two 1-year courses (one in construction and the other in manufacturing) which were designed specifically for the junior high school.

A. Industry — centered approaches:

    1. Alberta plan, University of Alberta (Canada):

        a. Seventh grade — electricity, graphic arts, ceramics, plastics, woods, and metals

        b. Eighth and ninth grades — power transmission, testing technology, electronic technology, power technology, mechanical technology, graphic communications, computer technology

2. American industry project, Stout State University: eighth grade — industry today, evolution of industry, organizing an enterprise, operating an enterprise, future of industry, distributing products and services, and the students' business venture

3. Enterprise — man and technology, Southern Illinois University:

   a. First course — experiences in the enterprise, electronics and instrumentation, visual communications, materials and processes, energy conversion, and power transmission

   b. Second course — advanced experiences in enterprise

4. Functions of industry, Wayne State University and the University of Illinois:

   a. Goods-producing activities — research, product development, planning for production, and manufacturing (unit and continuous)

   b. Goods-servicing activities — diagnosis, correction (adjustment, replacement, and repair), and testing

5. Industrial arts curriculum project, Ohio State University and the University of Illinois:

   a. World of construction

   b. World of manufacturing

6. Orchestrated systems approach, Indiana State University: product planning, manufacturing, assembling, packaging, storing, and shipping

B. Technology — centered approaches:

   1. Industrial arts as the study of technology (Olson) — manufacturing, construction, power, transportation, electronics, industrial research, services, and industrial management

   2. Technology as a discipline (DeVore) — production, communication, and transportation

C. Industrial arts as a method of individual development —
Maryland plan, University of Maryland:

1. Eighth grade — group projects and line production

2. Ninth grade — contemporary units, group projects, line
   production, research and experimentation, or individual
   or group technical development

D. Career — occupation emphasis:

1. Partnership project, Central Michigan University: ninth
   grade — industry and civilization; industry; organization;
   research, design, and development; planning for production and manufacturing operations; manufacturing;
   distribution; and service

2. Galaxy plan, Detroit public schools: business education,
   materials and processes, visual communications, energy
   and propulsion, personal services, and electronics

3. Introduction to vocations, North Carolina State Department: relating one's self to occupations; the economic
   system; manual and mechanical occupations; clerical,
   sales, and service occupations; professional, technical,
   and managerial occupations; and planning ahead and
   evaluating

4. Career development for children, Southern Illinois
   University:

   a. Seventh grade — economics and career planning

   b. Eighth grade — exploration and decision making
      related to educational planning which is consistent
      with personal characteristics and occupational goals

The popularlity of the Industrial Arts Curriculum Project
in career education exploratory programs appears to be due to
three major factors: (a) it has extensive and attractive curriculum materials for teachers and students which have been
actively promoted by the publishers and by several important
labor and industrial groups, (b) large numbers of teachers have
been carefully prepared to teach these materials, and (c) the
two courses have the same structural organization as the U.S.
Office of Education's fifteen career education clusters (and

they are identical in title to two of these clusters). The fact that the Office of Education supported the Ohio State-University of Illinois project long before the fifteen clusters were identified indeed suggests that the project may well have determined the predominant structure of the clusters along industrial (rather than occupational, instructional, or psychological) lines. In any case, the exact correspondence between the two project course titles and two Office of Education clusters has undoubtedly aided the acceptance of the project in career education.

Even more significant is that the Industrial Arts Curriculum Project fits career education so well, despite the fact that its initial development preceded by several years the development of the term "career education." This appears to give further support to our contention that career education components have been in existence for some time and that the principal task is to put them together.

The major problem with the industrial arts project of Ohio State-University of Illinois is that two years of one-hour-a-day course work is required to explore just two career clusters. Several different approaches have been used in an attempt to resolve this problem: (a) the total number of clusters can be reduced, thus making the project appear to cover, say, two-elevenths, rather than two-fifteenths, of the world of work, (b) each project course may be reduced in length from one year to one semester, or even to nine weeks, or (c) one or both of the project courses may be used as a *model* of exploration of the world of work. The latter approach appears to have considerable potential, at least for careers in agriculture, mining, fishing, transportation, communications, and power. With the aid of additional teacher-constructed materials, the format and materials of the industrial arts project could be used for career exploration purposes in several clusters. Each time the project emphasizes a concept or principle, the teacher-made materials could emphasize the applicability of the concept or principle to careers in other clusters noted above. The project format appears to be less directly applicable to careers in personal services.

The reader of the outline above is struck immediately by its absorption with manufacturing, and by the almost complete absence of concern with service and white-collar careers. Nevertheless, several of the structures shown in the outline appear to have greater "generalizability" to career awareness and exploration than does the Ohio State-University of Illinois project. "American industries" and "introduction to vocations," for example, cover several clusters which the project does not mention. Perhaps the most complete set of materials for industrial arts teachers who are interested in improving career education is available from McKnight Publishing Company (Bloomington, Illinois). It is to be hoped that other publishers will follow the lead of McKnight in making a broad range of junior high school-level career education curriculum materials generally available to teachers and students.

HOME ECONOMICS

There have been three major emphases in career education in home economics: careers in homemaking, dual careers of homemaking and wage earning, and careers in fields which use the knowledge and skills traditionally associated with home economics. These three emphases have been encouraged and faithfully chronicled in the *Illinois Teacher of Home Economics* (at one time called the *Illinois Teacher for Contemporary Roles*). This journal undoubtedly has more influence on public school curriculum development in home economics than any other source. Its articles and even complete issues on career education (e.g., November-December 1973) have influenced the contents of this book as well.

Despite the fact that a third of our paid labor force is female, the most pervasive career for women is homemaking. Almost every woman engages in this career on a full-time basis for one or more periods of her lifetime, and for many women it is the principal career throughout adulthood. Yet a number of influential persons have argued that homemaking is not a vocation and that it is impossible to have a "career" in homemaking. Their argument has been, ostensibly, that only *paid* employment counts in vocations and in careers, but there is at least a suspicion that male attitudes have been in part responsible for their conclusion. We are proud to have played a part in working for full recognition of the important role of homemaking in career education.

Nevertheless, homemaking education is not without its problems. For many years it has been a bastion of female influence, despite the fact that almost half of the homemakers are male (though studies of work in the home indicate that far more than half of such work is performed by females). There are few male homemaking students; and male students who do not take home economics rate such classes as the least popular secondary school subject. Yet the literature contains enthusiastic but scattered reports of successful home economics classes for boys, usually in cooking. Coeducational classes are almost as rare as male teachers of homemaking.

The dual-careers emphasis is also designed almost exclusively for females. It recognizes that when a woman works outside the home, she is expected to have a simultaneous career as a homemaker, and that the responsibilities of this dual career require special preparation. It would seem logical that more males than females should have preparation for dual careers, since more males than females work outside the home, but few if any dual-careers programs are designed for males... or for both sexes. An impressive exception is a program staffed by Weber State College (Ogden, Utah) which sends home economists into the community to train single men who live alone — most of them oldsters — to prepare nutritious meals for themselves and otherwise "keep house."

The third type of career education program offered by home economics teachers is based on the occupations and careers which emphasize the skills and knowledge normally taught by home economists. This may sometimes be used as a euphemism for "women's occupations," a term which, for obvious reasons, is no longer popular. But it goes well beyond such occupations, suggesting a rational use of home economics teachers in fields to which they can contribute most. Rotella (ca. 1971) suggests most such careers lie in the personal service cluster, and provides 81 carefully researched occupational briefs for the teacher. Other important clusters are environmental and human development services.

All three of these home economics-based career education programs have had some trial in middle/junior high schools.

By far the greatest emphasis, however, continues to be placed on homemaking careers for girls. This program is an important part of career education at any level, but home economics teachers can and should contribute to other career education programs as well. The American Home Economics Association is developing files of home economists employed in various types of work, including homemaking. The availability of such lists should aid teachers in locating valuable human resources in or near the school.

JOINT HOME ECONOMICS-INDUSTRIAL ARTS PROGRAMS

Teachers of home economics and industrial arts form a natural team for development of career education programs at the middle/junior high school level. Almost every such school has both fields represented. They often represent the only practical arts programs in the school, and their combination of required courses for girls and boys often gives such a team access to all of the students in the school.

Working independently, and with little aid from teacher education or professional associations, many home economics and industrial arts teachers have discovered the idea of exchange classes. This method has been used almost exclusively at the middle/junior high school level, and usually has resulted in boys moving to the home economics laboratory for a fraction of a year (usually six to nine weeks) at the same time the girls are shifted to an industrial arts laboratory. Many times a special program is designed for the boys, but the girls most often receive a portion of almost exactly the same industrial arts instruction normally provided to boys.

Several things appear to be questionable about such exchange programs in a career education program. In part due to their short length, these programs have even less individualization of instruction than regular classes designed for one sex. There is rarely any mention of careers, perhaps due to unconscious sex biases on the part of the instructors, and the advantages and disadvantages of coeducational practical arts classes appear not to have been considered. Sex-segregated career education programs are self-contradictory. How can awareness and exploration of careers be achieved in a setting which assumes that full awareness of and even minimal exploration of certain careers should be forbidden to students in a single-sex class?

Dzurenda (pp. 26–27) describes an approach involving home economics, industrial arts, science, health services, and business occupations teachers. Sixty students (boys and girls) were cycled through instruction in each of these areas during a voluntary summer school program.

An approach which seems even more satisfactory because it is on a continuing basis has been that of Maryland teachers who several years ago began developing career education programs by forming teams of home economics, industrial arts, and guidance personnel. These teams worked together at the local level, planning career education programs for the junior high school, and exchanging ideas across the state. A number of interesting approaches were developed, many of which are described later in this chapter. Using this team as the base, the next step was to add a well-respected academic teacher and then a representative of the school administration to the team. Teams constituted in this way indeed produce results.

Another excellent approach is that of the Occupational, Vocational, Technical Division of Pittsburgh schools. Their coeducational program for grades six through eight involves business education, home economics, guidance, and industrial arts. Ten areas are covered: manufacturing, information processing, construction, visual communications, power and transporting, merchandising, business communications, foods and nutrition, clothing and textiles, and home, health, and community. Four basic concepts are presented in each area: human relations, production, communications, and economics. Each also has five concerns:

(1) That the student know himself, his interests, and his potential

(2) That he recognize what is really involved in the world of work — business, industry, community, and home

(3) That he has opportunities to work with others — other students and teachers — as well as time to develop his own activity

(4) That he collect enough information to participate in decisions for his future

(5) That he have opportunities to use a variety of media and resources

Each student works with the guidance personnel to prepare an "activity-interest profile" which is designed to help in the selection of further educational and career activities. This approach has the advantage of not requiring major changes in existing course titles, and of not requiring involvement of teachers outside the practical arts area. In the long run, these might prove to be disadvantages, but this approach allows a small group of teachers to get something started immediately, and then to build on it later.

A major emphasis in joint industrial arts-home economics classes should be placed on male-female role reversal. The boy who plays the role of child-care aide and the girl who plays the role of auto mechanic may choose not to continue in that role, but both will have a better understanding of themselves, of sex biases in work, and of a wider variety of opportunities in the world of work.

THE FINE ARTS

Sar Levitan's excellent book, *Work Is Here to Stay, Alas* (1973), points out that work is a function of society's wishes rather than its needs. In 1970, Americans spent more (in constant dollars) on alcoholic beverages than on all goods and services in 1870. Even allowing for the sixfold increase in population during this period, it is clear that much of the increase in expenditure has been due to our wishes rather than our needs. Presumably in 1870, people had most of what they needed for survival. Now they have considerably more.

We now have more musicians than coal miners. Whether we choose to have twice as many artists as domestic servants or farmers is up to us, since only a relatively few poeple are needed to produce what we must have to survive. The decisions as to what we want, and hence how many people can find work in a given career field, are very much a function of advertising and education. This suggests that career education in the fine arts should concern itself not only with those who want to work in fine arts careers, but also with the forces which create opportunities for work in these careers. Neither of these emphases needs interfere with the other proper concerns of fine arts educators.

Dual Careers Involving the Fine Arts

In the section on home economics, we described the concept of dual careers for women (and men) involving both homemaking and employment outside the home. There is another type of dual career which often involves the fine arts. Many people sell services (such as insurance and banking) or products (such as appliances and automobiles) which differ little in quality. The emphasis, then, is on the salesperson rather than on what is sold. In order to become known and respected in the community, these sales people must engage in community activities, most of which bear no direct relationship to their primary careers. Singing in a church choir or in a barbershop quartet, being a song leader or playing the piano for a service club, designing and producing posters for some civic enterprise, or participating in a local drama group becomes not just an avocation but a vital adjunct to the person's primary career. Moreover, skill or lack of skill in this secondary career appears to be interpreted by potential customers as indicators of skill, or lack of it, in the primary career. Thus if a real estate agent volunteers to design booths for the Parent-Teacher Association carnival, and the booths he prepares show poor taste or lack of skill, the assumption is likely to be made that this person is equally unskilled at selling real estate. Therefore, because major sales organizations are only too aware of this relationship, they teach their employees accordingly. Career education programs in the schools may find that this adds another note of relevancy, particularly if a student's parents see no reason why artistic talents should be developed.

Music

Perhaps only physical education teachers have displayed less enthusiasm than music teachers for career education programs. Both involve fields in which there is a very large supply of highly capable performers, compared to the modest number of jobs which allow persons to earn a decent living as full-time employees. This may help to explain why these two fields traditionally have emphasized avocational and esthetic rather than career education objectives. In view of the importance of music in culture and as an avocation, the schools indeed are justified in stressing these two goals.

But there is another side to the coin. The high earnings and expansive life-style of a few individuals and groups of musicians are reported in great detail by a wide variety of news media. This notoriety extends not only to popular artists, but also to serious performers who are fortunate enough to win major awards or otherwise attract enough attention to deserve mention in national publications and to appear on network television. Naturally, many students begin to believe that if they work hard and have a bit of luck, they can live as well as the media suggest their idols do. Such publicity is seldom countered by facts, both good and bad, which would allow students to begin exploration of a musical career on a more rational basis. This would appear to be a major responsibility for career education in music in the middle/junior high school. Students need to know how the system works; how the arts are supported; the role of the various musician federations and unions; the role of agents, of experience in a variety of settings, of publicity, and of luck.

In spite of the general lack of noteworthy efforts in career education in the field of music, there are some exceptions. The best we have seen is the work of the music staff of the Presque Isle (Maine) public schools. This includes a complete list of occupations within the music career field, together with information about entry requirements, sources of education and experience, working conditions, and ways in which occupational experiences are typically joined to form careers.

But much more needs to be done. The person who has only mediocre musical talent or who lacks early professional music education is very unlikely to achieve success in any of the many musical careers. We have noted elsewhere in this book that most aptitudes and abilities are not established firmly enough by age fifteen to warrant serious encouragement or discouragement of individual occupational or career aspirations. There appears to be a major exception, however, in several fine arts areas, including music. In those fields, talent or the obvious lack of it is evidenced rather reliably at a very early age; and even more important, if development of this talent is not started early it is unlikely to reach full fruition. *Career Education for Gifted and Talented Students* (Olympus Publishing Company, 1974) explores this problem in some detail. This book also describes how a wide variety of levels of musical ability can be developed, using the District of Columbia school symphony orchestra as an example.

The goal of career education in music should be to expand the student's view of the career implications of music. Case studies of the types of dual careers mentioned in the preceding section would provoke interesting discussions of life-styles. Exploration of the growing interrelationships of music and technology (e.g., electronic organs, amplifiers, music synthesizers, computer composition of music, light boxes) will interest many students. Others will be interested in musicology, psychoacoustics, musical instrument repair, the relationships between drama and music, and how musical abilities can be measured. Each of these has obvious career implications.

Scherer and Clary (pp. 19–21) has a good bibliography of resource materials and a very good sample teaching plan for career education in music. This is one of the few discussions which mentions careers in music education, despite the fact that this is one of the largest sources of employment in music. The Music Educators National Conference has excellent materials covering this and other careers in music.

Career education in music deserves further development. Because so little has been done in the past, the relatively modest efforts of those enthusiastic and capable teachers who are willing to develop career education programs in music at the middle/junior high school level seem certain to deserve and receive national attention.

Art

It may seem at first to be an anomaly that art teachers frequently are much more enthusiastic in their support of and involvement in career education than are their fine arts counterparts in music. The reason seems not to be so much in the relative affluence of art teachers, many of whom have established parallel careers of teaching, producing, and selling art. Nor does it appear to suggest that art teachers are any more devoted than music teachers to the full range of educational goals. Rather, it appears to lie in the recognition of the "generalizability" of many art skills, knowledge, and attitudes to almost every conceivable career. Indeed it would appear that only oral and written communications are more generalizable than art to a broad range of careers.

Unfortunately, neither the art nor the pedagogical components of art teacher education programs teach about this breadth of generalizability or how to convey it to the public school student. In the absence of a series of studies which explore these problems, and a textbook to put them into practicable terms, the art teacher is not lacking in potential resources. A team of home economics, industrial arts, and art teachers can go far toward identifying the breadth of need and rational ways of meeting it. This would go one important step beyond the initial stages of the Maryland plan described above, since many art teachers have credibility in both the "academic" and "nonacademic" camps of teachers.

Some art programs in the middle/junior high school have assumed that the nearest commercial art teacher is the only source which needs to be used in building a career education emphasis in art. It may well be true that such a teacher, more than any other single person, can be of assistance, but the use of art in careers extends far beyond what is ordinarily emphasized in commercial art classes. It is difficult to conceive of a worker in any field whose career options would not be enhanced by a knowledge and appreciation of art or by skill in the processes commonly taught in art classes. The garbage collector who insisted on an attractive sign and color on his truck would get more business, have greater pride in his work, and add to the esthetic wealth of the community. The secretary who used principles of art in designing a brochure would have increased opportunities for promotion or for transfer into related careers. Conversely, the worker who does not have this knowledge or these skills finds some opportunities to be foreclosed as a result. Frankly, we do not know the full dimensions of the impact of the arts and esthetics on careers, but we know enough to be sure that this aspect of the arts is underemphasized. Smith (October 1973) suggests new approaches to this problem and new ways of understanding its importance in our lives.

An instructional approach which is entirely consistent with the career education philosophy is to study the community outside the school to better understand the applicability of art content. Student interviews with practitioners in a wide variety of careers, paid and unpaid, are one device for accumulating such information. If students prepare scripts and make audio or video tapes or motion pictures for reporting these data and use cartoons for commenting on them, we have the use of art forms to represent the uses of art. Other art forms can also be used for this purpose of course.

Bowling Green Junior High School (Kentucky) approaches the study of careers by emphasizing two or three of the Office of Education's career custers each year, beginning in the first grade. By the end of the seventh grade all students have studied all clusters. Since the fine arts and humanities cluster is taught in the seventh grade, art teachers have an especially easy task of helping students make the transition to the eighth and ninth grade program of individual review and hands-on exploration of clusters which are of especial interest to each student.

Another source of help is Scherer and Clary (pp. 21–23), which presents a sample teaching plan for the career of cartoonist and lists resource materials for several art-related careers. Mentioned, but not treated in detail, are careers in architecture, interior decoration, display art, fashion design, crafts, communication, advertising, and photography. Not mentioned, but equally important, are art careers in the various news media.

Fine and Practical Arts Career Education Activities

To avoid frequent and needless repetition in describing career education activities in the practical and fine arts, we have developed the following set of descriptions. Each item has been used in one or more subject fields at the middle/junior high school level. Items have been selected to represent excellent current practice in career education, though it is certain that additional, equally meritorious examples could have been selected. Each user of this list in invited to refine and extend it. Additional items may be found in Bottoms (1972) and Hurt (1973).

Career education activities have been grouped according to goal, and for each activity, the following data are included: (a) title, for identification purposes in the event that the reader desires to learn more about the activity, (b) group, indicating the target group or groups for which the process or procedure was designed, and (c) activities, a description in very brief form of what was done and how. In some cases this description will be enough to suggest to the experienced teacher diverse expansions and modifications of the original idea, but in many cases it might be well to get additional ideas from the school in which the practice was identified. For this purpose the name of the school is included as the last part of each item, though it is likely that activities similar to those described are being conducted in many other schools as well.

Goal: To Improve Career Education Instruction

A. Career education newsletter

1. Group: Teachers in Delaware career education programs, plus others who ask to be put on the mailing list

2. Activities: The newsletter is mimeographed on goldenrod paper, with the first sheet having a printed heading. Very short descriptions of teacher activities are given, with many names listed. Enough detail is involved so that you know if you want to check with the teacher to get more. There is an excellent column on questions parents ask, with suggested answers.

3. School: Milford, Delaware

B. Interviews instead of field trips

1. Group: Kindergarten through eighth grade students

2. Activities: Most field trips are oriented toward products or processes, but career education emphasizes people.

Instead of providing student tours of industrial and business premises, the Peoria Association of Commerce agreed to accept the school's suggestion that it provide one worker to be interviewed by each group of four to six students. Workers came from many levels of the organization, while field trips usually had been conducted by white-collar workers. Similar arrangements have been made for four hundred teachers to interview employees. (The interview guide is described in detail in Dugger and Pryor, pp. 48ff. It appears to be based in part on Wernick, director of Project ABLE, Northern Illinois University, DeKalb, Illinois. Unfortunately, the practical arts are not mentioned specifically.)

3. School: Peoria public schools, Peoria, Illinois

C. Community resources volunteer board

   1. Group: Community volunteers

   2. Activities: In addition to having a strong community advisory committee, one school district has a community resources volunteer board made up of people upon whom the school can call to get expert assistance with career education. Volunteers are classified according to their specialty, time available, and so forth. (Another school calls these people "adjunct instructors.")

   3. Schools: Osseo, Minnesota; Peoria, Illinois

D. Employment terminology crossword puzzle

   1. Group: Home economics class or any other class studying work

   2. Activities: A crossword puzzle uses words or names of concepts which should be understood as part of career education. Below the puzzle are phrases which define the words or concepts. For example, "a meeting between an employer and a person looking for a job" would lead to the student writing the words "job interview" in the crossword puzzle. Students could construct their own crossword puzzles.

3. School: Not specified. (This activity is reported in the May-June 1973 issue of *Illinois Teacher of Home Economics*, vol. 16, no. 5, pp. 366–67.)

E. Employment case studies for the classroom

　1. Group: Home economics classes or coeducational career education classes

　2. Activities: Brief case studies of problems related to work are presented and discussed by teacher and students. Although some of the case studies in these examples are too advanced for middle/junior high school students, they can be used as guidelines for writing case studies which are appropriate to the age group. Students could also experiment with writing case studies of work. (See Griggs, "Employment Case Studies," for examples.)

　3. School: Not specified

F. Career development subject teams

　1. Group: Junior high school teachers, students, and others

　2. Activities: A team is set up in each subject field to find ways in which that subject could be better related to careers and the world of work. Each team includes a teacher of the subject, a counselor, a volunteer, a parent, a worker in a field related to the subject, and two or more students. The team members choose ways which help students see: a) the broad range of these related occupations, b) the self-actualizing or debasing features of these occupations, c) leisure implications of the subject, and d) ways in which the subjects relate to personal goal identification and development.

　3. Schools: University of Minnesota (Tennyson *et al.*; and Hansen, pp. 243–50); the Milford, Delaware, schools and the nearby Kent County Vocational-Technical School are strong in this area of helping teachers identify the career implications of their subject and helping change teacher attitudes about vocational education and the practical arts.

G. Video tape project

1. Group: Junior high school students

2. Activity: Junior high school students video tape other students interviewing workers on the job. Tapes are stored and reused until a better replacement tape can be made by another class.

3. Schools: Hazelton, Pennylvania, in cooperation with their Votech Center

H. Career development guidelines

1. Groups: Kindergarten though fourteenth grades (K–3, 4–6, 7–9, 10–12, 13–14), and instructors

2. Activities: Several Wisconsin schools have developed fine career education or career development guidelines, outlining goals, activities, and resources. These produce an integrated program for kindergarten through grade fourteen, with a minimum of undesirable overlap.

3. Schools: Eau Claire, Racine, and Sheboygan public schools, Wisconsin

I. Fair Park Career Education Center

1. Group: Middle/junior high school students, grades six through nine

2. Activities: The state fairgrounds can be made available to the school district for six months each year. There are plans to bus middle/junior high school students there to supplement regular practical and fine arts courses.

3. School: Dallas Independent School District, Texas

J. School within a school

1. Group: Eighth and ninth grade hard-to-reach students

2. Activities: Four to six classrooms are set aside for use by project students. An additional classroom serves as a news media center. These rooms are near the home economics, industrial arts, and library complexes, which serve to provide support for the project. Teachers were trained as a group during the summer preceding the

project. Emphasis is on subject-teacher contracts, occupational cluster exploration, and individualized instruction.

   3. Schools: Central, Riverside, and Orchard Street schools, East Providence, Rhode Island

K. Mini-courses

   1. Group: Middle grades students

   2. Activities: North Carolina has developed several mini-courses which help to develop career awareness and to begin career exploration. Among these, the course in dental assistant-dental hygienist has been used with fifth graders in connection with a unit on teeth; the secretarial and receptionist courses have been used with fifth graders as part of a unit on language arts; and the home economics course has been used with fifth graders in a unit on nutrition.

   3. School: Raleigh, North Carolina

L. Guidance-oriented exploratory program

   1. Group: All middle school students, grades six through eight

   2. Activities: Each teaching team is composed of a business, an industrial arts, and a home economics teacher and a paraprofessional. Mixed groups of boys and girls have activities designed to develop interests, identify abilities, and acquire information and experiences relating to the spectrum of careers in the world of work. Each student assembles a personal portfolio related to interests and abilities which will be useful for educational and career choice decisions. At grade six, students are introduced to four elements of the world of work: human relations, production, communications, and economics. At the second level, about grade seven, ten broad areas are explored: manufacturing; construction; information processing; power and transportation; food and nutrition; visual communications; business communications; home, health, and the community; merchandising; and clothing and textiles. At the third level, about grade eight, the students explore three or four of the ten areas.

3. Schools: Washington Education Center and Chatham Elementary School, Pittsburgh, Pennsylvania

M. Program of education and career exploration

1. Group: Middle/junior high school students

2. Activities: Students explore six occupational areas. Real and simulated work experiences are used, followed by group guidance activities. A normal population is used because there is some evidence that work experience programs may have negative results if all or even most of the students are delinquents or potential dropouts.

3. Schools: Twenty schools in Georgia (Matheny, pp. 19–21)

N. Did you know!

1. Group: Coeducational career education classes or home economics classes

2. Activities: The objective is to provide some facts about women's lives and to show the pattern of change in women's life-styles. The teacher can provide a variety of 1920 data about women and ask students to estimate similar figures for 1970. (Both sets of data are provided by Griggs, "Did You Know!")

3. School: Not specified

O. Maze vs map for the future

1. Group: Seventh grade industrial arts students

2. Activities: Teacher and students developed a career game and constructed a "maze" vs "map" approach to planning career development. They clipped newspaper stories showing "success" and "failure" and discussed what these terms mean.

3. School: Calvert Junior High School, Maryland

P. Prevocational education

1. Group: Ninth and tenth graders

2. Activities: Sixteen classroom teachers wrote a pamphlet titled "Suggestions for Implementing and Organizing Prevocational Programs in South Carolina." It contains

equipment lists, prices, and suggested activities covering sixteen occupational units: agriculture, air conditioning, building construction, child care, cosmetology, graphic arts, distributive education, electricity, food service, health occupations, mechanical drawing, metal work, office occupations, power mechanics, sewing, and textiles. A unit on the world of work is also suggested.

3. School: State Department of Education, Office of Vocational Education, Columbia, South Carolina

Q. Project occupational versatility

1. Group: Junior high school students in three populous districts

2. Activities: Beginning and advanced industrial arts students, boys and girls, are put in the same classes. A student self-management and self-instructional system was developed, and students were encouraged to form teams to use and further develop this system. Students in this program were less dependent upon teachers, more willing to accept responsibility for their own learning, and had more positive attitudes toward planning than other industrial arts students.

3. Schools: Metropolitan Area of Seattle Industrial Arts Consultants, Seattle, Washington

R. Work with parents

1. Group: Parents of junior high school students in the inner city

2. Activities: Weekly parent meetings held on Wednesday mornings. Parents were informed of educational and job opportunities, and of ways of taking advantage of job opportunities. General discussions seemed profitable, especially when they followed speakers or films. Parents went on several field trips and were involved in a career night program and a mother-daughter night. A key factor in parent involvement was the work of a community aide.

3. School: Burroughs Junior High School, Detroit

Goal: Career Awareness

A. Mini-courses

1. Group: Fifth graders

2. Activities: Very short, transportable courses have been developed in three fields: secretary-receptionist, dental assistant-dental hygienist, and home economics. These have been taught as part of fifth grade units on language arts, teeth, and nutrition, respectively. Student and teacher responses have been excellent.

3. School: Middle grades counselor-coordinator, Raleigh public schools, North Carolina

B. Social Security numbers

1. Group: Sixth graders

2. Activities: Students applied for and received Social Security numbers. As simple as this idea sounds, it has generated great enthusiasm. Individual letters must be written and, most important, individual replies are received, each with a distinctive number. Securing a Social Security number is a type of initiation rite for entry into most paid employment.

3. School: Raleigh public schools, North Carolina

Goal: Career Exploration

A. Part-time cooperative education exploration

1. Group: Volunteer junior high school students

2. Activities: Coordinators of part-time cooperative programs in the nearby senior high school take volunteer junior high school students with them, one at a time, when they go out to visit business and industry. Each coordinator makes fifteen such trips a year.

3. Schools: Perry Hall Junior High School, Baltimore, Maryland; North Hartford Junior-Senior High School has junior high school students interview senior high school part-time cooperative students, and feels that they get as much or more from them as from adults.

B. Home economics career tree

   1. Group: Home economics class

   2. Activities: The teacher prepares a bulletin board or flannel board, showing the trunk of a tree, representing the field of home economics. As students explore the field, they add branches representing the broad areas of it. Then leaves are added to represent occupations or careers such as dressmaking, fashion designer, garment tester, and so forth. An overhead transparency with overlays may be used similarly.

   3. School: Hoopeston public schools, Hoopeston, Illinois

C. Pretechnical education project

   1. Group: All seventh and ninth grade students, plus some eighth grade students

   2. Activities: Required courses lasting seven weeks were developed in industrial arts, home economics, art, group guidance, and communications media. Each seventh grader took all these courses. In the eighth grade, an elective course on the free-enterprise economy was offered. In ninth grade the program was required; it included short courses in science, radio and television production, community services, manufacturing and construction, and business and industry. Emphasis was on exploration of educational requirements for careers.

   3. School: Bridgeport public schools, Michigan

D. Path to job success game

   1. Group: Home economics class

   2. Activities: A game board is prepared with 33 squares arranged to form an "S." Each square has a question to be answered, with questions chosen from local newspaper ads, the telephone book, and other local sources. From two to six students play in turn, answering questions lettered in the squares. The particular question is chosen by rolling one die of a pair of dice.

   3. School: Melvin-Sibley public schools, Melvin, Illinois

E. Analysis of an employment agency contract

   1. Group: Home economics class

   2. Activities: The teacher secures a sample contract from an employment agency which must be signed by each person seeking a job, and which obligates that person to pay a fee when a job is obtained. Students are asked to read the contract and answer certain questions, such as:

     a. If you take a job, but do not begin work, will you have to pay the service charge?

     b. If you are laid off after two months, are you required to pay a service charge based on what you would have earned if the job lasted twelve months?

     c. You turned down a job with "X" company after you learned of the job from the employment agency. But six months later, you learned from a friend of an unrelated job at the same company and were hired. Do you owe anything to the employment agency?

     d. If a job paid $2.00 an hour, and you secured that job through this employment agency, how many hours pay would you owe them?

   3. School: Melvin-Sibley public schools, Melvin, Illinois

F. Introduction to vocations

   1. Group: Eighth and ninth graders, usually, but some younger students

   2. Activities: Exploratory, manipulative, classroom, shop, and laboratory experiences. Students rotate through a series of courses in at least five occupational areas of health, manufacturing, business, marketing, and distribution. This is accompanied by a career guidance unit, "Know Yourself." Availability of a career resource center in the school district is a distinct asset, but it is essential that this program be followed by placement in more advanced training courses or on a job. If this is done, it can be of special assistance to the student who plans to drop out of school at the end of the eighth or ninth grade.

3. Schools: Various, especially in New Jersey (Gambino, pp. 56–57)

G. Career clubs

1. Group: All junior high school students

2. Activities: Taking mini-trips with data collected by camera, and audio and video tapes; role-playing of jobs; setting up and operating businesses; conducting surveys; visiting goal-oriented students in high school and in the community college; publishing a career newsletter

3. Schools: Various in New Jersey (Gambino, pp. 56–57)

H. Oaklyn introduction to vocations

1. Volunteer junior high school students, boys and girls

2. Activities: During a six-week summer session, students were cycled through home economics, industrial arts, science, health services, and business occupations activities, including field trips and manipulative and cognitive experiences. Shorter cycles were also included for fields which could be covered in one or two days (e.g., flower culture, shoe repair, and so forth). Nonpublic school staff and students were included. The best student in sewing was a boy, and the best in drafting was a girl. Interest in cooking was higher among boys than among girls.

3. Schools: Oaklyn Junior High School, New Jersey (in a report by Dzurenda, pp. 26–27). A similar program has been implemented in Indianapolis and Gary ("Talent Quest for Sixth Graders").

I. Cooking experiences

1. Group: Junior high school home economics class

2. Activities: Five resource people demonstrated and talked to the class on cooking ethnic foods, such as *poella, shu mai*, knife care, sugarballs Indian, and squash. Five occupations were represented: professional cook, rest-home cook, ethnic cook, hospital cook, and dietician. Students particularly enjoyed the demonstrations and were eager to try out the skills demonstrated.

3. School: Lawrence Cook Junior High School, Santa Rosa, California (Hartmann, no date)

J. Natural foods experience

1. Group: Junior high school home economics class (plus two other classes)

2. Activities: A health foods store proprietor talked to the class and responded to student questions: How old do I have to be to work in your store? Where does your food come from? Is it good for you? He suggested forming an organic gardening club, and offered to furnish seeds if the school would get a plot of ground. Math skills were learned by comparing prices and calculating nutritional values. Science skills were learned in the areas of health, nutrition, and geography. Social implications of changing occupations and advertising were studied.

3. School: Lawrence Cook Junior High School, Santa Rosa, California (Hartmann, no date)

K. Ecology experience

1. Group: Junior high school home economics class

2. Activities: A representative of a water-softening firm demonstrated the problems created by water pollution, what we can do about it, and what is being done by industry. Students were given a water test kit, tested their own sources of water, and were asked to name three instances of water pollution and three occupations that deal with or rely upon a supply of good water. Skills in mathematics were learned by testing water and by determining size of water containers. Science skills were learned through study of the effects of minerals and chemicals on the quality of water. English skills were learned through writing reports of water tests and reports on occupations related to water quality.

3. School: Lawrence Cook Junior High School, Santa Rosa, California (Hartmann, no date)

L. Building careers in foods

1. Group: High school home economics classes (but the

technique seems applicable to middle/junior high school students)

2. Activities: A bulletin board display shows "ground floor," "first floor," "second floor," and so forth. "Ground floor" has a hinged cardboard door which, when raised, displays the world of work competencies needed, plus directions for advancement to the "third floor" or "first floor" (education and work experience needed for movement to different steps on career ladders in foods). Nine groups of occupations are covered.

3. School: Tuscola High School, Tuscola, Illinois. (Further details may be found in McCormick, p. 368.)

M. Career exploration for related training

1. Group: All eighth graders, boys and girls

2. Activities: Five to six weeks in a program for all twelve hundred eighth graders, using resource persons from the community, audio-visuals, visits to jobs, and visits to the area Skills Center. During the summer, the students could spend two days in each of four career interest areas, getting hands-on experiences at the area Skills Center.

3. Schools: Eastern Upper Peninsula Independent School District, and Lake Superior State College, Michigan. "Career Quest" is a similar program for eighth, ninth, and tenth grade students in Gary, Indiana.

N. Whitaker outdoor living laboratory

1. Group: One hundred to 150 junior high and high school students per year

2. Activities: Students have helped to develop a game refuge, arboretum, Christmas tree farm, and water recreation area. They study earth and biological sciences, meteorology, state and local history, and job opportunities and requirements. They operate a weather station and monitor pollution. Teachers are trained on this same site.

3. School: Whitaker Middle School, Portland, Oregon

O. Junior high school interdisciplinary career education project

1. Group: All students in a junior high school which has many students from low-income homes

2. Activities: In the seventh and eighth grades, students received orientation to business communications, health, manufacturing, construction, transportation, and in personal and community services; in the ninth grade: choice of home economics-related occupations or of industrial arts curriculum project/world of construction or world of manufacturing. This instructional program is supplemented by a career information center which is well equipped and has a wide variety of resources on careers, and is staffed by a full-time career counselor who works with both staff and students.

3. School: South Junior High School, Colorado Springs public schools

Goal: Career Exploration and Skills Development

A. Careers in construction, building maintenance, and allied occupations

1. Group: Low-income middle/junior high school students

2. Activities: This is one of a cluster of vocational courses, each of which is available for one-fifth or two-fifths of the school year, which requires forty hours of instruction. Unlike most courses at this level, it is designed to give the student marketable, entry-level job skills. Parallel courses in related communications, mathematics, and science skills have been developed for those students who need them. Objectives are few, but specific, and are confined to safety, tools, materials, and job procedures.

3. School: Dade County public schools, Miami, Florida

B. Exploratory education

1. Group: Seventh graders

2. Activities: Students are paid at the prevailing wage rate

for their job classification during a mass production project, using tokens redeemable at the project's store, merchandise mart, or cafeteria.

3. School: Division of Occupational, Vocational and Technical Education, Pittsburgh public schools, Pennsylvania

Goal: Self-Exploration

A. Career exploration module

1. Group: Middle/junior high school students

2. Activities: Practice in decision making, simulation of job tasks, study of manpower and economic trends, use of career information centers, and classification of the world of work are suggested activities. Students can create a career development contract which: a) specifies tentative goals, b) determines where the student is now, c) points out what needs to be changed to get to where the student wants to go, and d) develops an action plan. Obviously this type of contract can be repeated later in life.

3. Schools: Newton, Massachusetts, and Marsall-University High School, Minneapolis, Minnesota, have career information centers. Schools which have other activities are not identified (Hansen, pp. 243–50).

B. Tentative career hypotheses

1. Group: Middle/junior high school students

2. Activities: "Examine and assess a tentative career hypothesis through case study, group approaches, autobiographical career lifelines, and group and individual counseling...test present achievements and goals in relation to tentative educational and vocational plans." This could be combined with Hansen's "broadening role models" if the tentative career hypotheses were in a nontraditional career; for example: black quarterback, female auto mechanic, male elementary school teacher.

3. School: Not specified (Hansen, pp. 243–50)

C. Strength group

1. Group: Middle/junior high school students

2. Activities: Once a week a coeducational group meets to identify and plan strategies for capitalizing on their individual strengths. Leaders could be paraprofessionals, counselors, or teachers who have been trained in both career development and group processes. A home room converted to a life-planning laboratory would be a good setting.

3. School: Not specified (Hansen, pp. 243–50)

D. Career education for the college bound

1. Group: Eighth and ninth graders in a highly selective college preparatory school

2. Activities: All of these students expect to go to college but need career education, especially with regard to self, values, and needs. A nine-week course plus semiweekly seminars was built around these concepts. Behavioral objectives were identified and achieved. Pre-enrollment interviews with students selected those most likely to profit from the program. Discussions used such vehicles as an abridgment of *Future Shock* and sections of a college-level personnel management text and a text for training counselors. Due to the high level of reading achievement of the students, no difficulties were encountered with the text material.

3. School: University High School, Urbana, Illinois. (For further details, see Smith and Davisson, pp. 342–50.)

Goal: Serving Discouraged Students

A. Hopewell Occupation Work Center

1. Group: Eighth and ninth grade, slow and discouraged students, ages fourteen through seventeen

2. Activities: Many of the students appear to be waiting for the age when they can drop out of school, and if this is the case, they would have no occupational preparation. At the center, students spend half-days and are assigned

to one of four areas: maintenance and repair, home economics, health occupations, or business education. Half-days at the home school are spent in related English, related mathematics, and physical education. Center staff emphasizes occupational, social, and personal adequacy. Students are encouraged to continue their education after they leave the program.

3. School: Hopewell public schools, Virginia

B. Career studies

1. Group: Elective for ninth grade junior high school students, boys and girls

2. Activities: Selection from students who apply is made by counselors and teachers on the basis of an existing problem in one or more of the following areas: retention, attendance, discipline, grades, achievement test scores, general attitude toward school, or maturity level. Project approach is used. Projects include: build a trash can oven to mold plexiglass and dry buttons; build electronic kits; dissemble and assemble a gasoline engine; design a beach house and build a model of it; design, silkscreen, and sell Christmas cards; make lap trays, wall plaques, puzzles, felt books, and stuffed toys for patients in a nearby state hospital; build a "haunted house" for the annual school carnival; survey and mark off the field for track events; serve as the school stage crew; use the public address system to produce live commercials to sell products of the line assembly project. Line assembly uses the Junior Achievement model (described elsewhere in the chapter on work simulation) except that the social studies class examined the corporate structure, and the mathematics department conducted a cost analysis, did the banking, and taught students about the stock market and the formation of contracts. Products were designed in the art and industrial arts classes, and prototypes constructed there. The English class became the advertising and publicity department. Products included yo-yos, wall plaques, buttons with contemporary inscriptions, and autographed books.

3. School: Perry Hall Junior High School, Baltimore, Maryland. (Similar programs are at Thomas Johnson Junior-Senior High School. The Milford Middle School, Delaware, makes and markets model wooden racing cars through a nationally known corporation.)

C. Junior education work training

1. Group: Junior and senior high school boys and girls, ages fourteen through seventeen

2. Activities: Academic instruction is provided in a self-contained classroom by a teacher/coordinator for half of each day. For the other half-day, students are employed in local businesses or in certain vocational laboratories of the local schools, including machine shops, graphics and mechanics, and commercial hospitality education foods.

3. Schools: Five schools in the Durham public school system, North Carolina

Goal: Measuring Knowledge of Career Concepts and Information

A. Career development status survey instrument

1. Group: Students in grades seven through twelve

2. Activities: The career development status survey instrument was developed in 1972 to measure students' knowledge of career concepts and information. It is being used as a pre- and post-test instrument for target and control group students.

3. School: Covina Valley Unified School District, California

SUMMARY

Practical arts teachers appear to be more involved in career education than any other group of teachers in the middle/-junior high school, but fine arts teachers, especially art teachers, have a great deal to contribute as well. It is encouraging to see groups of fine and practical arts teachers working separately or in concert with academic teachers to develop ways in which they can best contribute to a well-rounded program of career education.

The major element missing is a focus around which the career education emphasis can be built. Industrial arts has sought such a focus in industrial materials and processes, in industrial occupations, in industrial structure, and in technology. Home economics has sought it in homemaking, in dual careers of homemaking and paid employment, in careers for women, in personal service occupations, and in occupations and careers which use the content commonly taught by home economists. The latter approach is also most commonly used by music and art teachers. A promising emphasis which seems not to have been tried would focus on the role of the subject field in changing public demand for products and services in ways which could lead to improved opportunities for employment and improved working conditions.

It is too early to tell which focus will prove to be best, and whether the same focus should be used in each subject field as well as in unified programs. In the meantime, many unrelated but constructive activities aimed at career awareness and exploration are beginning to emerge from the work of individual innovative teachers and small groups of such teachers. But many of these activities are not known outside the walls of the classroom or laboratory. Many others are not known outside the school district.

This chapter has attempted to identify a variety of such activities as a beginning toward better understanding of what each teacher and each subject within the fine and practical arts can contribute to career education. A major portion of these activities, however, can be grouped together under the heading of work, work observation, and work simulation. These activities and their rationale form the next chapter of this book.

REFERENCES

Bottoms, Eugene; Evans, Rupert N.; Hoyt, Kenneth B.; Willers, Jack C. *Career Education Resource Guide.* Morristown, New Jersey: General Learning Corporation, 1972.

Dugger, Chester W.; and Pryor, Charles V. *Career Awareness and Exploration.* Peoria, Illinois: Peoria Public School District 150, 1972.

Dzurenda, Joseph V. "Summer School for Introduction to Vocations: A Voluntary Program Works." *American Vocational Journal* (December 1969).

Gambino, Thomas W. "Junior High: The Exploratory Years." *American Vocational Journal* (December 1969).

George Washington University. *Title III and the World of Work.* Washington, D.C.: National Advisory Council on Supplementary Centers and Services, Program of Policy Studies in Science and Technology, 1972.

Griggs, Mildred. "Did You Know!" *Illinois Teacher for Contemporary Roles* (May-June 1973), vol. 16, no. 5.

——————. "Employment Case Studies for the Classroom." *Illinois Teacher for Contemporary Roles* (May-June 1973), vol. 16, no. 5.

Hansen, L. Sunny. "A Model for Career Development through Curriculum." *Personnel and Guidance Journal* (December 1972), vol. 51, no. 4.

Hartmann, Ada. "Home Economics Experiences" in Sealand, *Report on Career Education in Sonoma County, California.* Santa Rosa, California: Sonoma County Office of Education (no date).

Householder, Daniel. *Review and Evaluation of Curriculum Developments in Industrial Arts.* Bloomington, Illinois: McKnight Publishing Co., 1972.

Hurt, Mary Lee; and King, Bertha G. "Selected Highlights in Vocational Home Economics Education." Mimeographed paper for the U.S. Department of Health, Education and Welfare, Office of Education, Bureau of Adult and Occupational Education, Washington, D.C., June 1973.

Kagy, Frederick D.; and Lockette, Rutherford E. "Guidelines for Industrial Arts in Career Education" (draft copy). Mimeographed paper for University of Pittsburgh, Department of Vocational Education, Pittsburgh, Pennsylvania, undated (ca 1972).

Levitan, Sar A. *Work Is Here to Stay, Alas.* Salt Lake City: Olympus Publishing Company, 1973.

Matheny, Kenneth. "The Role of the Middle School in Career Development." *American Vocational Journal* (December 1969).

McCormick, Kathryn. "Building Careers in Foods." *Illinois Teacher for Contemporary Roles* (May-June 1973), vol. 16, no. 5.

Ohio State University. *Review and Synthesis of Foundations for Career Education.* Columbus: Eric Clearinghouse on Vocational and Technical Information (VT 014805, no date).

Rotella, Salvatore G.; *et al. A Curriculum Model Designed to Orient Students to Personal and Public Service.* Volume 1. Springfield: Illinois State Board of Vocational Education and Rehabilitation, Division of Vocational and Technical Education, undated (ca 1971).

Scherer, R. T.; and Clary, Joseph R. *Middle School Curriculum Guide.* Raleigh: North Carolina State University, Center for Occupational Education, 1973. Monograph no. 3.

Simpson, Elizabeth J. "Home Economics at the Secondary Level — A Curriculum Model with Emphasis on the Occupational Aspect." Mimeographed paper for the University of Illinois, College of Education, Bureau of Educational Research, Department of Vocational and Technical Education, 1969.

Smith, Kathryn; and Davisson, Judy K. "Career Education for the College Bound." *Illinois Teacher for Contemporary Roles* (May-June 1973), vol. 16, no. 5.

Smith, Ralph A. "The Arts, Cultural Services, and Curricular Development." *Journal of Aesthetic Education* (October 1973), vol. 7, no. 4. (A special issue containing the Proceedings of the U.S. Office of Education-sponsored conference,

"The Arts and Career Education: Toward Curriculum Guidelines.")

Tennyson, W. W.; Klaurens, M. K.; and Hansen, L. S. *Career Development Curriculum: Learning Opportunities Packages*. Minneapolis: University of Minnesota, College of Education, Department of Distributive Education, 1970.

Toffler, Alvin. *Future Shock*. New York: Bantam Books, 1970.

Wernick, Walter. *First Steps: Planning a Career Development Activity in Your Classroom*. DeKalb: Northern Illinois University, ABLE Model Program, 1971.

6

Work, Simulated Work, Work Observation in the Middle/Junior High School

The centrality of work in career education makes an understanding of work essential for both teachers and students of career education. To understand and then to value work, they need to engage in it *actively*, not passively. Learning to work is like learning to swim... there is only so much you can learn from a book, and your rate of learning is increased by careful observation and expert instruction. Finally, learning is internalized and made personally meaningful only through experience.

There are those who have flatly said that our society will not allow students of middle/junior high school age to work. Such a statement ignores the fact that going to school in itself is work. But this chapter goes beyond this one type of work: It uses the research base of chapter 2 (plus studies from industrial psychology, plus experiences of middle/junior high school teachers) to describe some important aspects of work, and to show ways in which work can best be observed and experienced by students eleven through fifteen years of age.

229

Types of Work Experiences

Experience with work, paid or unpaid, may be categorized in a variety of ways. Among these are:

(1)   Participation: personal involvement/observation

(2)   Size of group: individual/small group/large group

(3)   Place: in school/at school (but not part of it)/out of school; at home/away from home

(4)   Role played: employee/independent contractor/-employer

(5)   Type of work: production/service; single/repetitive

(6)   Degree of reality: actual/simulated

Each of these dimensions should be considered in designing work experiences for middle/junior high school students and in planning ways to capitalize on the work which students do on their own — work in which the school is not directly involved. Each of these dimensions affects the other; thus a full description here of opportunities for learning about work is impracticable. This chapter suggests some of the directions in which planning can take place, points out some of the constraints imposed by society, and suggests some ways to avoid or minimize the undesirable educational effects of these constraints.

When the desirability of work experience for middle/junior high school students is presented to teachers, to parents, or to the students themselves, the usual reaction is: That would be great! But how can it be done? Rarely is there a suggestion that experience with work is *un*desirable. The value of work experience is almost universally accepted, and the discussion immediately turns to the means for accomplishing it.

In a society comprised of small communities, cottage industries, and farms, opportunities for observing work are present all around. If the farmer, the blacksmith, and the cobbler are nearby, they can be observed and sometimes questioned about their work. In the United States these opportunities began to disappear more than a hundred years ago. Factories were erected, and fences were installed and armed guards strategically placed to keep out the unwanted.

But this was not the only difference. The village (and later, the company town) offered few opportunities for choices among careers. While almost all of the occupations available for choice were observable, the total number of occupations available for choice was low. Such choice was further restricted by the custom of following the father's occupation (for boys) or the mother's occupation (for girls). This too began to change more than a hundred years ago. There has been a manifold increase in the number of occupations. And the availability of educational opportunities, plus the trend toward development of a meritocracy — advancement based on merit rather than on factors such as family background (which may be unrelated to productivity) — has made it possible for at least the more able youth to choose among thousands of different entry jobs and tens of thousands of careers. These added opportunities for choice occur despite entrance quotas imposed by agencies that range from local labor unions to state medical schools. Today, an individual can observe only a small proportion of the occupations from which choices could be made, even if employers were to pull down all their fences.

Thus far we have discussed opportunities for *observation* of work. There have been similar changes in the opportunities for actual *participation* in work. Child labor laws prohibit most employment of youth under age fourteen, and many states have laws which require special permission for employment of youth under age sixteen. Work on or around "hazardous machinery," including automobiles, is often prohibited for youth under age eighteen, unless they are involved in an educational program and are between ages sixteen and eighteen. This effectively excludes almost all youth of middle school age from participation in most manufacturing occupations. Fourteen- and fifteen-year-olds (eighth and ninth graders) can be employed in most states in daytime (nonschool) periods in most retail trade occupations. The laws of almost all states permit employment by family farms and businesses and permit youth to serve as "independent contractors" who operate their own businesses, such as delivering newspapers, mowing lawns, raising and selling animals, washing cars, shining shoes, running errands, entertaining, or selling "snow" cones, Christmas cards, or cosmetics. A relatively new business for youth is "house sitting." In communities where it is dangerous to leave a house unattended for even a few hours, students answer the telephone, take in newspapers and mail, turn on lights, and so forth, to let outsiders know the house is occupied. There are no laws prohibiting work in and around the home, paid or unpaid, if it is guided by parents or guardians.

Child labor laws came into being because of widespread exploitation of children in the early stages of industrialization. Some protections are probably still necessary, but these laws need to be reexamined to see if they are not actually impeding the career preparation of youth. Until changes are made, the middle/junior high school which desires to involve students in observing and performing real work must adapt to them.

In order to present a clearer picture of the relationship between involvement in work and observation of work, we have developed Figure 7 which depicts four states of observation and personal involvement in work. "Structured observation" means more than "watching"; it involves conscious, educated study of what individuals and groups do at work, what makes them satisfied and dissatisfied, what products and services they produce, and what route they follow in building careers. From the standpoint of career education, condition "a" is the most desirable: Each student is or has been working, and simultaneously is observing consciously the work he or she is performing as well as the work of others. Conditions "b," "c," and "d" are, successively, more and more undesirable. Condition "c" represents the situation of many adults (including some teachers who have not seriously studied what work means to the individual and to society). These individuals work, but they give no thought to work as work. They may be dissatisfied with their work but do not know why, or what can be done about it. They may be satisfied with their work and assume that anyone who is doing a different kind of work must be dissatisfied. Condition "d" represents a complete absence of involvement in and awareness of work. Fortunately, there are very few adults in condition "d," but until career education is more widespread through our education system, and until its graduates constitute a large part of the work force, it is probable that a large majority of people, both youth and adult, will be found in condition "c."

Students in the middle/junior high school are typically of ages eleven to fifteen. Despite the laws which severely circumscribe the types of paid work activity undertaken by those eleven through thirteen years of age and restrict work opportunities for the rest, a sizable portion of these youth do work for pay. There are hundreds of thousands of newspaper carriers, an even greater number of baby sitters, and significant numbers of youth who work part time at shoveling snow, baling hay, mowing lawns, pulling weeds, caring for neighbor's pets, driving tractors, housecleaning, walking invalids, washing cars, selling greeting cards, caddying at golf courses, and so forth. Millions more work at household chores, for which some are paid, and some receive "allowances," with the tacit or explicit understanding that chores will be done.

Although there are no estimates available, the number of middle/junior high students who work outside the school but do not receive pay must be extremely high. In addition to those who perform unpaid home chores, there are group (patrol) leaders in Scouts, Girl Scouts, Camp Fire Girls, Boys Clubs, and 4-H Clubs; leaders in student government; shop foremen in industrial arts classes; equipment managers for athletic teams and musical organizations; volunteers who work for community centers, hospitals, churches, libraries, cemeteries, and in fund collection, litter collection, paper drives, recycling programs; and a host of other activities. Students answer telephones, run errands, hand out announcements, arrange furniture, sweep and dust, tutor, supervise swimming and games, coach athletics, carry water and food, and set tables. In some communities they still dust erasers, clean chalkboards, feed the fish, water the plants, and otherwise assist teachers with school tasks.

Three things stand out when we look at the paid and unpaid out-of-school work of this age group. First, despite the modern stance that "chores" no longer need be done around the home, there is not only a wide opportunity for paid and unpaid work for youth, but also many opportunities for work experience that go begging. For example, what community could not use more workers to help with cleaning and painting, or caring for grass, flowers, and shrubbery in the city parks? Or what community is satisfied with the care provided for the very young, the very old, the convalescent, or the handicapped? Second, not only do these work activities occur outside the school, but the school is as completely oblivious to them as it is to most of the work which goes on within or just outside its walls.

A third point is closely related to the second: The worker also is often oblivious to the work, since these activities are not seen as work by the participants. Instead they are seen as opportunities to secure money (sometimes for luxuries, but surprisingly often for absolute necessities), or as fun, or as something adults feel ought to be done. Consequently these youth are in condition "c" (Figure 7). They are working, but they do not know that this work is a means of learning about work, of learning about other workers, or of helping to design better careers for themselves. Therefore they are not getting the maximum benefit from their work, though they are nevertheless far better situated than those in condition "d."

School Is Work

There is only one type of work activity which is nearly universal among middle school age youth: Almost all of them go to school. According to our definition, school is work, and hence school experiences ought to be analyzed and studied in much the same fashion as other types of work. One way in which schoolwork (note the use of the word "work" in this common phrase) differs from almost all other types of work is in the degree to which the rewards of that work are postponed. In most other types of work, paid or unpaid, the rewards come concurrently with or shortly after the performance of the work. Payday is closely associated with paid work. In unpaid work, the worker is almost always a volunteer; thus almost by definition, the unpaid worker experiences immediately the joys of working with others and the satisfactions of getting things done. If the tasks appear to be too unrewarding, the volunteer quits.

	Structured Observation of Work	
	Yes	No
Personal Involvement in Work Yes	a Learning to appreciate the full value of work to you and to others	c Learning the feel of work but unaware of what you and others really are doing through work or what work is doing to you
No	b Aware of others at work, but unaware of what work really is like for you	d Unaware that work is done and unaware of its value to you as an individual and to society

FIGURE 7. Personal Involvement with and Structured Observation of Work

But schoolwork in the middle school is unpaid *and* compulsory. (So are chores, in some families.) Some, but not all, students would attend school voluntarily if our compulsory attendance laws were repealed. Presumably they see enough reward, immediate or deferred, to cause them to be voluntary workers. But other students do not find enough reward to encourage them to work hard at the tasks of the school. One solution would be to abolish compulsory attendance laws and to pay schools on the basis of the proportion of students they could attract on a volunteer basis. Or we could pay children to go to school as we do certain unemployed adults who are being retrained. Career education suggests another, perhaps more feasible, solution: to increase rewards to students by showing them the relevance of school tasks as preparation for participation in the occupational society.

Capitalizing on Work Experience

The objectives of career education suggest that the school should capitalize on these work experiences by removing misconceptions about work, and by helping students to ask important questions such as:

(1) Why are almost all newspaper carriers male and baby sitters female?

(2) Which of your abilities are used in your work and which are not?

(3) What do you like and dislike about your work?

(4) What does your work contribute to your family and to society?

(5) Do you enjoy working by yourself, with a small group, or as part of a large group?

(6) How could you organize your work more effectively?

(7) What do you enjoy about being your own boss, as compared with being an employee?

(It is interesting that career education is accused by some critics of preparing everyone to work for the military-industrial complex, though child labor laws restrict much of the paid work experience of youth to settings in which the youth is the entrepreneur rather than the employee.)

Schools also have an obligation to educate parents in the means of providing work opportunities for youth. A number of good examples of such parent education activities have been noted in *Career Education and the Elementary School Teacher*. Newsletters to parents, advisory committees, and adult eduction classes in how to teach career education at home have been described. Other suggestions for parents are:

(1) Trading work to allow their children to work for neighbors instead of at home

(2) Assisting youth to accumulate capital for a small business such as lawn mowing

(3) Describing good and bad working conditions

(4) Involving youth in realistic tasks such as cleaning the home or family business, sorting business papers, and helping with tax forms

Above all, parents should learn that work, for youth, should be primarily a means of teaching them about work and only secondarily a means of getting work accomplished. The common statement of parents, "I'd rather do it myself instead of taking the time to persuade and teach him (or her) how to do it," completely misses the point. The basic reason for teaching a child to make a bed (for example) should not be to get cheap labor for bedmaking, but to teach important skills and attitudes which are likely to affect success in the world of work, and indeed, in all of life.

Another thing which parents and teachers should teach (so that youth can learn) is that work does not necessarily involve monetary pay. Even economists do not understand this fully, since unpaid work is not considered a part of the gross national product. Nevertheless, the housewife works. So does the volunteer voter registrar, the parent who supervises the student lunchroom, and the youth who puts away the dishes after the evening meal. All who produce goods and services primarily for others, rather than for their own pleasure, work and contribute to the welfare of society and to their own well-being. Work provides rewards in many forms, only one of which is money.

Once we get enough money to supply basic needs, the non-monetary rewards such as personal satisfaction and opportunity to create tend to become much more important.

School-Operated Businesses

Most schools operate a variety of businesses which provide opportunities for students to learn about work. School newspapers, yearbooks, magazine, and candy sales are quite common. Some schools even operate gardens or farms. It is rare, however, for these activities to be used for teaching about work. Instead, they are seen as ways of earning money for school activities, or as ways of saving money by producing needed goods or services more cheaply than they can be purchased on the open market. Where this is the case, actions should be taken to structure the opportunities for learning about work, and to provide a closer tie between this work and the other teaching-learning activities of the school. The number of opportunities for such work needs to be increased sharply. In most schools, only the "good" students or those who are part of the power structure are allowed to participate in these activities.

Sometimes the situation is worse than that described above. In many parts of the world where school gardens are operated, it is the general practice to sentence students who break school rules to spend a certain number of hours working in the garden. The result is easy to see: Students are taught that manual work is punishment to be avoided at all costs. If punishment is absolutely necessary, a more effective means is to require the student to sit and do nothing. Still better is to avoid punishment as much as possible and accentuate the positive by "allowing" students who do well in class to have time to work in the garden.

There is a built-in conflict between efficiency of production and efficiency of teaching which needs to be recognized by all who plan school-operated businesses. Many educational reformers of the eighteenth and nineteenth centuries recognized the need for youth to learn about work. They were also aware of the fact that when learning and work are related one to the other, learning occurs more rapidly. At the same time they were faced with the problem of inadequate funding for schools. A solution which was tried repeatedly was to turn the school into a producer of goods or services which could be sold to maintain the school. Similar experiments were tried in reformatories, mental hospitals, orphan asylums, and other educational or semieducational agencies which society needed but for which society was unwilling to pay.

These experiments have always ended in failure, though they are still being tried, especially in developing countries in various parts of the world. The reasons for failure always have been nearly identical, and knowledge of them can help us avoid the same mistakes in career education programs today. One reason for failure appears to be paramount: an inevitable conflict between production efficiency and efficiency of instruction.

A study of this difficulty is particularly instructive, for it applies to the career education of adults as well as youth. Every new skill takes time to learn. If we graph production vs time for a new worker to learn a skill, we get a learning curve. The length of time to learn complex skills is long, and the time required to learn simple skills is short, but the shape of the learning curve is nearly the same for all types of skills.

Figure 8 indicates that a great deal is learned between points A and B, for production rises rapidly during this period of time. The time period between B and C is about the same as between A and B, but the gain in production is much less from B to C.

If we are operating a school, we are likely to stop formal instruction in a skill at about point B. We do this because other skills need to be taught, and we recognize that the time from B to C will not result in a great deal of learning. Unfortunately, we sometimes teach a class as a unit instead of teaching individuals, and force our better students to mark time between B and C, while slower students are making progress between A and B.

On the other hand, if we are operating a factory, or a business, or a farm, we have a different point of view. The time between A and B is costing us money, because the production of the worker is low. We begin to make money at about point B, and can recoup the money we have spent on training only if the worker spends considerable time at full production. The

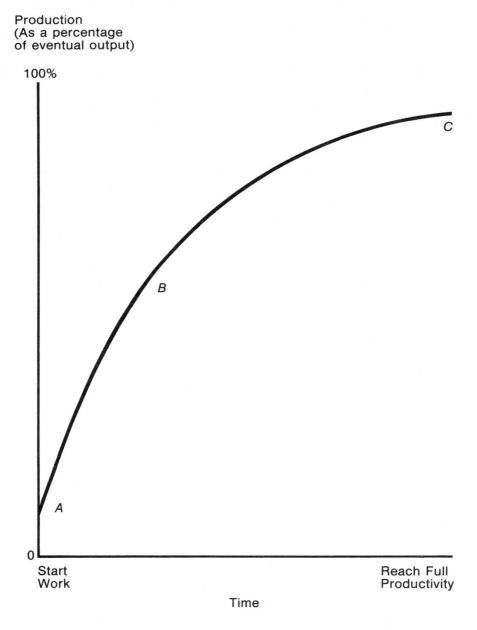

Production
(As a percentage
of eventual output)

100%

C

B

A

0

Start
Work

Reach Full
Productivity

Time

FIGURE 8. A Typical Learning Curve for a New Worker

longer we can keep a worker producing at full capacity, the more profit we will make. Therefore an employer will be reluctant to shift a worker to a new job, because this would involve starting the worker on a new learning curve. Of course, if a worker's production drops because of boredom, it might be desirable to shift him to a revised job.

The learning curves for cognitive knowledge have the same shape as the curves for learning skills, and it seems likely that the learning curves for attitudes are similar in shape.

These simple facts of learning theory and economics illustrate the principal difference between a school and an organization which has as its goal the efficient production of goods or noneducational services. Teachers want to get the student to point B as quickly as possible, and then start teaching something new; the factory or business is rewarded for getting a person from point A to point C as rapidly as possible and keeping him or her on the same task. Only when an employer can move a person from point A to point B more rapidly than can the school can we justify learning that particular skill on the job instead of in a school. It is a sad commentary on certain school programs that employers regularly can outperform the school, even though teaching is not the primary goal of the employer.

These same simple facts tell us why a school will fail if it tries to operate as a factory does and pay its own way. They also tell us that when schools operate businesses for the purpose of providing work experience for students, these businesses rarely, if ever, will be both efficient producers of profit and efficient learning sites. Schools should be, and often are, organized to promote efficiency in learning. When they are efficient at this task, they will be relatively inefficient as producers of goods or noneducational services, simply because they are unwilling to require that a student keep on performing the same task after he or she has learned it thoroughly.

For these reasons, the school should capitalize on the study of work which students do outside school (at home or in other part-time work), but the school should rarely operate a factory or business in competition with the private sector. Generally, the school should restrict the programs it operates to simulated work and to the work of the teacher and student *qua* teacher and student.

Simulated Work in the Middle School

More and more schools have been turning to simulated work, because it is sometimes more efficient for instruction than real work, and because many types of work for pay are prohibited for youth under age sixteen.

The borderline between real work and simulated work is not sharp and clear. Pay is not the criterion for dividing one from the other, because money is not a necessary motivation for some people or for some work. As noted earlier, pay is not received for many work activities, such as those of homemaker. Conversely, there are many make-work activities for which pay is received, but which are only poor simulations of work.

Work simulation involves the creation of activities which are designed for teaching about the production of goods and services, but which produce goods and services as byproducts of instruction, rather than as byproducts of profit making, or as principal ends in themselves. One example of work simulation is a mass-production project in which a class produces two hundred dolls made of beads and string, but the goal of the project is to teach about the effects of repetitive work. Another example would be a candy sales campaign in which the primary goal was to teach about selling, rather than to make money for the class. To be most effective, work simulation tasks should have the following characteristics:

(1) They should appear important to both teacher and learner. Digging holes and filling them is not ideal simulation, even if it teaches the use of a shovel. Whenever possible, there should be some use for the products or services produced. If you want to teach a person to use a shovel, tree planting would not only teach the skill, but many other things as well, including teaching that work can produce worthwhile results.

(2) They should be arranged in sequence as carefully as are other learning experiences. Progressions from the simple to the complex and from easy to difficult are

typical and logical. Too often, however, students are assigned to tasks in the order in which they are received from some outside agency (e.g., beginning typing students are assigned to prepare complex forms because these forms are needed in the school office), or are assigned to tasks in the same chronological order they would be performed by an experienced worker. (One caution should be observed, however: If the student is taught to do a simple task without understanding the complex task of which it is a part, it may have no meaning. For this reason, it may be advisable to introduce the student to the complex task before going back to teach thoroughly a simple part of it.)

(3) They should cover a wide range of types of work (white-collar/blue-collar; goods/services; indoor/outdoor; work with people/things/ideas; paced by machine/by the worker/by time studies/by others in a group/or by a supervisor.

(4) They should cover a wide range of types of organization for work (individual/small group/large group; artist/artist-craftsman/mass production; specialized/-whole function).

(5) They should cover a wide range of work roles (entrepreneur/employee; producer/inspector; buyer/seller).

(6) They should recognize work standards such as speed and accuracy which are required in real work, and apply these standards as rapidly as students can learn to cope with them.

Each simulation should be of interest to students, should be carefully planned in advance, and should involve all students in one way or another (but not necessarily all at the same time).

The Assignment

The oldest form of simulated work experience in education is the assignment. A student is asked to read, write, observe, or calculate, and then to produce a written or oral report which is checked for quality by a supervisor: the teacher. These are typical work activities performed by white-collar workers in a wide variety of fields, and illustrate the bias of the school toward preparing people for white-collar, but not blue-collar work. Although the assignment simulates fairly well many of the activities required of white-collar workers, it has lost its identity as a form of work simulation, and has come to be regarded by teachers and students alike as a purely academic exercise. Assignments frequently are carefully arranged in a sequence which is designed to increase learning efficiency, but they usually fail to take into account each of the remaining characteristics of good simulated work. They often do not appear important to the students, and they are almost invariably limited to white-collar, indoor services, are paced by the teacher, are produced one at a time in the manner of an individual artist, and are highly specialized rather than covering a whole function. They also cast the student in the roles of employee, producer, and seller. Many important work roles are seldom portrayed; e.g., those of employer, consumer of services to business, and buyer of products and services.

The Project

When the project method was introduced into schools several generations ago, few teachers saw it as an effective vehicle for simulating work. Instead, it was seen as a means of overcoming certain deficiencies of the assignment. In particular it was seen as a way of increasing the apparent relevance of instruction by assigning a group of tasks which formed a coherent whole. This has a partial parallel in the "job enlargement" efforts of the world of work, where periodic attempts are made to redesign jobs so that workers produce an identifiable product or service (e.g., a radio), rather than contribute such a small fraction of the whole (e.g., solder two wires) that each worker feels is irrelevant.

Another common goal of the project is to increase student creativity by leaving certain parts of tasks unspecified. As the student progresses to more and more sophisticated projects, the amount of creativity allowed or required can be increased. Ideally, by the time the student leaves school, she or he should be capable of initiating, carrying through, and evaluating projects with little or no outside assistance. This progression through a series of levels of creativity has a close parallel in most of the career ladders of the world of work. Each ladder begins with an occupation which requires (and allows) little creativity. Ideally, each step on a given ladder requires and allows more creativity as well as more responsibility.

It is clear that the project method can and should have considerable use in simulated work experience. Most middle/-junior high school teachers have had considerable experience with the project method; thus the transition should be easy for them. Indeed, all that is required is to identify and then to teach significant aspects of work, work values, and the world of work, using old, familiar methods in slightly different ways.

Junior Achievement

Perhaps the most well-known work simulation involving young adolescents is "Junior Achievement." It uses the project method, but rarely is taught within the school. For more than twenty years a national nonprofit corporation has arranged for local businesses throughout the country to sponsor groups of young men and women who are interested in learning more about how our business system operates.

The local sponsoring company furnishes an adult advisor, but the youth themselves elect officers, do market research, choose a product or service (usually from a list of examples which have been used successfully by other groups), sell stock, manufacture and sell the product or sell and perform the service, and liquidate the company, paying themselves and the stockholders from the proceeds. Products have covered a wide range, including the manufacture of perfume, greeting cards, fire extinguishers, golf tees, and wooden toys. Service activities include typing, advertising, and appliance repair. Some companies fail to make a profit, but a higher proportion of Junior Achievement companies succeed financially than do new businesses managed by adults.

The complete cycle from birth to dissolution of the company normally requires one school year. Nevertheless, these Junior Achievement corporations are rarely operated in conjunction with the school. This naturally raises the question: Why not?

One obvious reason is that many teachers feel that this type of activity, while it teaches things which are "nice to know," is not so important as the activities normally carried on during the school day. The rationale for career education suggests, however, that such learning *is* as important as the other functions of a school.

Other reasons for not including Junior Achievement in the regular school program are: fear that an activity which attracts volunteer, middle class students will not work with nonvolunteers; lack of enough sponsors to allow inclusion of all students; and fear that school-sponsored production and sale of goods or services will be opposed by local industries and businesses. There is also a fear that the free-enterprise system will not be examined critically by a sponsoring group which states clearly its intent to preserve traditional business structures and values. If this fear is real, it suggests that involvement of the school could provide a more balanced program.

It may not be possible to provide Junior Achievement-type activities for all students immediately, but a gradual introduction of this concept into the school will provide opportunities for experimentation to determine the best form for each community. One change which should be considered is the inclusion of simulation of collective bargaining. Incorporating this into the school will require the use of class advisors from organized labor, business, and industry, and could serve as the basis for regular exchange of personnel between schools and the remainder of the world of work.

Mass Production Projects

An instructional device which is feasible in any school, and which is being used with increasing frequency in the middle/junior high school, is the mass-production project which has some of the same goals as Junior Achievement. Many industrial arts classes and a few home economics and art classes include at least one mass-production project, in which the entire class (or some significant portion of it) is organized into production units that undertake to produce a quantity of identical products or services. Students may or may not be involved in the design, market research, tool design, or distribution of these products, or in the choice of the services to be produced, but there are excellent reasons for teaching them through involvement. Usually enough units are manufactured so that each student can keep one, and additional units may be given to charitable or other nonprofit organizations. Products which have been manufactured include: wooden toys, coat hangers, dictionary racks, bookends, circuit testers, pen sets, birdhouses, bird feeders, high-intensity lamps, carbon dioxide-powered model race cars, model rockets, wall plaques, autograph books, and yo-yos. Dozens of other examples could be given.

In its more elaborate forms, the mass-production project very much resembles the Junior Achievement program. Usually, however, the mass-production project uses hand or power tools which are available in the art or industrial arts laboratories, rather than using equipment borrowed from Junior Achievement industrial sponsors, is less likely than Junior Achievement to sell the products, and places more emphasis than Junior Achievement on acquisition of technical skills.

The prime goal of the mass-production project is almost always to simulate the manufacturing industry so that students can learn, in concrete form, the meaning of such key concepts as interchangeability of parts, specialization of labor, and economy of scale. Many industrial arts teachers also include a goal of occupational exploration which is, of course, vital to career education. With this in mind, teachers allow the students to volunteer for positions as foremen, inspectors, machine operators, and assemblers. Periodically, workers are shifted, and effects on product quality and quantity are noted. Alert teachers also call attention to effects on worker's morale and interest.

The important distinction between many such projects of the past and those designed for career education lies in the emphasis on personal involvement. Maximum benefits for career education arise when the student sees what it means for his individual career, rather than seeing it as an elaborate charade which has meaning only for others. Similarly, a sense of individual involvement increases the likelihood that the student also will learn the noncareer education concepts which the teacher seeks to convey.

Unfortunately, the mass-production project is not as adaptable to teaching about the production of services as it is for teaching about manufacturing. It is possible, however, to introduce malfunctions into several one-cylinder gasoline engines and apply specialization of labor in servicing them. Car washing, lawn care, and household repairs for the elderly and disabled are other services that have been performed by practical arts classes. Dr. Jacob Stern, of the University of Illinois, has designed a unique teacher education course which uses a business structure for goods servicing. His graduates teach courses which combine some of the best features of Junior Achievement and mass production.

The One-of-a-Kind Project

Practical and fine arts classes have used the custom-designed, one-of-a-kind project method with great success in teaching the use of materials and tools and as a motivational device for encouraging other learnings. Each student is assigned or selects some material object to be produced; it may be a cake, earrings, a tie rack, a chisel, a drawing, a sculpture, and so forth. The student completes the project, usually working alone but receiving periodic instruction in the use of the tools and materials required by the project. The project usually is judged not only in terms of its quality, but also in terms of the processes used to produce it.

In the world of work, efforts to reduce the use of the kinds of work which are analogous to the individual project have been intensifying for many years. Hairdressing, television repair, performing in theaters, housecleaning, and a few other similar service activities still employ sizable numbers of people, but the numbers should decline as ways are found to serve more people at less cost (through increased productivity). In the meantime, our society is so wealthy that some people are willing to pay for individualized products or services.

Career education suggests that when the teacher uses the one-of-a-kind project method, he should be sure that the student understands:

(1) That this method of producing goods and services is likely to decline in importance in the work force

(2) That few people are able to earn high pay in this kind of work

(3) That it allows freedom from supervision and opportunities to create work of high quality which are very satisfying to many people

This typical relationship between low pay and a low number of products produced per man-hour, and the trade-off between the desire of the artist to produce high-quality work, and the low pay per hour for most (but not all) artists are vital understandings which are a part of career education.

OTHER PROJECT STRUCTURES

It is desirable in some classes to have the one-of-a-kind project involve a group activity and for mass-production projects to be produced by an individual. Most complex, custom-made products, such as residences, do involve a group of workers, and the artist-craftsman may produce a hundred rings before going to a new design.

Figure 9 illustrates some of the relationships between size of work group and quantity of product or service. The important point for career education is that if instruction in the fine and practical arts uses the custom-designed, one-of-a-kind project to the exclusion of the mass-production project, students will have been unable to explore a major aspect of careers. Similarly, if students always work alone on projects, rather than working for a major portion of their time in teams of two or more, another major aspect of career exploration will have been omitted.

Home economics classes which have units on foods or clothing almost invariably stress individually designed, one-of-a-kind products. Quantity food preparation is stressed in the few home economics classes which still are involved in school lunch programs, but almost everyone agrees that such involvement is undesirable. Besides, the food is not esthetically very pleasing. It is rare for a clothing class to produce, say, fifty

	Individual Working Alone	Group Work
Single Product or Service	One worker completes all or a major portion of one product or service which will not be duplicated. Typical occupations: painter, typist, hairdresser, cabinetmaker, tool and die maker	Several workers each complete a small part of a product or service which will not be duplicated. Typical work settings: residential construction, chorus, football game
Multiple Products or Services	One worker completes all or a major portion of several nearly identical products or services. Typical occupations: artist-craftsman, mimeograph operator, teacher in self-contained classroom, window washer	Several workers each complete a small part of many nearly identical products or services. Typical work settings: assembly line, medical clinic

FIGURE 9. Size of Work Group and Quantity
of Product or Service

blouses, all alike, in order to better understand the occupations in garment work.

Similar biases appear to exist in most fine arts classes. The design and production of unique jewelry, painting, and sculpture are emphasized far more than the work of the artist-craftsman, who may spend even more time on design but will produce several dozen or several hundred articles all alike. Unique performances of music and drama are stressed, rather than video or audio recording, which makes a performance available to a considerably larger audience — and incidentally employs more people in the arts. It would appear that many teachers of fine and practical arts tend to associate quantity with mediocrity. Project methods which illustrate that this relationship is not necessarily true have considerable importance for consumers as well as for participants in careers.

Work Experience and Career Exploration (W.E.C.E.P.)

The work experience and career exploration program is designed for potential dropouts of age fourteen and fifteen at any grade level. Some five hundred schools in eleven states served more than eight thousand students in 1971–72, and the program is growing rapidly. Some states will fund the program only in schools which have a high average dropout rate.

The program uses federal vocational education funds in a part-time, cooperative education program. The teacher-coordinator selects and places students, chooses work stations for them, visits the students on the job, and teaches the two-hour daily in-school related class. Indeed the program is similar to the high school-level, part-time, cooperative program, except that the high school program often serves only the best scholars from among those who apply.

Two school districts in Joliet, Illinois, and one in Maywood, Illinois, have excellent sets of goals, forms, rating sheets, and descriptive materials for a work experience and career exploration program. Another in Dundee, Illinois, is working with migrant students and has established control and experimental groups, with the latter receiving the program. Almost all of the comparisons strongly favor the experimental group. For example, four of the control group dropped out, compared with none of the experimental group, and the latter had slightly more than half as many days absent as did the control group (Brown and Wright, 1972). Individual cases of almost unbelievably dramatic character were frequent in the experimental group.

Because of their age, students in this program cannot be employed in certain occupations, and their minimum wages are sometimes specified. However, federal regulations are much more flexible for students in the program than for other fourteen- to fifteen-year-olds, because they are in a vocational program which is carefully supervised by the school. Section 520.21 of "Employment of Student Learners" describes federal regulations, but state rules may apply as well; therefore it is desirable to check with the state director of vocational education before proceeding with this type of program.

Dundee, Illinois, has an interesting innovation on pay. They want students in the work experience and career exploration program to be paid the minimum wage, but some employers objected that these potential dropouts were not worth that much. An agreement was reached that the school would pay the difference between the minimum wage and that which the employer felt the student was worth. Seventy percent of the employers are now paying the full wage.

The program was conceived as a three-year experiment to determine whether a combination of work experience and career exploration would produce desirable effects for fourteen- and fifteen-year-old potential dropouts. As is often the case in field studies of this type, some of the members of the control group have been affected by the experiment, demanding equal instruction or seeking information and experience on their own. And few schools have undertaken studies as carefully as Dundee. Still, it seems clear that the basic thesis of the program has been proved: With good teacher-coordinators and close cooperation of school and community, many potential dropouts can be salvaged, and contributing members of the community can be prepared through the work experience and career exploration program.

The Work Simulation Package

A number of people have begun to develop prepackaged programs or kits which are designed to provide a type of work simulation for individuals or for small groups of students, without requiring much teacher involvement in designing the experience. Perhaps the simplest and most effective of these are the "occupacs" developed by Marla Peterson and her associates at Eastern Illinois University. Each "occupac" is a medium-sized box which contains a number of role-playing aids and a script which helps a student explore the occupation through simulated work activities. The landscape gardener kit, for example, allows creation of a miniature park, complete with plants and trees. The nurse kit has a thermometer, bandages, and the like to create a simulation of treatment of a sick child.

A more elaborate and considerably more expensive simulation device has been created by Singer-Graflex. This has several work stations which allow students to use tools and other equipment to assemble or service real objects. By rotating through each of these work stations, the student experiences a bit of work performed by people in a number of occupations. Still more elaborate are the simulation experiences provided in the Industrial Arts Curriculum Project courses in construction and manufacturing. These are described in chapter 5 of this book.

It seems odd that business education, which has developed the most complete and sophisticated work simulation programs in office practice at the senior high school level, appears to have made little use of simulation in the increasingly common junior high school courses offered under such titles as "Introduction to Business" or "Personal Typing."

Work Observation

Almost every career education program makes extensive use of work observation. This activity should be planned for maximum educational effectiveness.

Career educators recognize that work observation does not have the educational potential of work, or even of work simulation, simply because it is difficult to get active learner involvement in work observation. This does not mean that work observation is not useful. It means that active learner involvement in work observation is highly desirable, and it means that work observation should be used when work and work simulation are not practicable. The typical program of work observation involves class visits to places where work is done, but this is not the only or even necessarily the best way of observing work.

Earlier, Figure 7 illustrated that it is possible for an adult worker to go through life without ever carefully observing the work that he or she has been doing. Most people observe certain aspects of work, and can tell who is working effectively, who learns a new task rapidly, and who is well paid. But often other aspects of work are not observed carefully. There is a typical tendency to underrate the skills of others and to assume that whatever makes a worker satisfied or dissatisfied will affect the job satisfaction of others in the same way. One of the skills that career education should teach is that of observing one's own work as well as that of his or her peers. To increase learner participation in work observation, some teachers encourage students to develop rating scales for describing and evaluating different jobs in terms of how they relate to the student's own preferences and values. Typical items in working conditions to be observed include the following (judged in terms of "what suits me"):

(1) Sometimes too hot; usually not too hot or too cold; sometimes too cold

(2) Too much physical activity required; usually about the right amount of physical activity; too much sitting around required

(3) Too dangerous; usually about right; too little risk

(4) Too exacting; usually about right; too boring

(5) Too little responsibility; usually about right; too much responsibility

(6) Too dirty; usually about right; too clean

(7) Work with too many people; usually about right; work with too few people

When students design and complete checklists of items such as these or answer questions contained in an observational guide, they are likely to learn far more from observing work than they would learn on a typical tour. One thing they will learn when they compare results is that some of the qualities of a job which most repel some students are the very qualities which attract others. This is one of the most important truths which people can learn about work, for it helps to explain why and how the work of the world gets done.

The business or factory tour needs careful preparation if it is to have maximum value in a career education program. Certain problems in arranging tours are difficult to avoid.

(1) A considerable amount of time must be spent in planning.

(2) Other teachers become unhappy because students must miss their classes while on tour, if the tour taken requires more than one class period. (In the middle/-junior high school this disadvantage can be turned into an advantage if the teachers work cooperatively on career education.)

(3) A tour costs money: for the school, for the students, or both.

Answering the following list of questions will help to minimize these difficulties:

(1) What do you want to accomplish? Can it be done best by a field trip? Why not use work simulation, a film, or some other method prior to or instead of a field trip? Can you accomplish your goals by visiting a mass-production unit in the school industrial arts laboratory? Or a typing class, a home economics class, or an art class?

(2) Do you know the school rules for field trips? If there are no rules, help to develop some.

(3) Exactly what do you want students to observe? Plan the trip with this in mind. Where is the best place to go? Don't forget to consider whether all students can afford to go, if the trip is a long one.

(4) Have you secured the approval of school authorities, officials of the agency you plan to visit, and parents of your students?

(5) Have you discussed the goals of the field trip with the agency you want to visit? Otherwise they will give you

the tour they have designed for the general public or for specialists who are already familiar with processes that are involved.

(6) How can you best prepare the students for the trip? They should know exactly what they are to observe (an observation guide or rating sheet is helpful), and they should be expected to report orally or in writing on the results of their observations. Students can help to develop the observation guide.

(7) What key points do you want to include in the discussion of what has been learned? What career ladders were observed? What working conditions? What entry level training requirements?

(8) How can you evaluate the trip? Did you accomplish your goals? Do you want to use a similar trip again? What can be changed to make the next trip better?

(9) What is the best way to thank everyone involved, including the other teachers whose classes you have disrupted? A follow-up letter will not only aid you in the future, but will assist other teachers who want to take field trips.

(10) What advance plans do you want to make for next year? Try to get funds allocated so work observation becomes a regular part of education, rather than an afterthought.

It is not necessary that all work observation be done in groups. A general rule is that if all students in a group can learn from a particular type of observation, then group observation is desirable. If only a few in the class will find a field trip or other large group observation useful, then individual or small group observation is preferable. Examples of desirable group activities are:

(1) The social studies class visits an assembly line and an artist's workshop to compare work styles.

(2) The homemaking class views a film comparing food preparation for a meal on a camping trip, in a home, a restaurant, and a frozen foods factory.

(3) The industrial arts woods class is assigned to watch a television program that deals with timber farming and conservation.

Individual or small group observation of work can be done in a variety of ways:

(1) Permission is secured to allow one, two, or three students to visit a worker on the job, interview her or him, and report back in oral or written form. Student-made movies or video tapes offer an interesting way of reporting. (Sixth-graders are capable of writing scripts and shooting excellent films.) Color slides and cassette recordings are even easier, and these can be combined to make slide-tape presentations. Everyone likes to know where and how the work was done.

(2) A high school coordinator of cooperative education takes one or two junior high school students along on visits to high school cooperative students on the job. A report back to the junior high school class will often be in order.

(3) Parents are encouraged to secure permission for a son or daughter plus a friend to observe them on the job.

Worker Models

It is common for students to choose certain adults or peers as models, though this choice may not be verbalized. For career education purposes it would be helpful if students chose worker models, preferably in the home or community. Some may object that students should not be allowed to use models from a disadvantaged community. This is incorrect, for two reasons: first, some students will choose such models, and it is better to discuss the advantages and disadvantages of such a choice, rather than pretending that it does not exist. Second, in *every* community, no matter how poor or crime ridden, there are persons worthy of emulation. Those who urge that models be chosen from outside a ghetto, for example, often equate success with earning enough money to flee the ghetto. Surely success includes more than this. The choice should be based not just on occupation, but on work-style, life-style, career progression, and a variety of other attributes which can be observed, analyzed, and evaluated. Students should be encouraged to compare these models with other workers, and with the student's own characteristics (abilities, interests, education, personality, and so forth). Some students will wish to identify their models by name, while others will prefer to keep the models anonymous. Anonymous models should be real persons, however, rather than phantasies.

When possible, models should know that they have been selected. Some of them may wish to assume a big brother or sister role, or at least allow themselves to be observed. Being chosen as a model by a student is very flattering to most people, but it also imposes major responsibilities which are too seldom realized by models.

In all communities, but particularly where there are sizable amounts of illegal activity, some students will occasionally choose models who are regarded by the teacher as undesirable. Some teachers may forbid such choices by students, but if a student is sincere in the choice, the teacher's prohibition may be ineffective. Perhaps the best reaction for the teacher is to help the student to analyze objectively the illegal life-style of the model together with its consequences. Such discussions will help all students to better understand the nature and meaning of work.

Periodically, perhaps each semester, students may wish to consider changing models in order to learn from a variety of people. If students wish to change more or less frequently, however, this should be permitted.

Career Clubs

The junior high school years are not too soon to begin the development of career clubs. Future teachers' clubs, for example, can be quite satisfactory. Many of the high school-level career clubs (future farmers, future business leaders, industrial clubs, and so forth) tend to discourage students from joining unless they are enrolled in vocational courses, while others such as the Junior Engineering and Technical Society tend to discourage membership of pre-high school students. If state and national rules cannot be changed, there is nothing to prevent the establishment of allied clubs which are related to local high school-level clubs. High school students and teachers can provide some of the programs for junior high school career clubs, and learn a great deal while doing so.

Existing clubs can be encouraged to add career awareness and exploration to their present activities. Clubs devoted to astronomy, chess, drama, music, and many other subjects frequently overlook the career aspects of their specialty while concentrating on other important goals.

Junior high school club leaders or organizers should be particularly alert to a problem which plagues high school-level career clubs. Membership in high school clubs is often contingent on the student's being enrolled in a particular class. Because it is often difficult for the student to transfer from one subject to another, it is also difficult for him to change from one career club to another. Indeed, it is usually easier for an adult to quit one career and take up another than for a high school student to shift from one career club to another. Obviously this would be even more indefensible for junior high school clubs.

Clubs at the junior high school level have a problem in meeting after school because of transportation difficulties. Ideally, clubs should meet during the school day, and on a staggered schedule so that students could meet with two or more career clubs without conflict.

Career clubs often will want to join together to plan programs of mutual interest. Sponsorship of a school-wide career day is one good joint activity which encourages cooperation among clubs. It also serves as desirable work simulation for student leaders as they acquire skills through arranging the program with outside individuals and with groups such as employment agencies, businesses, cooperative extension service, Manpower Development and Training agencies, etc., which offer or evaluate preparation for careers.

Summary

Because work is what careers are all about, the study of work is a key portion of career education. The best ways of studying work include work experience, but experience alone is not enough. The best combination includes personal experience, plus structured observation, plus systematic study of work, work values, and the world of work.

A variety of laws restrict the kinds of work that youth of middle/junior high school age can do. A surprising proportion of them work part time, however, as "independent contractors" or at tasks around the home. Many others work as unpaid volunteers. These types of work deserve recognition and systematic study.

Equally deserving of recognition is the fact that students work at school. Although such work is unpaid and compulsory, it deserves reward which can come in part through recognition of its relevance.

Schools could provide additional experience by operating businesses which compete in the private sector, but this is rarely successful due to inherent conflicts between efficiency of production and efficiency of instruction. The standard learning curve points out this conflict vividly, since efficient instruction moves students rapidly through the early stages of learning a large variety of tasks, while efficient production attempts to avoid the early stages of learning and to secure continued output from individuals who have learned a task thoroughly.

Simulated work offers excellent opportunities for career education. But simulation activities require as careful design as other types of teaching. The assignment and the project are methods which can be used effectively to simulate nonschool work.

Junior Achievement and the mass-production project can be particularly satisfactory simulations. However, it is important to be sure that simulation covers a variety of types of work. Among the important categories are production of goods/production of services; custom (one-of-a-kind)/duplicate (several or many identical products or services are produced); and individual worker/team of workers. Traditional school programs often concentrate on production of only a single item, designed and produced by a person who works alone. But mass-production projects often overlook kinds of work such as a team constructing a unique building, or the artist-craftsman producing one or two hundred identical pieces of high-quality jewelry. Most middle/junior high school programs pay too little attention to the rapidly growing world of service work.

Work observation plays an important role in career education. Both individual and group observation should be used, and students can play an important role in improving the quality of observation and reports of what was observed. Modeling of workers in the community can be a useful form of observation, and career clubs can provide a good vehicle for teaching.

REFERENCES

Boocock, Sarane S.; and Schild, E. O. (Editors). *Simulation Games in Learning.* Beverly Hills, California: Sage, 1968.

Bottoms, Gene; and Matheny, Kenneth B. "Occupational Guidance, Counseling and Job Placement for Junior High and Secondary School Youth." Atlanta, Georgia: Georgia State College, 1969. Mimeographed.

Brown, Edward E.; and Wright, Maurice. *Evaluation of W.E.C.E.P.* Dundee, Illinois: Community Unit School District 300, 1972. Mimeographed.

Career Studies. Perry Hall Junior High School, Baltimore, Mayland.

Eau Claire Public Schools Career Development Curriculum Guide, Junior High School 7-9. Eau Claire, Wisconsin.

"Employment of Student Learners." Section 520.12, Title 29, Part 520, Code of Federal Regulations. Washington, D.C.: United States Department of Labor, Employment Standards, Administration, Wage and Hour Division. (W. H. Publication 1343 Revised.)

EPDA Career Experience Evaluation Forms. Santa Rosa, California: Sonoma County Office of Education, 1973.

Floyd, Gladys L. *WECEP Guide Book*. Joliet, Illinois: Joliet Public Schools, District Number 86. Undated (ca 1972).

Johnson, Richard. "Simulation Techniques in Career Development." *American Vocational Journal* (1970). vol. 45.

Hoyt, Kenneth B.; Pinson, Nancy M.; Laramore, Darryl; and Mangum, Garth L. *Career Education and the Elementary School Teacher*. Salt Lake City: Olympus Publishing Company, 1973.

Katz, Martin. *You: Today and Tomorrow*. Princeton, New Jersey: Educational Testing Service, 1957.

Krumboltz, John D.; and Bergland, Bruce. "Experiencing Work Almost Like It Is." *Educational Technology* (1969), vol. 9, no. 3.

Law, Gordon, Jr. *Simulations and Career Education*. Trenton, New Jersey: Department of Education, Division of Vocational Education, Bureau of Occupational Research Development.

Simpson, Elizabeth J. "The Home as a Career Education Center." *Exceptional Children* (May 1973).

Stern, Jacob. *Functions of Goods-Producing Industrial Establishments*. Unpublished doctoral dissertation, 1964. Wayne State University, Detroit, Michigan.

Varenhorst, Barbara. "The Life Career Game: Practice in Decisionmaking" in Boocock and Schild, Editors, *Simulation Games in Learning*. Beverly Hills, California: Sage, 1968.

_____; Gelatt, H. B.; and Carey, R. *Deciding: A Program in Decision Making for Grades 7-8-9*. New York: College Entrance Examination Board, 1972.

Work Study Program, Progress Report Number Four. Kansas City, Missouri: Kansas City Public Schools, 1967.

York, Edwin; Walsh, Priscilla; Kapadia, Madhu; Law, Gordon Jr.; and Richards, Leo. *Grades 7, 8, and 9 Learning Resources for Career Education*. Edison, New Jersey: Occupational Resource Center, 1973.

Organizing
Career Education in
the Middle/Junior
High School

Those middle and junior high schools desirous of installing career education programs are faced with three key operational questions. First, how should personnel and resources be organized for career education? Second, how should the content of career education be organized for presentation to students? And finally, how should career education programs at the middle/junior high school level be evaluated? There exists no clear consensus among those who work in career education regarding any single way in which each of these questions should be answered. We do not say that we have final and definitive answers to any of them. But because none of these questions can be ignored, we do feel a responsibility for sharing some of our current thinking on these topics with readers of this book.

We will begin by summarizing view of others for whom we have developed great respect. Following this, we will present our own current views, which admittedly are presently incomplete and tentative. It is our hope that with this kind of content organization, readers may find a basis for developing answers that will work for them in their own particular middle/junior high school setting. .

Summary of Views of Selected Leaders in Career
Education Program Organization

Drier has provided a comprehensive summary of the organizational process used in implementing career education programs in Wisconsin (pp. 39–41). He describes the organizational process as it operated at the state level and was later transported for use in local school systems. Because of the systematic way in which organizational and content programs were approached in this effort, it deserves description in some detail. The essential strategies used in Wisconsin were:

(1) Developing a general set of background, conceptual materials at the state level for delivery to local school systems

(2) Leaving the development of program specifics to local schools so that individual staff members could become deeply involved in the planning process

(3) Providing schools with eighty hours of in-service workshop assistance aimed at developing local programs

Each of these three general strategies seems to us to be extremely wise. The in-service workshops involved school administrators, student services personnel, educational technicians, teachers, and students. No mention was made of involvement of either parents or members of the business-labor-industry community in these workshops.

The content of the programs was organized around sixteen career development concepts, each of which is given one of three priority orderings — introduce, develop, or emphasize — in the scope and sequence matrix developed at the state level. The suggested middle/junior high school content, in terms of these priority orderings, is as follows:

Career Development Concepts	Grades Four through Six	Grades Seven through Nine
1. An understanding and acceptance of self is important throughout life.	Develop	Emphasize
2. Persons need to be recognized as having dignity and worth.	Develop	Emphasize

Career Development Concepts	Grades Four through Six	Grades Seven through Nine
3. Occupations exist for a purpose.	Develop	Emphasize
4. There is a wide variety of careers which may be classified in several ways.	Develop	Emphasize
5. Work means different things to different people.	Develop	Emphasize
6. Education and work are interrelated.	Develop	Emphasize
7. Individuals differ in their interests, abilities, attitudes, and values.	Develop	Emphasize
8. Occupational supply and demand have an impact on career planning.	Introduce	Develop
9. Job specialization creates interdependency.	Introduce	Develop
10. Environment and individual potential interact to influence career development.	Introduce	Develop
11. Occupations and life-styles are interrelated.	Introduce	Develop
12. Individuals can learn to perform adequately in a variety of occupations.	Introduce	Develop
13. Career development requires a continuous and sequential series of choices.	Introduce	Develop
14. Various groups and institutions influence the nature and structure of work.	Introduce	Develop
15. Individuals are responsible for their career planning.		Introduce
16. Job characteristics and individuals must be flexible in a changing society.		Introduce

During the in-service workshops, staff members from each school worked on identifying and describing specific behavioral objectives, activities, resources to be used, and expected outcomes at each grade level in ways that assured that duplication and overlap would not occur. Drier reports that with this kind of general strategy, 35 local schools were able to develop comprehensive career development programs for themselves.

Drier does not specifically address himself to evaluation questions because, as a part of the general strategy, development of specific evaluation methods was an integral part of local school program planning. However, he does refer to evaluation of the total Wisconsin effort in this way:

> *Worth the time and money?* After the field test, observers repeatedly raised the question: Is career development worth the 383,000 hours and $90,000 investment? It may be considered a cheap investment if the 75,000 students enrolled in the field test schools understand themselves better, realize the potential of the world of work, and acquire the ability to carefully plan and prepare for their work roles.

Thus it would seem that Drier is emphasizing three primary evaluative criteria: increases in student self-understanding, increases in knowledge regarding the world of work, and increases in student ability to plan and prepare for a work role.

In an immensely thoughtful article dealing specifically with the middle school environment, Matheny (pp. 18–21) comments on the content to be imparted to middle school age youth:

> In summary, while the middle school has special responsibility for teaching basic habits of industry, it shares with elementary and senior high schools the responsibility for teaching decision-making skills. The middle grades should be a time for self- and occupational exploration, for becoming planning-oriented, acquiring decision-making skills, and learning the habits of industry. Except for a few early-school leavers, the selection of a specific occupation should be discouraged.

Matheny suggests a number of practices to be incorporated at the middle/junior high school level: (1) emphasizing career implications of all subjects, (2) using the total community as a learning laboratory, (3) real and simulated work experience, (4) use of career games and kits, (5) group counseling, and (6) teaching decison-making skills. In commenting on suggested procedures for use in evaluating effectiveness of results, he says:

> The evaluation task is more difficult for middle schools than for senior high schools, since there is a lack of terminal criteria such as employment or enrollment in post-secondary institutions. For the most part, evaluation in the middle school will be concerned with measuring the increased vocational maturity of students.

He then describes a number of currently available instruments used in measuring vocational maturity. Those readers who seriously consider Matheny's recommendation with respect to evaluation are urged to study and reflect upon the following quotation from Super before moving in this direction:

> There are now in existence four types of measures of vocational maturity.... None have as yet progressed even from the experimental to the developmental stage, and certainly none are yet ready for use in practice.

Our biases are consistent with this viewpoint. Despite this one basic disagreement with Matheny, we urge readers to study Super's article as well (pp. 9–14). There is much of value in it.

An article especially significant in its discussion of personnel resources required in a career development effort was written by Tennyson (pp. 54–58), wherein his rationale for career development — based on relationships between work and play — recognizes that worker alienation is a problem within as well as outside the school setting. This too is consistent with the rationale we would use for justifying the entire career education movement. The article is recommended in its entirety for all who read this book. For our purposes here, special attention is called to his observations of personnel requirements for organizing and implementing career development concepts. The following excerpts from Tennyson deserve careful attention:

> At the moment, there is in most states a leadership void with respect to career development in the schools.

> It is uncertain whether the needed leadership is to be found within the ranks of school counselors, industrial arts teachers, other vocational educators, or some new functionary yet to be trained and perhaps called a career development coordinator.... [T]he task will be accomplished best by leadership teams composed of vocational educators, counselors, and academic teachers.... Both the vocational educator and the school counselor have unique contributions to make in promoting the career development program. The vocational educator's leadership potential lies in his knowledge of the world of work, the counselor's in his understanding of human behavior.... Leadership for career development is largely a matter of consultation.

We applaud Tennyson's emphasis on consultative teamwork and his recognition that a wide variety of kinds of expertise is required in organizing and implementing a career development program. Since career education is broader than career development, the breadth of expertise for the former is greater as well.

We urge readers to refer to chapter 3 for further recommendations and practices in organizing career education programs and to chapter 2 for examples of possible evaluative criteria. With this urging and the examples presented here, we now turn to our own thoughts regarding the three key questions raised at the start of this chapter.

ORGANIZING PERSONNEL AND RESOURCES FOR CAREER EDUCATION AT THE MIDDLE/JUNIOR HIGH SCHOOL LEVEL

Our general point of view is in agreement with Drier's three basic strategies outlined above that call for the presence of some substantive content in career education for personnel to learn, for the availability of in-service time and resources required to learn and assimilate that substantive content and plan to put it into practice, and for allowance of maximum freedom and flexibility for individual staff members to be as creative and innovative as they can be in translating this substantive content into action program steps. We will comment extensively on substantive content in the next section of this chapter. Here, we concentrate on the other two basic strategies described by Drier.

It is expected that at some point in time, teacher education institutions will change their preservice curricula so that it will reflect the presence and importance of the career education movement. While a few have already begun to do so, most have not. Thus career education finds itself largely dependent on in-service education of presently employed school personnel for program formulation and implementation. Such in-service education cannot be accomplished in only one or two days, as some school administrators seem to have assumed. In a one-day workshop, we find ourselves moderately successful in "selling" the career education concept. After all, as a very broad generic concept, career education (as we see it) is simply helping our students understand the importance of our subject matter in terms of ways in which they might use it in their work. This concept is no more difficult to "sell" than mother-hood, God, or research; i.e., some may not "buy" it, but it is unusual for many to stand up and argue against it!

As a generic concept, career education has already been "sold," as is evidenced by the Gallup poll of public attitudes toward education (pp. 38–50). Under the heading "More Emphasis to Career Education," results are reported for five samples which show responses to the question: "Should public schools give more emphasis to a study of trades, professions, and businesses to help students decide on their careers?" There was greater agreement among all groups surveyed for this question than for any other question in the entire survey. Ninety percent of the total national sample, of the sample of adults with no children in school, of the sample of public school parents, and of the sample of professional educators chose the "Yes, more emphasis" response to this question. Of persons in the remaining sample (private school parents), 89 percent chose the "Yes, more emphasis" response. Certainly the desir-ability of career education, both in the eyes of the general public and as viewed by professional educators, is eminently clear.

We know of no single best way — nor of any simple way — to provide the in-service education necessary for career education. We have observed it being accomplished by a variety of means. The middle/junior high school, perhaps more than any other level of education, is in an ideal position to encourage teams of teachers to join together in joint education projects for their students. That is, many such schools find teams of teachers (within each school faculty) meeting regularly to plan together. Unlike the compartmentalized elementary school and the highly departmentalized senior high school, middle/-junior high schools seem to have often been organized in ways that promote and encourage cooperative efforts among several teachers. In schools where this is the case, the regular planning meetings of such teams of teachers may prove to be a desirable vehicle for planning activities for implementation of career education. This does not, however, answer the questions concerned with how to provide such teams of teachers with the needed in-service education.

Some school systems (e.g., Anne Arundel County, Maryland), using local funds, have released a number of key teachers for a full year or more and assigned them responsibility for gathering the substantive content of career education, packaging it in a form that other teachers can use, and serving as in-service resource guides for teachers throughout the system. We consider this an excellent approach, but recognize that few school systems will feel they can afford it.

Where this cannot be done, we favor an in-service approach such as that which was used during the 1972–73 school year in Sonoma County, California. There, the in-service career education program began with a short workshop (less than one week). At the workshop, each teacher was helped to develop one career education learning package that he or she could implement in the classroom immediately. This was followed by monthly meetings held during a school day (substitute teachers were hired for this day) in which, once again, each teacher constructed a career education learning package — or, in many cases, more than one. A key feature in the program was the presence of three paraprofessionals called "career education specialists" who helped teachers secure needed community resources and contacts for implementing their ideas. The advantages of this approach include the fact that it can be accomplished on a "volunteer" basis, with no teacher or school feeling pressured to participate, and the equally important fact that local resource persons are made available whenever needed.

Since 1970, the Maryland State Department of Education, under the leadership of Niel Carey and directed by Nancy Pinson, has been conducting in-service education for middle/-junior high school teachers in career education through the use of summer workshops, followed by systematic follow-up visits to participating schools during the next school year. The central idea behind this approach was to provide in-service education to members of a school "team" and then to provide on-site assistance to that team as it attempted to implement career education activities in its school. In 1970, three-person "teams," consisting of a counselor, an industrial arts teacher, and a home economics teacher from each middle/junior high school, were formed. These teams, while they tried hard, were not too effective in securing school-wide adoption of the career education concept during the 1970–71 school year.

In 1971, two additional persons — one a math teacher and the other a teacher from any other subject matter area the school selected — were added to the three previously named kinds of team members, and another summer workshop was held for these five-member teams, each representing a different middle or junior high school. Still not satisfied with the results, the 1971 workshops added a sixth member — the school principal. With this addition, much more positive results were observed during the 1972–73 school year than during any of the preceding years. At this point, elementary schools and high schools were also allowed to send participants. Beginning with the summer of 1972 and continuing in the summer of 1973, one more element was added — a separate workshop for county-level supervisory personnel from the county boards of education in which participating schools were located. This too has proved to be an effective addition. With this kind of support, follow-up visits to participating schools during the school year after the summer workshop appear to be generally productive and beneficial learning situations for those making the visits, as well as for those being visited.

A great deal of in-service education in career education has been carried out in a learning-by-doing context. Teachers have learned how to make career education learning packages by getting an idea and then determining for themselves how to implement it. By trial and error we have learned how (and how *not*) to conduct field trips to business and industrial settings, to build a cadre of career education resource persons from the business-industry-labor community, and to involve parents in the total career education program by recognizing the need for such activities and trying to meet that need with locally devised programs in local schools. Teachers have learned career implications of their subjects by participating with their students in field trips and by using occupational resource people in their classes. The self-discovery approach to learning has proved to be as exciting and interesting for teachers as it is for their students. While admittedly inefficient and sometimes embarrassing because of mistakes that are made, it is also very reinforcing both in the degree to which retention of learning occurs and to which teachers become committed to the learnings they attain.

We emphasize the learning-by-doing aspect of in-service education here because it is essential to some of career education's most basic assumptions. Career education seeks to reduce "worker alienation" among teachers by providing teachers with the freedom and the autonomy to become as creative and as innovative as possible. To do so, we must: (1) trust and believe in teachers more than many school systems have, (2) abandon the notion that teachers can learn only through "spoon-feeding," (3) free teachers from the educational "assembly line" where they are trapped by strict curriculum guides and enslaved by the textbooks others have said they must use, and (4) allow teachers to help their students learn in the broader community as well as within the walls of the school itself. The term "in-service teacher education" doesn't always have to mean something that we do *to* teachers. Career education places high priority on a concept of in-service teacher education that frees teachers to learn for themselves.

The in-service education required for career education extends to the business-industry-labor community and to parents. If we expect educators to learn how to work with the business-industry-labor community, then we must also expect persons from that community to learn how to work with educators in career education efforts. A leadership role here has been taken by the U.S. Chamber of Commerce, beginning with the national conference on career education it hosted from February 28 to March 1, 1973. One outgrowth of that national conference was a handbook of action suggestions regarding ways in which school personnel and personnel from the business-labor-industry community could work together in a total career education effort. While obviously only a beginning, the handbook is deserving of careful study by all who work in career education. A subcommittee on career education was recently established by the U.S. Chamber of Commerce to further follow up on its national conference. It is hoped that many other elements of the business-labor-industry community will see fit to join with the Chamber of Commerce in this effort. In addition, we very much need groups such as the National Congress of Parents and Teachers, along with affiliated state and local associations, to join in this effort. Some beginnings have been made.

Questions continue to be raised regarding who should be appointed as the local coordinator of career education. With establishment of the Center for Career Education within the Bureau of Occupational and Adult Education of the U.S. Office of Education, one possible pattern of organization has been set. Depending on the extent and the rapidity with which federal funds for career education are channeled from the Office of Education to state and local school systems, this pattern may extend down to the state and local levels. It is important to recognize, even at this initial point in time, that the Center for Career Education is one of two major components of the Bureau, with the other being the Center for Vocational, Technical and Manpower Education. Thus within the Office of Education, career education is clearly viewed as an entity in itself, not simply as a part of or an extension of vocational education. While in our opinion career education has not been ideally placed within the Office's framework, it has been established, staffed, and recognized as an integral part of the total educational process.

Within local school systems, it is our hope that a school *system* coordinator of career education will be appointed under arrangements which permit her or him to report directly to the superintendent of schools. Because career education extends from the preschool years through all of adult education, because it involves activities and actions of all school personnel, and because it involves extensive relationships between the local education system and the broader community within which the school system operates, it seems to us that this organizational pattern makes a great deal of sense. Most communities should be able to afford one such person, with adequate supporting staff, at the school system level.

At the *building* level, it seems to us that the school principal should assume the role of coordinator of career education. We say this for two basic reasons. First, the kinds of changes called for by career education are basically those that must be approved by the school principal. These include changes in scheduling, in curricular organization, in relationships with the broader community, and in ways in which school personnel work together on joint efforts. Because career education represents a total school effort, it seems to us that the person bearing basic responsibility for the school's total operation should take the leadership role in career education. That person is the school principal. We have seen, in the experiences of the Maryland schools, how ineffective the original teams of industrial arts, home economics teachers, and counselors were in implementing career education within a given building. We have also seen how much faster and more effectively such implementation took place when the principal was added to the team. We have seen both how much the principal can hurt development of career education by his lack of involvement and how much he can help when he assumes an active leadership role. It is neither proper nor possible for someone to take this role away from the school principal. Thus it makes sense to us if this role as coordinator of career education is assigned to the principal as coordinator of all eduation within a given school.

Our second reason for recommending that the principal assume this role is simply a matter of money. Career education cannot and should not wait for massive infusions of new funds for implementation. It does not need a new breed of staff specialists at the building level in order to be effective. It is our firm belief that if we were to create and fund such a new kind of staff at the present time, we would have difficulty implementing career education as a responsibility of all school personnel. New money for career education is not now generally available, nor are large sums needed at this time. What is needed most is a professional commitment and dedication to the goals and objectives of career education. It is our feeling that this can best be accomplished by designating the school principal as coordinator of career education within his or her school.

We do recognize and support the need for the employment of paraprofessional personnel and a great increase in the use of parents and volunteers from the business-labor-industry community. Whether the needed paraprofessionals represent new personnel or come from the current allotments for teacher aides will of course be a question of local financial resources. At any rate, the financial cost will not be high. It is our feeling that while the roles of the teacher, the school counselor, and the curriculum specialist will all change with the advent of career education, it is not necessary to think about hiring still more professional specialists to work with such personnel. To do so would retard the kinds of role changes we are seeking to bring about within current personnel.

Similarly, it is our feeling that currently existing physical facilities, with slight modifications, can be used effectively as career education programs are implemented at the middle/-junior high school level. We need three basic kinds of facilities for career education at this level. First, we need a career education resource center for use by teachers and students. A portion of the school library or an adjoining room can be converted for the use of students and teachers. In addition, many middle/-junior high schools already have teacher curriculum planning facilities within their buildings which can easily incorporate career education materials. Within a given classroom, many teachers are collecting and storing career education materials needed for use in the learning packages they are constructing. While there may well be a central career education learning resource center operating at the school system level, we do not see the need now for such a center as a building addition in junior high schools and middle schools.

The second kind of physical facility needed by career education at the middle/junior high school level is space for work simulation activities and projects. Again, it is our feeling that, in most schools, existing facilities can be adapted for this purpose. This is especially true of facilities currently built for purposes of teaching art, industrial arts, and home economics. Where extensive equipment is not required in the work simulation effort, facilities within the regular classrooms can easily be used for work simulation exercises. As discussed in chapters 3 and 5, facilities of area vocational schools are currently being used by some middle/junior high schools for work simulation projects. Again, while it would obviously be easy to visualize a new wing of the schoolbuilding being constructed as a comprehensive work simulation center, we do not believe this to be a prerequisite for effective implementation of career education in most middle/junior high schools.

A third kind of facility is required to provide some opportunity for students to engage in hands-on basic vocational skills training as part of the career exploration process. Again, existing facilities in industrial arts, in home economics, and in area vocational schools contained within or adjacent to the school system can and are being effectively used for this purpose. Some schools are engaging in a limited amount of hands-on basic vocational skills exposure through the use of portable carts containing basic tools and machines that can be moved from classroom to classroom. We see no need to engage in construction of building additions in order to provide this kind of facility.

On the question of costs required for mounting and implementing career education at the middle/junior high school level, we are asking neither for large numbers of new professional staff specialists nor for new school construction. Specialists in educational finance tell us that 90 percent of the education budget is devoted to some combination of building and personnel costs. If this is so, then, since we are asking for neither buildings nor for new professional personnel, we are certainly not asking for large increases in local school budgets in order to implement career education.

Some funds will be needed, of course. At the beginning of a new program, most of these expenditures are needed to support in-service education efforts of teachers. Some should be allocated for employing at least one paraprofessional in career education for each middle/junior high school. A small amount will be needed for career education materials. By and large, these funds can be provided through reallocation of current school budgets. The total amount of new monies required to organize and implement a career education program should not, in our opinion, exceed more than 1 percent of the current total operating budget at the middle/junior high school level. In making these statements, we are not saying that we wouldn't welcome modest new financial support, or that we would be unable to effectively improve our career education efforts were it to be made available. We merely say that we believe a middle/junior high school can operate an effective career education program without greatly increased financial resources. The career education movement asks schools to change because they *should* do so, not because they will receive new state or federal education dollars if they do. We think the changes that result from this strategy will be more long lasting than those that occur when a few schools are in effect "bribed" to change by those who offer them financial assistance for doing so. Sizable payments to only a few schools have a further undesirable effect because they give the remaining schools an excuse for doing nothing. Fortunately, increasing numbers of schools are refusing to use this excuse, but are proceeding on their own.

In this and previous chapters, we have indicated that we feel the school principal should be designated coordinator of career education when a middle/junior high school is organizing for career education. With the principal in the pivot position, he or she could work with counterparts throughout the school system and with a person designated coordinator for the entire school system, beginning with preschoolers and continuing to adults in adult education. It is essential that the career education program at the middle/junior high school level be coordinated in scope and sequence with programs in elementary and senior high schools.

It is equally essential that some kind of organizational framework be established for implementation of career education at the individual school level. Three kinds of organizational efforts seem to us to be minimally essential. First, we suggest establishment of a "career education content committee" (any similar title would do) whose membership includes a school counselor, an industrial arts teacher, a home economics teacher, and one other teacher from each grade level who is actively engaged in career education activities. We think Tennyson's article, referred to earlier in this chapter, makes a good point when it points to the need to use both the expertise industrial arts and home economics teachers have regarding the world of work and the expertise the school counselor has in human understanding and decision making. The expertise of the classroom teacher who has learned how to infuse career education into the teaching-learning process is equally essential. The "content committee" should provide the school principal with the basic background, knowledge, and support he or she requires in order to effectively serve as coordinator of career education for the school.

Second, it is our feeling that career education committees composed primarily of classroom teachers should be set up by grade level, not by departmental organization. We say this because of the great need and potential of career education for helping teachers work together in activity projects that extend over several subject matter areas simultaneously. The "content committee" can serve effectively as consultants to these teacher committees operating at each grade level, thus relieving the school principal from what would otherwise be an exceedingly time-consuming activity.

Third, it is our strong belief that each school should establish a "career education resource and advisory committee" whose membership would include parents, representatives from the business-labor-industry community, civic organizations, and students. Such a committee is needed both to help the school obtain *resources* required for career education and to provide *advice* with respect to how the school can collaborate with the broader community in a total career education effort. The resources include donated equipment and materials, adult volunteers who will assist career education efforts both within the classroom and outside the schoolbuilding, and information regarding sources of data, work experience opportunities, and field visit site opportunities that can be used in the career education program. The advice needed concerns itself primarily with how best to work with the broader community in ways that will increase both the effectiveness and the acceptance of the career education movement.

In summary, our key concerns in this section have been directed toward the vital importance of in-service education for career education and toward the necessity for organizing staff and assigning responsibilities in the career education effort. We have tried to present suggestions for positive actions in ways that do not demand substantially increased financial resources.

SUBSTANTIVE CONTENT OF CAREER EDUCATION AT THE MIDDLE/JUNIOR HIGH SCHOOL LEVEL

Confusion seems to exist among those who to date have attempted to formulate career education concepts around which comprehensive career education programs can be organized. As noted previously, because the generic goals of career development are almost identical to the generic goals of career education, most of those who have attempted to formulate lists of "career education" concepts have used a "career development" conceptual framework for doing so. To the extent that common lists of career development concepts still reflect confusion between "careers" and "occupations" and to the extent that the other components of career education are overlooked, such lists have some serious deficiences when used in organizing the substantive content of career education programs. This represents a problem that has caused considerable misunderstanding. A second problem has been a rather routine failure to consider formulating career education programs around the variety of work values that exist in our present culture. A third problem has been our widespread failure to differentiate the terms "work values," "work ethic," and "work habits." It is our purpose here to attempt to alleviate these problems by formulating a sightly different organization for the conceptual framework and substantive content of career education.

The most comprehensive attempt to summarize and categorize career development concepts formulated by others was reported by Bailey (pp. 24–28). Because of the procedures he used and the problem with which he was concerned, his article is reviewed here in some detail.

Bailey was interested in assessing the relative importance professional leaders in four associations gave to each of a number of common career development concepts. The organizations were: the National Vocational Guidance Association, the National Employment Counselors Association, the American School Counselors Association, and the American Vocational Association. To carry out this study, Bailey first identified a total of 240 career development concepts in the professional literature. He was able to quickly reduce this number to eighty by eliminating duplications and those concepts he considered to be unimportant. These eighty concepts were then sorted into four categories. A final list of forty concepts — ten in each of the four categories — was chosen for use in the study by selecting those with the highest category reliability. These forty statements were then sent to six leaders from each of the four professional groups, and each respondent was asked to rank the concepts in the order of their importance. Bailey was thus able to obtain a mean rank ordering for each of the four associations and a cumulative rank ordering that represented the judgments of all respondents.

His findings indicate that of the four associations, only the American Vocational Association leaders tended to assign equal importance to each of the four categories. Except for the American School Counselors Association, the others assigned the highest priority to the "general" category of concepts. The leaders of this association assigned their highest priority to concepts in the "psychological self-reference" category. The highest agreement in rank orderings was found to be between leaders in the National Vocational Guidance Association and the National Employment Counselors Association, while the lowest rank order correlation was found to be between leaders in the American School Counselors Association and the American Vocational Association. The three organizations representing divisions of the American Personnel and Guidance Association (that is, the National Vocational Guidance Association, the National Employment Counselors Association, and the American School Counselors Association) agreed more with each other than they did with leaders in the American Vocational Association. In view of the obvious need for counselors and vocational educators to work more closely with one another in comprehensive career education efforts, these findings are significant and deserving of careful thought.

The forty career development concepts, together with their composite rank orderings based on all respondent replies, are presented below. For purposes of brevity, many of these concepts have been paraphrased.

Concept	*Rank*
A. Economic:	
1. The major reason why most people work is for money.	13.5
2. The need for security causes many workers to keep the jobs they have.	20.0
3. Work gives us personal satisfaction in the achievement itself.	24.0
4. The law of supply and demand creates new jobs and eliminates others.	24.0
5. Work is a way of winning economic independence.	27.0
6. Economic development in a community creates new work for some and more work for many others living in that community.	30.0
7. Higher pay comes when needed jobs are in short supply, and those in such jobs can charge directly for their services.	33.0
8. Labor market demands are such that some people must take jobs that are available rather than being able to choose their vocations.	35.5
9. "Economic security" is often in first place in job satisfaction studies.	38.0
10. If every kind of discrimination in occupational entry could be removed, giving people proper information about wages would result in the right people and the right number of people in each occupation.	40.0

Concept	*Rank*

B. "General":

1. People are different in abilities, attitudes, and aspirations. — 1.0
2. The occupation one is in affects his or her total life-style. — 5.0
3. Job satisfaction is a combination of: a) the work environment, b) opportunities for recognition and advancement, and c) intrinsic work aspects of the job. — 8.5
4. There is no single "best" motive for choosing a career plan. — 10.0
5. Vocational choice is determined by social, individual, and economic factors, each of which may operate independently on one. — 15.0
6. Occupations are ranked according to duties, difficulty in obtaining the job, rewards one gets from the occupation, and social prestige. — 18.0
7. Workers don't value what they do as much as they value the conditions under which they work and the rewards they get from work. — 20.0
8. Leisure will become as satisfying and respectable in the future as work has been in the past. — 28.5
9. The personal dignity and significance of work have declined for many occupations. — 32.0
10. The work a man does tells more about him that is significant, in this culture, than any other single item of information. — 24.0

C. Psychological self-reference:

1. Worker satisfaction is directly proportional to the extent to which work helps the person implement his self-concept and satisfy his major personal needs. — 2.0
2. People with different personalities choose different occupations. — 3.0

Concept	*Rank*
3. Worker satisfaction depends on the extent to which one's work allows him or her to play the kind of role he or she wants to play.	4.0
4. A satisfying and rewarding work may bring self-fulfillment to one.	6.5
5. Motivation to work and capacity for work are greatly influenced by early childhood experiences.	11.0
6. Choosing an occupation is a way of establishing who you really are.	16.0
7. Work achievement brings personal satisfaction to the individual.	24.0
8. One has to set life goals before occupational goal selection becomes truly meaningful.	26.0
9. When one refuses to work or to do his best, he may be expressing hostility.	34.0
10. The number of occupations providing personal satisfaction to the worker is slowly but surely declining.	39.0

D. Sociological:

1. Personal relationships with fellow workers are important to job satisfaction.	6.5
2. Worker success depends in part on cooperating with others.	8.5
3. Occupational experience is a part of induction into one's culture.	12.0
4. Work is a way of becoming part of a group.	13.5
5. Much of one's total life routine is organized around the work one does.	17.0
6. Work is a means of acquiring social status and prestige.	20.0
7. Work is a means of developing satisfying social relationships.	28.5

Concept	*Rank*
8. Work organizations are human organizations.	31.0
9. Most of us spend our lives serving and in the service of others.	35.5
10. The only hope for man to be fulfilled in a world of work is that he get along with his fellow man.	37.0

A 1967 monograph of the Texas Education Agency contains reference to what we consider to be an excellent list of career development concepts which, according to the document, were taken from a publication by Ms. Lee Laws titled *Elementary Guide for Career Development* (Ridener, 1967). The following concepts are reported to be those at the elementary school level and further developed at the junior and senior high school levels:

1. There is dignity in work.

2. Work is important to the worker and to society.

3. People work for various rewards or satisfactions.

4. School is part of the preparation for a life of work.

5. Workers need some kind of special training for most jobs.

6. There is a wide variety of jobs.

7. To work effectively, one needs the ability to get along with people.

8. There is need for cooperation in work.

9. Some workers produce goods; other produce services.

10. Specialization leads to interdependency.

11. Many jobs are related.

12. Occupations are grouped in job families.

13. Supply and demand help determine occupational choice.

14. Chosen occupation affects the worker's total life.

15. Finding out about one's self — interests and abilities — is important in decision making.

16. Different jobs will exist in the future from those found at present or in the past.

17. A person may find many jobs which are suitable for him.

18. Geographical location determines kinds of work found therein.

19. Technological progress changes, eliminates, and creates work.

The sixteen career development concepts referred to earlier in this chapter from the Wisconsin State Department of Education are reproduced here for purposes of keeping the various listings in a single portion of this chapter. They are:

1. An understanding and acceptance of self is important throughout life.

2. Persons need to be recognized as having dignity and worth.

3. Occupations exist for a purpose.

4. There is a wide variety of careers which may be classified in several ways.

5. Work means different things to different people.

6. Education and work are interrelated.

7. Individuals differ in their interests, abilities, attitudes, and values.

8. Occupational supply and demand have an impact on career planning.

9. Job specialization creates interdependency.

10. Environment and individual potential interact to influence career development.

11. Occupations and life-styles are interrelated.

12. Individuals can learn to perform adequately in a variety of occupations.

13. Career development requires a continuous and sequential series of choices.

14. Various groups and institutions influence the nature and structure of work.

15. Individuals are responsible for their career planning.

16. Job characteristics and individuals must be flexible in a changing society.

The Anne Arundel County (Maryland) Career Development Task Force — referred to earlier in this chapter as composed of a selected group of educators given one full year to develop a conceptual framework for their career education program — arrived at five major conceptual statements along with a number of subconcepts. These are reproduced below:

A. Self — Self-understanding is vital to career decision and work performances.

   1. A positive concept of self enables the individual to enter and function in the working world.

   2. A person's work may contribute to a positive concept of self.

   3. An individual may be suited for numerous different occupations.

   4. There are identifiable attitudes and behaviors which enable one to obtain and hold a job.

   5. The individual's perception of his environment affects his attitudes toward work.

   6. Value judgments influence vocational choice.

   7. Each individual has a contribution to make to the world of work.

   8. Knowledge of one's self in relation to work is a continuing process.

   9. The individual's perception of people affects his ability to work cooperatively.

B. Technology — Man and technology are continually interacting in his work.

   10. Through technology man uses his creative ability and resources in a work setting.

11. Man uses technology to satisfy his needs and to achieve his desires.

12. Technological developments cause a continual change in the emergence and disappearance of jobs.

13. Technology has unlimited implications for man's work and leisure time.

14. Technological development has been one of slow change until recent times.

15. Man must learn to use technology to his advantage.

C. Economics — Man's livelihood depends upon the production, distribution, and consumption of goods and services.

16. Man's work contributes to a nation's wealth and productivity.

17. The economic system structures incentives for man to work.

18. Our economic system influences work opportunity.

19. Understanding economics helps man to function effectively and make choices and decisions consistent with his needs and resources.

20. Man's work affects his standard of living.

21. Economic fluctuations influence occupational choice and opportunity.

22. Geographical settings affect work.

D. Society — Society reflects the creative force of work.

23. Society is dependent upon the work of many people.

24. The customs, traditions, and attitudes of society affect the world of work.

25. Societal needs determine vocational opportunity.

26. Society provides rewards for work.

27. Society enacts laws to protect the individual as a producer and consumer of goods and services.

E. Career — Career education prepares man for the world of work.

  28. Career choice is a developmental process.

  29. People do many kinds of work.

  30. A person may have many careers.

  31. Hobbies and interests may lead to a vocation.

  32. There are job clusters within occupational areas as well as across occupational areas.

  33. Career areas have a hierarchical structure.

  34. Basic education enhances job performance.

  35. There is a specific knowledge for each career area.

  36. Vocational preparation requires skills development.

  37. Work experience facilitates career decision making.

  38. Workers may need vocational retraining in the course of a lifetime.

  39. Transferable knowledge will facilitate retraining.

In 1971, the California State Department of Education published a monograph which includes the career development concepts derived by a task force (*California Model*, 1971). The concepts formulated by that task force include:

A. Career planning and decision making:

  1. Individuals differ in their interests, aptitudes, abilities, values, and attitudes.

  2. The understanding, acceptance, and development of self is a lifelong process and is constantly changed and influenced by life experiences.

  3. Environment and individual potential interact to influence career development.

  4. Individuals must be adaptable in a changing society.

  5. Career planning should be a privilege and responsibility of the individual.

B. Education, work, and leisure alternatives:

6. Knowledge and skills in different subjects relate to performance in different work roles.

7. There is a wide variety of occupations which may be classified in several ways.

8. Societal expectations influence the nature and structure of work.

9. There is a relationship between the commitment to education and work and the availability and use of leisure time.

10. There are many training routes to job entry.

C. Life-styles and personal satisfactions:

11. Work means different things to different people.

12. Job satisfaction is dependent on harmonious relationships between worker and work environment.

13. Job specialization creates interdependency.

It is obvious, upon examining these lists, that a substantial degree of agreement exists among the groups who formulated them. While varying considerably in organizational patterning, they have many of the same basic concepts which are repeated in each. Those responsible for constructing the lists have devoted thousands of man-hours to this task. The result has been the kinds of broad, general concepts illustrated by items on the lists themselves. Those who examine the basic documents in which the lists appear will find, almost without exception, that they are intended to represent broad guidelines for the scope and sequence of career development concepts which are to be imparted to students in a career education program. Teachers using such lists as a basis for constructing career education learning packages use a broad concept as a starting point. From this, they typically choose one or two particular subconcepts to be emphasized in one learning package. The total number of possible career education learning packages which could be used to teach the subconcepts developed from the lists would be manifold. By developing subconcepts from these broad lists, the teacher has some assurance that the content being taught has some validity. In addition, the teacher can see how what is being taught fits into a broader pattern.

If the concepts are examined carefully, it can be seen that they cover a number of areas that could be considered to be included in the substantive content of career education. Some schools may find it a useful in-service exercise to try to classify each of the concepts presented in these lists into one of the following classifications:

   I. The World of Occupations
  II. Work Values
 III. Work Habits
  IV. Occupational Satisfaction and Adjustment
   V. Occupational Decision Making
  VI. Career Decision Making

Those schools who follow this suggestion will discover that the lists of concepts placed under each of the above headings vary greatly in length. Very few will appear under the heading of "work habits." Those that appear under the heading of "work values" will be discovered to represent only part of the totality of work values now existing in our society. Those related to "occupational decision making" will be almost as numerous as those classified under "career decision making." Thus if one views these lists in the perspective of the review of research generalizations found in chapter 2, it is obvious that not nearly all of these concepts are appropriate for use at the middle/-junior high school level. Those working at this level will need to examine these concepts carefully in order to determine those that seem most appropriate to introduce, to develop, or to emphasize with the students in a particular school.

We believe that it would be appropriate to consider the following kind of classification for *primary* emphasis at the middle/junior high school. In making these suggestions, we wish to emphasize that we are not recommending an *exclusive* emphasis at any one grade level.

Grades five and six: primary emphasis on work values (awareness) and work habits

Grade seven: primary emphasis on the world of occupations

Grade eight: primary emphasis on work values (exploration)

Grade nine: primary emphasis on career decision making

Of the six classifications developed above, it can be seen that in our opinion, no *primary* emphasis should be placed at the middle/junior high school level on either "occupational decision making" or on "occupational satisfaction and adjustment." We would consider it proper to introduce concepts related to occupational satisfaction and adjustment in grades five through seven when pupils are being introduced to the broad scope, general nature, and necessity for existence of an occupational society. Similarly, we would consider introducing the concepts of "occupational decision making," in a very broad way, at grade nine when "career decision making" concepts are used as a primary focus of emphasis.

EVALUATING CAREER EDUCATION AT THE MIDDLE/JUNIOR HIGH SCHOOL LEVEL

When persons operating any educational program ask: When should we start evaluating our efforts? the most appropriate answer to give is: It's already too late! Evaluation is a topic that should be of central concern from the time consideration is given to initiating a career education program at any level in any school system. While this is not the place to discuss the topic of evaluation in detail, it would be inappropriate for this chapter to conclude with no mention of the topic. Therefore, we present here in very broad form our current thoughts regarding evaluation of career education programs at the middle/junior high school level. We agree with Drier's statements that the specifics of evaluation should be developed at the local level as part of the school's efforts to design and operate a career education program unique to their needs (pp. 39–41).

It is our feeling that full-scale evaluation efforts, based on a well-formulated design for a comprehensive career education program, are premature for installation at the middle/junior high school level at the present time. This is because the formation and application of evaluative criteria based on such a model necessarily would have to assume the presence and active implementation of career education both at the elementary and at the senior high school levels as well as middle and junior high school settings. Very few career education programs are currently set up and operating in such a comprehensive fashion. The gap is particularly acute at the senior high school level where very little has yet been done to initiate career education. Formulation of a comprehensive evaluation system for career education at the middle/junior high school level would, if done correctly, include several measures of a developmental nature to be assessed later at the senior high school level, with findings from middle/junior high being used in the total package as baseline data. Until some indication is given that career education will be an integral part of the senior high school's operation, it is difficult to justify collecting such baseline data.

Similarly, a comprehensive evaluation design at the middle/junior high school level would necessarily be predicated on career education activities carried out in feeder elementary schools. So far as we know, there are no middle or junior high schools operating today whose pupils have been exposed to a systematic and comprehensive career education effort since they were in kindergarten. Here, too, we find it difficult to justify a very sophisticated program of evaluation to be applied at the middle or junior high school level at this time.

Because of lack of assurance of the presence of a school system-wide program of career education, it is our feeling that an emphasis on product evaluation would be generally inappropriate for use at the middle/junior high school level at this time. In addition to the lack of comprehensive career education efforts at other levels, we also feel that, at present, most of our product measures are not sufficiently well developed or validated to justify extensive use with middle or junior high school students now.

As an example, let us consider use of measures of vocational maturity such as suggested by Matheny earlier in this chapter. Readers will recall Super's warnings regarding the use of such measures in their present state of development. It is our feeling that, in addition to Super's warnings regarding the lack of readiness of current instruments purporting to measure vocational maturity, we have much yet to learn before we fully comprehend the meaning of the concept of "vocational maturity" itself. Logically, it would seem to us that a "vocationally mature" adult, as opposed to a "vocationally immature" adult, would more often enter occupations for which he or she has been trained, would be more certain of his or her occupational choices once in that occupation, and would be more satisfied with the occupation he or she finally enters. We have seen no measures of vocational maturity that have reported even *attempts* (let alone successes!) to use such criteria in validating their measures. To be sure, much good work is being done in this area at the present time. Once such work has been completed, perhaps it will be appropriate to use these kinds of measures. In our opinion, their use at this time is premature.

We could consider evaluating career education in terms of the degree to which students have assimilated career development concepts such as those listed in the preceding section. It would not be difficult, and certainly not entirely inappropriate, to assess the extent to which students know and comprehend the meaning of such concepts. In the long run, of course, the proper question to ask is not: Do students know the concept? but rather: How do they implement the concept in their lives? Here, at the middle/junior high school level, we will find ourselves facing severe problems justifying the practical implications of whatever means we use to answer this second question.

In our opinion, perhaps the most appropriate approach to evaluation of career education programs at the middle/junior high school level could presently be centered around obtaining answers to three questions:

(1) To what extent are the five components of career education in place and operating? (See chapter 1 for specification of these components.)

(2) To what extent do teachers, students, parents, and the business-labor-industry community seem satisfied with career education activities?

(3) To what extent can career education efforts be shown to be related to increases in pupil achievement?

Our first concern in evaluation must, it seems to us, be directed at knowing something about the nature of the program whose behavioral results are to be evaluated. How many teachers have made career education learning packages? In how many classrooms have such packages been used? How many field trips have been conducted? How many parents have been involved in the program? How many students have been exposed to a general nature of the world of work? To actual work experience? To systematic instruction in decision making? What processes seem to work well, and which need further modification? These are but a few examples of the kinds of specific questions appropriate for use in approaching this first evaluative concern. To answer such questions, obviously, tells us nothing about the quality of the effort or about the results obtained from it. It *does* define the nature and degree of effort being exerted. We would consider this an essential prerequisite to other evaluation approaches. That is, there is no point in attempting to assess the worth of a particular effort unless one can first define its nature and scope.

Second, we would suggest evaluation approaches aimed at assessing the degree to which career education efforts appear to be meeting with acceptance on the part of teachers, students, parents, and the business-labor-industry community. If such groups are resistive to or even unsupportive of career education concepts, the program will surely fail. It seems to us particularly important to search out and discover persons or groups of persons who are suspicious, resistive, or antagonistic to career education. We need to listen to objections such persons have. Where such objections are based on misunderstandings, we can clear them up. When they are based on mistakes we have made, we can use them positively to correct our mistakes. Career education is not something that can be effectively forced on any group. We hope that by systematic and conscientious effort aimed at this second concern, attempts to do so will not be tried.

Finally, we strongly feel that evaluation of career education, no matter what else it includes, must surely include careful attention to questions relating to the effect the career education effort is having on student academic achievement. One of the most basic assumptions underlying the entire career education movement is that if students can see a relationship between what they are being asked to learn in school and what they might do with it when they leave, they will be motivated to learn more of the academic knowledge teachers are trying to impart. This is an assumption that can and must be tested very early in the operation of a career education program. There is a natural temptation on the part of some teachers to become so interested in career education activities and projects that they tend to forget the importance of the subject matter students are supposed to be learning. Nothing could kill the career education movement faster than to find that students exposed to career education are learning less subject matter than those who are not. Nothing can boost career education faster than to demonstrate that when a career education approach is taken, students learn more subject matter than when traditional classroom procedures are used. Even if our evaluations were to show no differences in academic achievement between students in career education, as opposed to traditional, classroom settings, career education would survive, provided both students and teachers are enthusiastically in favor of a career education approach.

Opportunities for using this third approach to evaluation are plentiful in most schools. It is rare to find that in a particular school, all teachers of all subjects embrace the career education concept simultaneously and are implementing it into their classrooms. More typically, a few teachers start it while most other teachers continue with their traditional approaches to teaching. In such situations, we often find easy and natural ways of comparing these two approaches to helping students learn academic content. Many schools administer standardized achievement measures routinely to all students. In such schools, the possibilities of a "before and after" approach to evaluating the effectiveness of a career education effort clearly exists.

It is our feeling that at the present time and in the present stage of development of the career education movement, these three approaches to evaluation are those that are both proper and possible for use by any middle/junior high school. While we would like to see all three used, we want to emphasize that we consider the third to be the most important.

Summary Statement

In this chapter, we have tried to speak to the "nuts-and-bolts" aspects of career education programs at the middle/-junior high school level. The three major topics discussed here concern themselves with: (1) organizing for career education, (2) the substantive content of career education, and (3) evaluation of career education. Our purpose has been to provide a broad overview of each of these three topics. We have made no attempt to discuss any one of them in a completely comprehensive fashion.

For the organizing of resources for career education, we have placed our primary emphasis on efforts to provide in-service education for participants in the career education program — including persons from outside as well as those employed in the school. We have tried to provide a special emphasis to the possibility of "self-learning" on the part of teachers who learn by doing in career education. We have made strong, assertive statements to the effect that at the building level, the principal should serve as coordinator of career education and that the need for large amounts of new money for career education is not great. While many will disagree, we hope our rationale and reasoning is clear.

Our discussion of the substantive content of career education at the middle/junior high school level is admittedly incomplete. It is included primarily as a stimulus for local schools to think about the content they feel to be most appropriate for use in their particular setting.

We conclude with a short section on evaluation of career education at the middle/junior high school level. Once again, we have tried to "lay it on the line" in terms of our current biases. Our prime point is that career education must, at this initial point, be able to demonstrate that it has a positive effect on student achievement.

REFERENCES

Bailey, John A. "Career Development Concepts: Significance and Utility." *Personnel and Guidance Journal* (1968), vol. 47.

California State Department of Education. *Career Guidance: A California Model for Career Development, K–Adult.* Sacramento: California State Department of Education, 1971.

Drier, Harry N., Jr. "Career Development Activities Permeate Wisconsin Curriculum." *American Vocational Journal* (1972), vol. 47, no. 3.

Gallup, George H. "Fifth Annual Gallup Poll of Public Attitudes toward Education." *Phi Delta Kappan* (1973), vol. 55, no. 1.

Matheny, Kenneth B. "The Role of the Middle School in Career Development." *American Vocational Journal* (1969), vol. 44, no. 9.

Ridener, John. *Career Development: A Paradigm.* Austin: Division of Guidance Services, Texas Education Agency, 1967.

Super, Donald E. "Vocational Development Theory in 1988: How Will It Come About?" *The Counseling Psychologist* (1969), vol. 1.

Tennyson, W. Wesley. "Career Development: Who's Responsible?" *American Vocational Journal* (1971), vol. 46, no. 3.

United States Chamber of Commerce. *Career Education and the Businessman: A Handbook of Action Suggestions.* Washington, D.C., 1973.

Career Education among Reform Initiatives

Reform and innovation are everywhere in the educational environment. Where it was commonly said that fifty years was the normal time for inculcating any substantial reform into the education system, experimentation, at least, is now a popular undertaking. Permanent changes appear to be taking hold and spreading with unprecedented speed, though the system is large and permeation still requires substantial time. Career education should be viewed as part of this reform atmosphere. It also has implications for other reforms, and they for it.

If one's imagination were allowed to run free with some dreamers about the educational future, that future would have little linkage to the past. One could foresee, with George Leonard in *Education and Ecstasy,* noncompulsory schools limited to age ten occurring in "gleaming geodesic domes and translucent tent-like structures scattered randomly among graceful trees." Students would meet and learn in encounter group sessions or meditate by themselves with the stimulation of an electronically controlled environment. Students would be "free learners" wandering where and doing what they wanted about the school grounds. They would have — along with CAI (computer assisted instruction), OBA (ongoing brain analysis), and CAD (computer assisted dialogue) — CMSR (cross-matrix stimulus response), and DBM (direct brainwave manipulation).

At age ten, formal education would cease and lifelong learning begin through adult education, periodic return to school, and work-study-recreation centers for all ages. Laymen and businessmen would set up their own schools, and parents would design their homes as learning environments. Youth would move from one learning environment to another as apprentices, volunteers, and paid workers in personal service activities.

Illich too would abolish schools after an early age, hoping for a freer, more exciting, and "natural" learning environment. Toffler sees education reacting to "future shock" by elimination of formal schools, relying more on home instruction by parents, aided by computer-assisted instruction and electronic video recordings. Mobile education would take students out into the community to learn by observation and participation in community activities. They would learn directly from those who know and do through visits to architectural offices, medical labs, broadcasting stations, and so forth. Discussion centers would bring students together with engineers, businessmen, public servants, among others, in lieu of certified teachers. "Cope-ability" for a world of continual change is to be the primary educational objective.

Other futurists suggest "thinking caps" that teach knowledge by electronic brain connections or intercranial hookups among students and between students and teachers. Electronic simulation and mind-altering drugs are suggested as educational tools.

But all of that is over the horizon (some would suggest *just* over). The administrator and teacher must deal with the here and now on the way to the future. The present is sufficiently permeated with educational reforms that one does not need to wait for the more dramatic promises. Our book ends with speculation on these major current innovations. Are they and career education compatible? How can career education contribute to them and they to it? Our final concern is: What are the next steps for the middle/junior high school administrator, teacher, and staff?

CAREER EDUCATION AND CURRENT INNOVATIONS

Flexibility, freedom, and individuality seem to be the key elements of current educational experimentation. While no attempt is made to be exhaustive, brief comments on each of several important innovations may make the case that though career education can and does work in traditional settings, it is most compatible with a more open system.

Accountability

One of the most controversial words in education, and for good reason, refers to the general concept of holding the schools responsible for student accomplishment. Schools have, until recent years, been judged primarily on their inputs rather than their outputs — how many books in the library and what the teacher-student ratio is, rather than how well the students can read and write. Students, parents, poverty, minority background, or some other force outside the school was always responsible for the failure of the child to learn. Now, young adults have even sued school boards or administrators after finding themselves unprepared to compete in the world outside the classroom.

Accountability is a concept no one can adequately refute. Everyone should be accountable for accomplishing what he was paid to do. The problem is how to measure and enforce it — how to decide when performance has been adequate or inadequate and how to reward or punish in accordance with it. Performance contracting is an intriguing approach to accountability, but one which until now has not fulfilled its promises. The notion is a simple one: Define specifically the outcomes desired in student reading levels, math ability, or some other measurable performance objective, contract with a private firm to accomplish the objective for an agreed-upon price, and pay only if or according to the extent to which the objective is achieved. That the earliest attempts found some firms teaching students mainly to pass the required tests and other contractors unable to outperform the schools is no cause for discouragement at this point. The two most serious challenges are (1) to devise a system for holding taxpayer-supported public schools accountable, and (2) to develop measures of performance in the affective, as well as the cognitive and psychomotor domains, recognizing that schools have socializing as well as knowledge and skill goals.

Performance evaluation holds multiple advantages for career education. These include (1) the opportunity for college-bound students to explore occupational education without being "locked in" by strict, Carnegie unit requirements of so-called "college prep" courses, (2) the opportunity to extend educational credit for student learning that goes on beyond the four walls of the school, without detracting from the worth of the credits that are granted, and (3) the opportunity to allow students some voice in determining their unique educational goals under a system whereby they can see how they failed to meet goals established by and for other persons.

Career education should be an accountable system. Its goals are clear and measurable but very long range — a satisfying lifelong working career. But it is not easy to hold a system accountable if a forty-year longitudinal follow-up study is required to measure its effectiveness. A shorter term objective could be successful job placement upon leaving school. One of the principles prescribed in chapter 1 is that the school should maintain responsibility for the student until he is placed in a job which gives promise of permanence or of providing a useful next step on the career ladder. But the elementary, middle, and junior high schools are only intermediate steps several years away from that limited though important objective. Even the senior high school is four years away for that portion of the graduates who choose baccalaureate programs. Another problem is the large number of variables involved. This limits one's ability to measure the contribution of the schools to success or failure. Therefore, measuring performance, at least at the middle/junior high school level, requires development of measures of change in knowledge and attitudes toward the world of work and of the extent to which career education motivated better academic performance. At least it is clear that career education is compatible with and contributes to accountability, even if all of the needed measures are not now available. Career education readily accepts the dictum that "if the student has not learned, the instructor has not taught successfully."

Competency-Based Education

Closely allied to the notion of accountability is the concept of measuring educational achievement not by the credits, grades, or hours of instruction absorbed but by demonstrated competence in what the school is assigned to teach. Ideally, if the skills, knowledge, and attitudes which the school sought to purvey could be listed and measured, those who entered with some portion of that competence could be credited with it, and all could advance as rapidly as they could demonstrate competence. At the vocational or professional level, it is conceivable that credit and credentials could even be given for demonstrated competence without school attendance. Since career education's objectives and goals are more definable than those of many other aspects of education, it lends itself well to this approach. The challenge again is in finding ways first to define and then to measure changes in attitudes and values concerning work. A great deal of longitudinal research is needed to learn what type of treatment and content during the school years contributes most to career success throughout life.

Of course, if competency-based education is good for the student, it should be good for the teacher. The state of Oregon has chosen to put its career education on a competency base for teachers as well as for students. Each teacher is expected to be able to:

(1) Identify the careers represented among the parents of students

(2) Use learning activities that foster wholesome attitudes regarding the worth and function of work in all fields at all levels

(3) Understand the total career education program within school districts and identify his or her role in the total program

(4) Help students realize that responsibility and decision making are part of career development

(5) Identify people in the local community who are willing to talk to students about their occupations, and keep a directory of contacts made

(6) Analyze the direct relationship between competencies developed while in school and those needed in occupations, as well as in citizens', avocational, and family life roles

(7) Identify organizational patterns and levels of jobs in industries and business in the community

(8) Identify major occupations and characteristics of jobs in each cluster area

Differential Staffing

More efficient use of staff at lower cost, it is believed, can be achieved by use of a hierarchy of teachers at various levels of skill, experience, and pay. An experienced and highly trained master teacher can supervise journeyman teachers, interns, and teacher aids, spreading the rarest and most expensive human resource and, it is hoped, obtaining better teaching and more individual attention. Educational preparation can range from less than a bachelor's degree for the aides to a Ph.D. or Ed.D. for the master teacher.

An obvious career education use and contribution would be to challenge the strict credentialism which now prevails in some states at the elementary and secondary school levels. Effective teaching requires knowledge and ability to transmit it. For every subject, or at least some part of every subject taught in the school, there are people in the world outside the school with greater knowledge than that of the teacher. Teaching ability can be taught in college, but many have as much teaching ability intuitively or by trial and error experience in teaching learners on the job. Whenever that combination of knowledge and teaching skill can be identified, why should it be denied to the students because the holder of it has not completed the formalities of education and certification? It should be a truism that the teacher cannot know as much about any occupation, except teaching, as some of the people actually engaged in it. Use is made of visitors to the classroom, of course, but it should be possible for knowledgeable persons to undertake classroom responsibilities or to bring learners to their workplace without the intervention of the teacher. If this technique can improve teaching and learning about a scientist's work style, why can it not improve the teaching of the academic tools he requires on his job? And if alright for career education, why not the same principle for all of academic learning? Therefore, an important reform required is to make it possible for some persons without standard teaching certificates to teach in our elementary and secondary schools. Some of the skills required in effective career education programs are those learned in the "school of hard knocks." Exchange programs should be established between professional educators and employed persons from the world of work outside education. The school could gain doubly: first-hand teaching by experienced people, and work experience for the teacher.

Team Teaching

Differentiated staffing is a form of team teaching, but in general, the team concept is employed horizontally rather than vertically; that is, teachers at the same level but of different competencies combine to take advantage of their respective specialties. At times, it may be teachers who can present different emphases within the same subject matter. More usefully, the team is interdisciplinary, lending itself to a project approach which extracts various learnings from a complex activity more like the real world. Persons with world of work knowledge teamed with specialists in academic subject matter comprise an ideal career education approach. Not only the occupational usefulness of certain knowledge and skills, but the concept of specialization of labor and interdependence of occupations and tasks come through more strongly in the project setting.

Individualized Instruction and
Nongraded Classrooms

The classic ideal of the school as one teacher, one student, and one log has always fallen before the realities of school finance. Individualized instruction is an attempt to retain the economies of scale of teaching in groups while adapting to individual differences. What is sought is a curriculum which will allow each student to advance at his own rate, usually by establishing specific behavioral or performance objectives, providing materials and locations for individual study, and having available teachers and other resource persons for consultation and evaluation. It does not necessarily mean one-to-one instruction. The lecture can still be used along with other techniques. However, the essential component is that the student be able to proceed individually and get individual attention when he or she needs it.

The nongraded classroom can be both an application of and alternative to individualization. Students are grouped according to their ability in various subjects rather than by age. Each individual can move at this own pace, progressing upward into various groups as his abilities improve in each subject, regardless of whether individualized instruction is available. For career education, individualized instruction carries the same advantages and costs as for all education. Individual attention is the ideal, but career education can function in the traditional groups. The nongraded situation facilitates recognition of various levels of vocational maturity among students, allowing developing awareness to continue for some, while others are engaged in exploration or even making and expanding upon vocational decisions when conviction is strong. Computer-assisted instruction, programmed learning, and simulations are devices and techniques used to facilitate individualized instruction. For career education, there is the added gain of exposure to careers which use these devices, as well as the opportunity for individualized exploration of career clusters and simulated models of the real world for demonstrating the long-range implications of short-range decisions.

Open Classrooms and Alternative, Informal, and Free Schools

The open classroom is a different concept from the nongraded classroom. The latter presupposes a prescribed subject matter which the individual surmounts at his own pace. The open classroom allows students to identify and pursue their own interests in their own way, with the teacher acting primarily as facilitator. Advocates state it as a situation in which the student as a person takes precedence over subject matter, while opponents argue that it does the individual a disservice in failing to provide subject matter knowledge he does not yet know he needs. Alternative schools are developed to meet the special needs of students who do not fit into, succeed in, or accept the majority patterns and interests of the regular school. Emphasis is generally upon areas of unique interest to a group, rather than the individual autonomy (and eccentricities) of the open classroom. "Free school" is a term often applied to both of these concepts, particularly when the school is formed outside the public school system. The informal school, or "school without walls," uses the community as a classroom, with the students learning in public and private nonschool buildings, such as museums, business firms, and so forth, but under school direction and coordination. The subject matter can be individualized or common to a group.

Obviously, career education can be an individual interest in the open classroom or the unique interest of an alternative school, and can be conducted without walls. It assumes that each student needs to learn certain concepts about work and formalizes the curriculum to that extent; but the student chooses those occupational clusters and areas which he wishes to explore. There is of course more which can be learned of the world of work outside the classroom than in it, so long as there is some structure and direction to the learning process. Not only does career education lend itself to openness and flexibility, it can also serve as a focal point and core to prevent the study of its attractive concepts from degenerating into anarchy and unproductive chaos.

Extended Year, and Day and Community Schools

As a heritage from our agricultural past, expensive but non-air-conditioned school buildings lie idle a fourth of each year. The normal six-hour school day also hardly exhausts the potential services of these institutions. Widely advocated but rarely adopted is the year-round school and the school as a community center with functions beyond the school day. The community school notion contemplates the school as a center for all sorts of community initiatives going far beyond formal education, even beyond that including adult and continuing education.

In the year-round school both students and teachers attend classes on a staggered basis throughout the full twelve months of the year. The year-round school offers many advantages for all education, but it is important to career education primarily for two reasons. First, it can help to avoid "dumping" large numbers of graduates on the labor market once a year, a practice that guarantees continuing employment problems for school leavers. Second, it provides an excellent opportunity for teachers to use part of their time during the year to gain experience in the world of work outside education without burdening employers with large numbers of such teachers only during the summer months.

An eighteen-hour school day and the six-day school week would be of benefit in many ways, and for career education, would have three significant advantages. First, it would allow much more flexibility in establishing work experience and work-study programs for secondary school students. Second, it would allow the public schools to make significant contributions to adult education, including the need for retraining and upgrading of both unemployed and underemployed adult workers. Finally, it would allow a much more efficient use of school facilities that would permit the expansion of vocational education shops and laboratories without huge additional school construction costs. The community school concept would include addressing the concepts of career education to the out-of-school population, facilitating remedial employment preparation, upgrading, changing career directions, and preparing for retirement.

Modular and Flexible Scheduling

Flexible scheduling allows variation in daily instruction, recognizing that all knowledge does not adapt itself to the traditional 45 or 50-minute classes. It allows varying the length of classes and labs to fit the instruction to be given. Modular scheduling involves breaking down information and instruction into small but discrete units. These can be offered in various sequences that are inflexible within each module, but added together, provide a flexible curriculum. Mini-courses are one form of modular instruction, lasting an hour, a day, or a week but concentrating on a limited concept. Career education's need to be integrated into the subject matter and to take the classroom out into the world and bring the world into the classroom works best with such scheduling flexibility.

Other Innovations

One aspect of career education which has contributed to its growing popularity is its flexibility and utility. It can be introduced into the most rigid and traditional setting or the most unstructured open classroom or alternative school. It can fit comfortably there and can contribute to any type of education activity. Along with its flexibility, career education's rapid growth depends upon the support of a dedicated cadre of school personnel, especially classroom teachers, who become excited with its possibilities and the reactions to their students. Thus career education promises to become an effective vehicle not only for its own reforms, but for bringing other proved innovations into the mainstream of American education.

This book cannot begin to present a complete inventory of the many stimulating career education ideas which will occur to alert classroom teachers. Only illustrations of the myriad possibilities have or can be given.

Simulated corporations have been established by math, English, social studies, and industrial arts students to sell stock, produce products, maintain books, write business letters and reports, transact business, role-play labor-management relationships, and so on. Parents and other workers have been observed on the job and invited to class, after which vocabulary development, letter writing, reading, and creative art were structured around the experience. Career fairs, simulated employment services, and group guidance activities have resulted.

Profitable field trips have been made to power plants, construction sites, industrial plants, vocational schools, colleges, restaurants, laundries, airports, auto dealers, hospitals, government agencies, shopping centers — wherever people are being trained or are working. Entire classes can participate, or individuals or small groups can visit and report to the class. Cameras and tape recorders are standard equipment for the small group visit and report. Advance study of the industry or site, post-trip analysis, thank you letters, charts, and such all add to the value.

Interviewing skills can be developed, and the career potential of such skills can be explored. Questionnaires can be developed for field trips, work observation, and classroom visitors. Students can learn interviewing techniques from newspaper articles and television shows. That the best research is from primary sources — the individual with first-hand knowledge — is a likely conclusion. Interviewing sessions can be role-played, taped, and critiqued.

Every school should have an organizational center to coordinate career education activities. Students can learn by participating in its design. Career kits for each subject area or mobile resource units circulating among small schools or classrooms can be products of such centers. Newsletters, bulletin boards, tele-lectures by persons unable to visit the school are all possibilities.

Teachers and students can play "What's my line?" or role-play real jobs. They should be alerted to the fact that they are already workers in the school, the home, and elsewhere, even if not employed, and should be taught to analyze their own work values and experiences. They can construct a model community, prepare a slide program of community resources, and read selections from literature that describe how people feel about their work. Students can compare the role of work in different cultures and the influence of geography on the occupational structure of different areas. Job applications can be simulated and reviewed, community job surveys made and ranked by attractiveness, the history of changing occupations studied, people interviewed to identify the factors which attract and hold them to their jobs. The list of possibilities is endless. All that is required is imagination. It is not easy, but the rewards are considerable — excitement for both student and teacher.

Most education reforms require major inputs of money and policy decisions by legislators, school boards, and administrators. Career education could profit by these inputs, but it can and ultimately must come into being by the decision of any teacher in any classroom.

FUTURE IN EDUCATION

The education system has been accused of concentrating upon the production of people as fodder for the industrial machine. Job training has been particularly characterized as teaching discipline and good behavior to subordinate and repress more natural instincts and interests (Reich, pp. 99, 142). People, it is alleged, are required to fit into careers rather than careers fitting peoples' preferences, talents, and life-styles. They supposedly work only for external reward without internal satisfaction. On the other hand, education is accused of giving too little attention to occupational concerns and failing to prepare people adequately for employment. Career education must walk carefully between these extremes, helping youth develop their own work values, making sure that they know the alternatives before them and the consequences of choice, and that they have what it takes to facilitate whatever choices are made.

Some aspects about the schools of the near future are foreseeable because they are here in the more advanced applications. Dissemination rather than innovation seems to be the need.

Scheduling will be more flexible, both in varying the length of lessons and in adding to the amount of unscheduled time. Schools will be open year-round and for longer periods of time each day. Students will move at their own pace, contracting to achieve performance objectives, studying independently, and reappearing when they need the teacher's guidance, approval of assignments completed, or new assignments. More learning will occur in the community and be brought back for reporting to the classroom. Students will also teach each other, both by the more advanced tutoring others and by discussion groups exploring and learning together.

There will be increasing use of technology, not only in individualized techniques such as computer-assisted instruction but by mass media as well. Classes will be more pupil centered and less teacher centered, with the teacher increasingly acting as a manager of techniques, subject matter, and materials all centered on effective learning by the student. With formal teaching becoming less important than independent learning, the students' responsibility will rise relative to the teachers'. The curriculum will be redesigned for active learning through student involvement. Knowledge will be discovered by the student more than transmitted by the teacher. Since learning will occur within and outside the school, traditional subjects will be redesigned for more active involvement outside the classroom.

There will be a closer and more deliberate connection between the school and the community. The school will no longer be isolated. Not only will students learn from and within the community, they will serve the community and learn from those service activities.

The academic subject matter courses will change with less emphasis on presentation of content and more on assuring that the essentials are learned. Science will become more field oriented and tied closer to the real world. Textbooks will become looseleaf manuals for continued updating, or annual supplements will be issued. Science classes will be linked to the computer centers and will also maintain closer liaison with industry.

Math will shift from teaching abstract concepts to stressing utilitarian applications. More self-instruction by students will allow the teacher time to emphasize and use case studies of application. English will take as its emphasis literature related to modern life and its problems. There will be more systematic training in research, the use of libraries, and so forth. Students will learn communications skills by communicating subjects which interest them. There will be further compromises between the standard forms and styles of communications and the dialects and idiosyncracies of various groups.

Social science will become more interdisciplinary, using as a basis for instruction real problems which are not easily dissectable into single disciplines. More learning will occur in the community dealing directly with problems. With satellite television and relatively inexpensive jet travel, the world *can* become the campus. A shift in all learning from teaching information to teaching by experience will encompass this.

Physical education will shift in the direction of self-expression. Youth will become less concerned for competitive sports, and coaches and parents will face that disappointment. Team sports will decline in favor of meeting individual needs. With drug experimentation, earlier sex activity, a growing interest in physical gratification, and a rising concern for the problems of aging, health will increasingly become a more important subject.

Despite these shifts in the handling of individual subjects, the tendency will be away from them. The trend will be to a core curriculum which teaches the same basics to all but is supplemented by a range of options for each student directed toward his interests and abilities. Among these will be emphasis on equipping him to earn a living and to enjoy leisure profitably. The elementary school must begin with a full common core of required skills and knowledge, but options will increase until the high school program is at least 50 percent elective, with many learning activities occurring outside the school, making full use of community facilities. The core approach will encourage interdisciplinary involvement.

Through all of this, career education will continue to rise in importance. It provides an objective to which all students can relate. It offers real world themes which can provide a common thread through a body of knowledge and experience. It both motivates and offers a learning vehicle. Career education is not supposed to be the universe, but its attractiveness is meant to be universal. Few are not interested in their future careers. For the middle/junior high school group especially, career education offers a vehicle for exploration of the really vital questions, ones in which even adults would find consternation if they dared ask themselves: *Who am I? Why am I? What can I become?* Career education cannot supply all the answers, but it may be next best to theology in pursuing them.

THE IDEAL MIDDLE/JUNIOR HIGH SCHOOL CAREER EDUCATION PROGRAM

It would require more courage and wisdom that we can collectively muster to present an ideal model for a career education program in the middle/junior high schools. But we can suggest some attributes. Since it is a process or approach underlying the whole instructional program rather than an addition to the curriculum, the ideal career education program would occur within the ideal middle school or junior high. That school would have clearly formulated its goals and objectives, and some but not all of those goals and objectives would relate to the students' future working careers. Every aspect of the curriculum, every learning experience — whether cognitive, psychomotor, or affective — would be judged by the potential answer to the question: What kind of human being will emerge from this process? Since the combination of exploration and self-discovery is the common concern of the age group, that would be the priority goal for this stage of education. Knowledge and skills would not be neglected, but they would emphasize exploration of the society in relation to self and of self in relation to society. Since all knowledge and skills cannot be taught in the time available, contributions to exploration and self-discovery would be the criteria for selection.

In effect, the curriculum would be competency based insofar as it is possible to determine the competencies required at this stage of life, though specific performance objectives might be more appropriately developed and applied to the teacher than to the student. Accountability would be in terms of these teacher and institutional performance objectives. Individualized instruction, team teaching, differentiated staffing, flexible scheduling, a nongraded school, and all of the technological gadgetry would be present, but the specified goals and performance objectives would exclude much of the directional permissiveness of the open classroom or free school.

For career education this would mean several things. The school administration would be enthusiastic in promoting the program. Someone in the school would have the assignment and a major portion of time free to promote and coordinate career education. It would require teachers trained either in-service or preservice in career education techniques. After undergoing such training, each teacher would develop and use career education learning experiences adapted to the subject matter and the students in the classes he or she teaches. The teacher would keep clearly in mind the priority assignment to teach the subject matter which, after thought and study, has been decided to be critical to the student's development, with career education techniques used to motivate and to illustrate. Subject matter would not slip into second place among priorities.

Each member of the administration and staff should recognize and pursue those responsibilities within which his or her specialties and background can make the greatest contribution in the middle/junior high school. Overall leadership and initiative is, of course, the responsibility of the principal. Every teacher has the assignment of incorporating career education concepts and materials into the subject matter of each course taught.

Each school should have at least one staff member, probably a counselor, who is the in-house expert on career development. He or she should be thoroughly conversant with research results and practice pertaining to career development for pre- and early adolescents, such as summarized in chapters 2 and 3. That knowledge would be used not only in counseling contacts with students but also in interaction with other staff. Part of the counselor's responsibility should be to alert and remind teachers of the career development needs of their students and consult with them on ways to adapt their instruction to meet those needs. The counselor is in an advantageous position to provide factual information and suggestions of ways in which students can be introduced to the occupational world and help teachers become familiar with the career implications of their subject matter. It would also be logical for the counselor to join with the industrial arts and home economics teachers, particularly, in a primary leadership and coordinating role in three vital career education responsibilities: (1) establishing and maintaining liaison with the business-industrial-labor community for interchanges between the school and the workplace, (2) developing and conducting work simulation projects, and (3) helping the youth to see the meaningfulness of and extract work values from the many work tasks the youth undertakes in school, at home, and in the community, often without defining them as work.

The industrial arts and home economics teachers are most likely to have an understanding of and contacts with the employing community outside the school. They along with the counselor should develop and exploit these contacts on behalf of their students. This trio is also the logical team to take the leadership in interdisciplinary projects combining academic and career activities. For instance, the hands-on nature of home economics and industrial arts can effectively provide the core of activities around which the math teacher can develop problems, the science teacher illustrate principles, the social studies teacher guide the students in exploring social implications, and the English teacher assign appropriate reading and report writing.

The home economics teacher is also the most obvious liaison between the home and the school, pointing up and recruiting parents to cooperate in teaching consumer education and homemaking skills (for both boys and girls). The industrial arts instructor can also teach homemaking skills (do-it-yourself repairs, crafts, and so forth), take a lead role in developing work observation opportunities, and provide the hands-on component for integrated academic and career education projects. The home economics and industrial arts teachers should emphasize that parenthood and homemaking are also work roles, that they are productive and satisfying, and that they can and should be completely shared in by both sexes.

The practical arts teacher should take the lead position in developing work simulation activities through which students familiarize themselves with production processes. Where business education is part of the curriculum, that teacher's role can be identical with industrial arts but emphasize white-collar production and skills. Music and fine arts teachers share the academic and practical arts role. They can teach career relevancy of their subjects, and they can also supply music and fine arts activities as the hands-on component of interdisciplinary projects.

With the physical education and health teacher emphasizing the physical requirements for successful careers, with the school custodial, maintenance, and school bus staff accepting responsibility for demonstrating the nature and meaning of their roles in the world of work, everybody is in the act. All of this in short is the prescription and the only requirement for a model middle/junior high school career education program.

REFERENCES

Illich, Ivan. *Deschooling Society.* New York: Harper & Row, 1971.

Leonard, George. *Education and Ecstasy,* New York: Dellacorte, 1970.

Reich, Charles A. *The Greening of America.* New York: Random House, 1970.

Toffler, Alvin. *Future Shock.* New York: Bantam Books, 1970.

Index